Realism and Antirealism in Kant's Moral Philosophy

Kantstudien-Ergänzungshefte

Im Auftrag der Kant-Gesellschaft
herausgegeben von
Manfred Baum, Bernd Dörflinger
und Heiner F. Klemme

Band 199

Realism and Antirealism in Kant's Moral Philosophy

New Essays

Edited by Robinson dos Santos and
Elke Elisabeth Schmidt

DE GRUYTER

ISBN 978-3-11-068523-7
e-ISBN (PDF) 978-3-11-057451-7
e-ISBN (EPUB) 978-3-11-057234-6
ISSN 0340-6059

Library of Congress Cataloging-in-Publication Data
A CIP catalog record for this book has been applied for at the Library of Congress.

Bibliographic information published by the Deutsche Nationalbibliothek
The Deutsche Nationalbibliothek lists this publication in the Deutsche Nationalbibliografie; detailed bibliographic data are available on the Internet at http://dnb.dnb.de.

© 2019 Walter de Gruyter GmbH, Berlin/Boston
This volume is text- and page-identical with the hardback published in 2018.
Printing and binding: CPI books GmbH, Leck
♾ Printed on acid-free paper
Printed in Germany

www.degruyter.com

Table of Contents

Preface —— VII

Antirealist Interpretations of Kant

Frederick Rauscher
Transcendental and Empirical Levels of Moral Realism and Idealism —— 3

Melissa Zinkin
Kantian Constructivism, Respect, and Moral Depth —— 21

Realist Interpretations of Kant

Christoph Horn
Kant's Theory of Historical Progress: A Case of Realism or Antirealism? —— 45

Patrick Kain
Dignity and the Paradox of Method —— 67

Lara Ostaric
Practical Cognition, Reflective Judgment, and the Realism of Kant's Moral *Glaube* —— 91

Elke Elisabeth Schmidt & Dieter Schönecker
Kant's Moral Realism regarding Dignity and Value. Some Comments on the *Tugendlehre* —— 119

Something in Between

Stefano Bacin
Moral Realism by Other Means: The Hybrid Nature of Kant's Practical Rationalism —— 155

Jochen Bojanowski
Why Kant Is Not a Moral Intuitionist —— 179

Oliver Sensen
Kant's Constitutivism —— 197

Subject Index —— 223

Index of Persons —— 231

Preface

This volume aims to clarify whether Kant is a moral realist, an antirealist, or something in between. Obviously, the answer to this question presupposes an understanding of the terms "realism" and "antirealism." Considering the current literature in metaethics, one finds that the topics of moral realism and antirealism have been broadly discussed for decades, and well-known (and, of course, also less well-known) philosophers have contributed ideas to this debate, including such scholars as David Brink, Christoph Halbig, Christine Korsgaard, Franz von Kutschera, Thomas Nagel, John Rawls, Peter Schaber, and Russ Shafer-Landau, to name but a few. Central questions in this debate are: What *are* moral realism and antirealism, and how can we define them? What are moral facts? Are they natural facts or not? Are they objective or subjective? Are moral facts subject-dependent or not? In the final analysis, is there something like one and only one form of realism or antirealism? Current debates do not show a unified or consistent terminology. Different philosophers use the terms quite differently and even new terms have come into play. So the debate concerns not only "realism" and "antirealism," but also forms of "strong," "weak," or "moderate" realism or antirealism. Furthermore, mediating positions have arisen such as "objectivism," "constructivism" (not only as a form of antirealism), "constitutionism," and "idealism." Again, all of these terms are used repeatedly with different meanings in different contexts, and there is no homogenous terminology. Between the positions of a strong moral realism, which is based upon God's existence, or on the existence of Platonic Ideas, and a non-cognitivist, antirealist understanding of morality, it seems that everything is possible in principle and named differently by different authors.

What probably is common to all moral realists is the claim that there are answers to at least some moral questions and that a moral judgment is true when it corresponds to the relevant moral facts. But here the agreement seems to end, and in order to distinguish a moral realist from a (cognitivist) antirealist, one has to ask what exactly these moral facts are and how they are to be understood in an ontological way. For classical antirealism (like relativism or subjectivism), the point seems to be that moral facts are completely dependent on subjects, who just *decide* what is morally right and wrong. According to this view, there are no necessary or universally binding norms or values, but only contingent ones. At the same time, strict realists hold moral facts to be absolutely independent of any subjects and their beliefs – and therefore they are necessary and universally binding. Yet again, this is not the whole story, for there is a wide range of positions between classical antirealism and strict realism.

So to decide whether one should label Kant's ethics "realism" or "antirealism", one has to do at least two things: explain what one means by those terms and argue for why Kant has to be subsumed under one category rather than another. The possibilities concerning the classification of Kant's metaethical position are, of course, numerous. One possible way to argue would be to emphasize the fact that the categorical imperative springs from and therefore depends on human reason, and that only human beings and their actions have moral value. In this respect, Kant could seem to be an antirealist, since morality would depend on human beings. On the other hand, one could argue that Kant claims his ethics to be universal and a priori because it is not dependent on any specific subjects and their desires or preferences, which seems to indicate that he is a proponent of moral realism. Yet these two views represent the limit positions, and mixed positions may be found in-between. For instance, one could point out that for Kant morality is indeed dependent on the *existence* of beings that possess pure practical reason, but that as long as these beings really exist, morality really exists and is therefore not only "real" but also objective and universal, and in no way up to individual or even arbitrary choices.

All the authors of this volume take up the task of classifying Kant's ethics metaethically, though they do it with different intentions and purposes, and they come to quite different conclusions. Hence it is no surprise that the ambiguity of terminology in the current metaethical debate is mirrored in this volume as well. There is no agreement among the authors of this volume on how exactly to define realism and antirealism (and their variants), nor is there agreement among them on whether Kant belongs to one or the other camp. In any event, all authors introduce and defend their terminology. Every paper is preceded by an abstract, and as one can see, all camps in the metaethical field have their inhabitants: Fred Rauscher and Melissa Zinkin belong to the primarily antirealist group; Christoph Horn, Patrick Kain, Lara Ostaric, and both Elke E. Schmidt and Dieter Schönecker read Kant as a fairly strong realist; Stefano Bacin, Jochen Bojanowski as well as Oliver Sensen take somewhat middle positions – or so *we* would classify their approaches.

A short note on the genesis of the volume at hand: This project was initiated at the conference "*Realismo e Anti-realismo na Filosofia Moral de Kant: Dignidade, Valor Moral e Reino dos Fins*" held at the Federal University of Pelotas, Brazil, in 2014. The group met again in 2015 at the University of Siegen to further discuss the topic, and the papers generated from these discussions are collected in this volume.

We would like to thank all the authors for their contributions and the many productive discussions in Pelotas and Siegen. We also would like to thank Richard Capobianco, Professor of Philosophy at Stonehill College, for polishing the English texts of non-native speakers; Nicholas Walker for translating the text of Christoph Horn; Jonas Höhler for formatting the texts; and Andreas Bender for taking care of the indices. Moreover, we are grateful to *Thyssen*-Stiftung and *Philosophische Fakultät* of the University of Siegen for funding this project.

Last but not least, our special thanks go to our dear friend and *fundamentalista*, Dieter Schönecker, for helping realize this project in many ways.

Robinson dos Santos and Elke Elisabeth Schmidt
Pelotas and Siegen, Oktober 2017

Antirealist Interpretations of Kant

Frederick Rauscher
Transcendental and Empirical Levels of Moral Realism and Idealism

Abstract The question "Was Kant a moral realist?" is sharpened by the two-level account provided in theoretical philosophy between the transcendental conditions for possible experience and actual empirical experience. In moral philosophy, at the transcendental level one determines the conditions for the possibility of moral agency as such, which for Kant includes: a free will, reason that provides universal law, an ability to choose ends, and an identification of absolute value. A moral realist holds that some conditions are independent of the conception of the moral agent, an idealist that all conditions are dependent. The empirical level refers to the realization of these conditions in actual individuals, and the dependence is upon the actual moral agent. Using this distinction, one might call Kant a transcendental realist but an empirical idealist about, e.g., the moral law, since it depends upon the rational moral agent as such, independent of particular moral agents.

* * *

This paper is not intended to answer the question of whether Kant was a moral realist or a moral idealist (or antirealist) but to provide a better understanding of the question itself. The mere question "Was Kant a moral realist?" viewed as a simple yes/no dichotomy is based on a failure to account for the complexity of Kant's moral theory in three ways, the third of which is the subject of this paper.

First, one must have a firm definition of "moral realism" at hand appropriate to Kant's philosophy. The term "moral realism" is relatively recent in the development of philosophy, a product of the twentieth-century analytic identification of metaethics as an area of philosophy distinct from normative ethics. The definition of realism most widely used has two main elements: 1) that moral claims literally construed are either true or false, and 2) that some are literally true.[1] This approach essentially equates moral realism with the acceptance of

---

[1] Geoffrey Sayre-McCord (1988, p. 5) uses this definition for his overview of moral realism. He also briefly mentions that one might contrast realism with idealism based on the issue of mind-independence of moral claims but brushes over the importance of this distinction by noting that both imply cognitivism and hence, on his definition, realism (1988, pp. 14–16).

the truth of moral claims and thus consigns moral antirealism to the rejection of the validity of morality.² It thereby sidesteps a traditional understanding of realism in contrast to idealism that focuses on the mind-dependence or -independence of certain aspects of experience. Kant's philosophy is most famous for insisting on this distinction and coming firmly down on the side of mind-dependence of synthetic a priori truth in theoretical philosophy. A definition of moral realism that takes into account the importance of mind-dependence would be better suited to assessing the issue in Kant.³

Second, one must specify the particular elements of moral theory at issue, e.g. "Was Kant a realist about moral value" and "Was Kant a realist about the moral law" might have different answers, making Kant a realist in one case and an idealist in another. Sometimes claims regarding Kant and realism are in fact made with regard to specific elements but generalized as if they covered Kant's position as a whole. Of course sometimes claims about particular elements of Kant's theory are appropriately limited to one element of Kant's ethics or do distinguish among various elements.⁴ I take as uncontroversial the claim that a proper answer to the question of whether Kant was or was not a moral realist requires an explicit delineation of the specific elements of Kant's ethics and an assessment of alleged realism with regard to each element independently. Only then can a judgment be made about Kant's overall position.

But there is a third, more controversial way in which the question "Was Kant a moral realist" is overly simplistic. In his theoretical philosophy Kant not only presents his position regarding the status of space and time in terms of mind-dependence, he also distinguishes two levels for understanding the reality of space and time, transcendental and empirical.⁵ He also employs the term "transcendental" in other contexts, as for example when he separates general

---

2 Sharon Street (2010, p. 370) makes essentially this same point when she notes that under such a definition even a subjectivist who takes moral truths to be relative to each subject would count as a moral realist.

3 I offer and defend in detail such a definition in an early article (Rauscher 2002) and revised it in my book on realism in Kant (Rauscher 2015). The version in the book defines moral realism as the position that "the moral principles, properties, or objects of the world are independent of the transcendental or empirical moral agent" (Rauscher 2015, p. 14). Moral idealism is correspondingly dependence on the moral agent. The current paper is a detailed argument for the value of the transcendental/empirical distinction that I employ in that book.

4 Patrick Kain distinguishes various elements in his various articles on Kant and moral realism, for example when discussing moral legislation in Kain (2004). Robert Stern is also careful to separate various elements of Kant's ethics in Stern (2011).

5 See KrV: A28/B44 and A35–36/B52. For the list of abbreviations of Kant's works, see the "Literature" section of this paper.

logic from transcendental logic,⁶ empirical deduction from transcendental deduction,⁷ empirical illusion from transcendental illusion,⁸ etc. Kant does not employ such language in his ethics outside the topic of freedom, but I contend that a similar distinction between empirical and transcendental is applicable to ethics and helps to illuminate the inquiry into answering the main question about Kant and moral realism.⁹ Indeed it can be so useful that it can even dissolve some of the disagreements about the issue. For example, Kant could turn out to be a transcendental idealist and at the same time an empirical realist about some elements of his ethics, showing that both realists and idealists are correct in compatible ways.¹⁰

The paper will first discuss Kant's usage of the transcendental/empirical distinction in theoretical philosophy to show that the way I am using the distinction in ethics is grounded in Kant's overall philosophy. I will explain how this transcendental/empirical distinction for realism/idealism applies to Kant's moral theory. I then apply this to the moral law and moral value to show exactly where the fault lines are drawn between different claims when using this distinction. I also review some of the ways in which other commentators' take on the issue of moral realism in Kant could be clarified or improved by using such a distinction.¹¹

---

6 See KrV: A55/B79–80.
7 See KrV: A85/B117.
8 See KrV: A295–296/B351–352.
9 I set out this distinction in Rauscher (2015, pp. 19–22) but provide a more focused and detailed explanation in this current paper.
10 When combined with my earlier point about individuating various elements of Kant's ethics for separate analysis, the possible configurations of moral realism and idealism in Kant multiply into the dozens. Luckily Kant can be construed as consistent in his approach to ethics, so some general principles can help to narrow the range of plausible interpretations. No one, for example, could plausibly hold that Kant is a transcendental realist about the value of contingently chosen ends of particular empirical agents.
11 I must admit that in my earlier work I myself assessed moral realism without using this distinction. My article (Rauscher 2002) invoked Kant's transcendental idealism as prima facie reason to think that he was not a moral realist but in the end gave more attention to the empirical by focusing on the human mind. I defined moral realism as "the belief that some of the moral characteristics of the world are independent of the human mind" (Rauscher 2002, p. 482). My focus on the human mind tended to embrace the empirical – such as my interpretation of the fact of reason as our actual experience of the categorical imperative – and bring in transcendental considerations only from that perspective – such as the way that I had claimed that practical reason is only posited on the basis of that experience. I failed to give due weight to the transcendental conception of a moral agent and even conflated the two levels. Only in the intervening years have I realized the utility of making the distinction.

I Empirical and Transcendental Levels

Although Kant presents the distinction between empirical and transcendental as both metaphysical and methodological, I will stress the methodological aspect. These two explanations of the difference between transcendental and empirical work together in a way that will apply well to the question of moral realism. In discussing the methodological distinction, I do not mean a full interpretation of transcendental idealism as methodological rather than metaphysical but only an explanation of the nature of the transcendental method in philosophy. There are two key elements to the transcendental method that I want to examine.

First, the transcendental method is itself only a way to defend a priori claims but not directly to provide a priori knowledge. As Kant explains in the *Mrongovius Lectures on Metaphysics* in 1782: "Transcendental philosophy [...] does not say something a priori of objects, but rather investigates the capacity of the understanding or of reason to cognize something a priori" (MM II: 784). In other words the a priori claims have their origin elsewhere but are justified using the transcendental method. Before presenting the transcendental deduction of the categories in the *Critique of Pure Reason* (in both editions), Kant explains the difference between the empirical and transcendental deductions as the difference between tracing the source of a concept and justifying the concept.[12] To illustrate an empirical deduction Kant cites Locke, who traced all concepts, or in his terminology "complex ideas," in the mind to specific sensations (or inner reflections), "simple ideas." Concepts are all given this sort of explanation without exception in Locke. A transcendental deduction, on the other hand, does not ask for the origin of the concept but only for the justification of its use a priori.

Second, the transcendental method does not require that the thinker, or the cognitive faculty of the thinker, who uses a priori principles or concepts be independent of empirically real nature. To put it simply, the transcendental cognizer is not required to be a transcendent being. It is merely the conception of the necessary structure of cognition required for a certain kind of experience. Kant is not entirely clear about this. On the one hand he says that the a prioricity of the concepts subject to transcendental deduction precludes those concepts from being derived from experience, while on the other hand he does admit that "we can search in experience" for the source of these concepts (KrV: A86–87/B118–19). By this he means that we would not succeed in deriving the concepts *from intuitions*, although we might be able to find some intuitions

---

[12] See KrV: A85–87/B117–119.

that *trigger* our minds to *generate* and employ the a priori concepts. The thinker can be understood entirely as a being in nature who relates to objects in two ways, first purely receptively through sensations and second actively through the concepts that the thinker's mind employs in processing those sensations. Some of those concepts would be a priori and derived not through sensation but through mental activity. That a thinker in nature has the a priori concept and uses it is implied by the justificatory role of the transcendental deduction. With the conception at hand, the question becomes whether any, and which, actual flesh and blood empirical beings instantiate that transcendental structure.

Both of these aspects show that the transcendental method would be able to show the required cognitive capacity of a being subject to certain conditions. Given the condition that Kant uses in the transcendental deduction of the categories – the requirement that a being is able to represent an objective experience – a transcendental deduction would show that some particular a priori concepts would have to be employed by any being who would satisfy the conditions. Those concepts would be transcendentally justified, and we could call the resulting picture of a cognizer who must employ those conditions a conception of a transcendental cognizer. Once we have the conception of a transcendental cognizer, we can ask the further question of which beings in nature actually embody that conception. We could know that any actual empirical being who will represent an objective experience will embody that conception, whether we are asking about alien life on other planets or beings who might evolve on earth. There is then a distinction between the conception of a transcendental cognizer and the different conceptions of empirical cognizers who might have awareness and mental life, only some of whom might embody the conception of the transcendental cognizer by being able to represent an objective experience.

This distinction applies easily to ethics. Kant himself does not explicitly employ the distinction between the transcendental and the empirical in his ethics, with a few exceptions regarding transcendental freedom. But his work in ethics follows the pattern. The main approach is to distinguish between transcendental and empirical *moral agents*. A transcendental moral agent is the conception of a moral agent that embodies all the necessary conditions for moral agency. An empirical moral agent is an actual flesh-and-blood individual. The best way to identify the particular issues regarding moral realism and idealism in Kant is to see the relation between all the various elements and aspects of morality such as value and the moral law on the one hand, and the moral agent as subject on the other hand. Any elements and aspects of morality that are dependent upon the moral subject would be to that extent ideal, any independent of the moral subject, real.

The transcendental moral agent would be determined by asking the practical analogue of the theoretical question "what are the necessary conditions for the possibility of a being able to represent to herself an objective experience?" Answering the theoretical question brings in the necessary cognitive structure of the cognizer as subject and the necessary conditions for the objects that such a subject would represent. In the practical case the question is related to *moral* experience: "what are the necessary conditions for the possibility of a being able to have valid moral experience?" When I use the term "moral experience" the term "experience" is not restricted to Kant's sense of experience of outer objects. I mean in it a broader sense in which conscious agents face moral decisions, deliberate, recognize or assign value, are aware of any moral standards, make moral judgments, feel pride or guilt, and the like. Human beings in Kant's theory certainly do all these things with conscious awareness. Moral experience is the experience of moral *agents*. Answering the question about the necessary conditions for a valid moral experience would involve any necessary structure of whatever faculties that agent has that concern morality as well as any properties that the world must exhibit to make that kind of agent possible.

The term "valid moral experience" already shows a distinctly Kantian approach to the issue because the focus of the question is on experience of a being, in this case a moral agent, rather than on something that is conceived in another way. Examples of other kinds of questions about morality that do not emphasize first-person experience would be "what are the necessary conditions for the existence of the good?" or "what are the necessary conditions for a stable society?" In the first case the answer might not even require a moral agent at all, as in G.E. Moore's intuitionism and the sheer existence of the good. But the question that I take Kant to be asking is one that does focus on the possibility of moral agency.

The reason for this focus on moral agency is that for Kant, philosophy is primarily a human-oriented activity. He defines philosophy in the *Critique of Pure Reason* as "the science of the relation of all cognition to the essential ends of human reason" of which the highest is the "final end" (*Endzweck*) or "vocation" of human beings (KrV: A839–840/B867–868). The most significant division in philosophy is between theoretical and practical philosophy understood in terms of theoretical knowledge of what is or what is given to us and practical action aimed at what ought to be or what is possible for us to create through freedom. Since the theoretical question for transcendental philosophy is about the conditions for knowledge of what is, the practical question for transcendental philosophy is about the conditions for action regarding what ought to be that we can create through freedom, which is what I mean to capture by saying: "the necessary conditions for the possibility of a being able to have valid moral experience."

The transcendental level of analysis, then, focuses on the conditions for moral agency. How Kant determines these conditions is not merely through transcendental deduction. In theoretical philosophy Kant also lays out some of the transcendental conditions for experience without using a transcendental deduction when he identifies the twelve categories of the understanding in the *Metaphysical Deduction*. This is a legitimate part of the transcendental assessment of the conditions for experience because it provides the content for what is subject to transcendental deduction. In ethics Kant similarly provides an analysis of the nature of morality before asking whether it can be confirmed through a transcendental deduction. The first two sections of the *Groundwork* function to identify and explain the nature of moral duty and of the moral law. This provides a transcendental conception of the moral agent as one who is subject to an autonomous moral law that stems from the agent's own will (as practical reason) accompanied by the determination of the objective value of humanity as an end in itself. In the *Groundwork* Kant stresses the identification and explanation of the moral law as a categorical imperative valid for finitely rational beings. In the *Critique of Practical Reason* he spends more time looking at the way in which finitely rational beings are aware of the moral law and how they would be able to act from the moral law in the face of non-rational inclinations. The second *Critique* also looks at the broader needs of a finitely rational moral agent who requires that the highest good be possible; the postulates of practical reason are analogous to the theoretical ideas of reason that are required for a coherent, systematic experience.[13] Since there is no explicit identification of the transcendental moral agent in Kant, we have to work through his arguments to identify what he takes to be the necessary conditions for the possibility of a valid moral experience. Some of this work is itself the subject of debate among interpreters, such as the precise scope of autonomy, the metaphysics of value, and the status of the postulates.

The empirical level of analysis asks about actual moral agents in empirically real nature. Given the conception of the transcendental moral agent, which is a conception of a particular structure of moral faculties and capacities and not a transcendent being in itself, the question can be raised which empirical beings in nature possess these structures and so instantiate transcendental moral

---

13 See KrV: A670/B698.

agency. In Kant's case we can ask, roughly, whether human beings possess an autonomous moral law that stems from the agent's own will (as practical reason) and humanity to make them objectively valuable as an end in itself. And do they possess the other attributes necessary for moral agency, such as a free will, consciousness of the categorical imperative, a belief in the highest good, etc.? Since these elements of transcendental moral agency are linked, the empirical being in question is likely to possess all of them or none.

The transcendental methodology Kant uses to discover and justify the necessary conditions for the possibility of representing experience and of moral agency results in an identification of two levels of analysis: the transcendental and the empirical. But Kant uses the terms "transcendental" and "empirical" to mark a metaphysical distinction as well, one that has implications for the use of these terms regarding moral realism and idealism. In the *Transcendental Aesthetic* Kant holds that space and time themselves are (merely) forms of intuition used by human beings rather than objects in themselves or relations among objects in themselves.[14] In this way space is transcendentally ideal rather than transcendentally real. But Kant still insists that space is empirically real and in fact a necessary form of human experience. Kant summarizes the status of space this way:

> Our expositions accordingly teach the reality (i.e., objective validity) of space in regard to everything that can come before us externally as an object, but at the same time the ideality of space in regard to things when they are considered in themselves through reason. We therefore assert the empirical reality of space (with respect to all possible outer experience), though to be sure its transcendental ideality, i.e., that it is nothing as soon as we leave aside the condition of the possibility of all experience, and take it as something that grounds the things in themselves. (KrV: A27–28/B43–44)

This passage brings out the metaphysical difference between empirical and transcendental realism and idealism. Something is ideal if it is dependent upon the subject, otherwise it is real. At the transcendental level, space is ideal if it is dependent upon the subject as a necessary condition for experience, but real if it is seen as a property of objects independent of any cognitive requirements of the subject. At the empirical level, space is real if it is objective, which can be understood as not being dependent upon anything contingent about the empirical cognizer, and space is ideal if it does depend upon something contingent about the empirical cognizer.

---

[14] See KrV: A26/B42.

There is a closer relationship between transcendental methodology and the metaphysics of empirical realism with the category of causality. Cause and effect is identified as a category[15] that is then justified through the transcendental deduction[16] and later given particular justification as the second analogy as temporal sequence of causality, where Kant is clear that the objects of experience are possible through causal law independent of our subjective perceptions.[17] Causal relations are empirically real as relations among empirical objects in space and time. We are able to know that these causal relations must hold of the objects of our experience because cause and effect is a transcendental condition for the possibility for us to cognize an objective experience. Our cognitive systems must process perceptions using cause and effect, *and* the empirical objects themselves must embody cause and effect independent of our perceptions. Because transcendental method identifies this latter as well as the former as a requirement for experience, the metaphysical claim about empirical objects is justified in addition to the claim about the cognitive system of the being having the experience.

Empirical reality in relation to objects can be understood in two different ways, both of which are relevant to ethics. First, empirical reality can be seen as the objective validity of a judgement. The spatiality of empirical objects is understood by Kant in relation to objective validity in the passage I quoted above: "the reality (i.e., objective validity) of space" (KrV: A28/B44). On this basis one might interpret Kant's empirical realism about space to refer only to the necessity of all human-like intuitors to use these same forms of intuition. A second understanding of empirical reality is more metaphysical: the independent existence of objects or properties of objects in space independent of the empirically conscious subject. This view is used by Kant most clearly in the *Refutation of Idealism* where Kant claims to prove "the existence of objects in space outside me" on the basis of a subjective consciousness inside me (KrV: B274–279). Here transcendental arguments support a metaphysical claim about empirical objects themselves in space, not merely a judgement about them. When in my previous paragraph I discussed the nature of cause and effect, I took the claims to objective causal law and causal relations to be an empirical realism in this metaphysical sense.

In a parallel way, elements of morality that are seen as transcendental conditions for moral agency will be empirically real. For if the element is

---

15 See KrV: A80/B106.
16 See KrV: A128, B162–163.
17 See KrV: B232–234.

understood to be a transcendental condition, then it is independent of the existence or thoughts of individual particular moral agents. (If there were no empirical moral agents at all, of course, then there would be no morality, just as if there were no beings who must use space and time as their forms of intuition, there would be no space and time.) And like theoretical philosophy, in practical philosophy there are two senses in which something might be empirically real. If a transcendental condition for moral agency identifies something that is a requirement for the mental processes of a moral agent, then empirical moral agents who possess that mental process are embodying those transcendentally valid processes, and any a priori principles stemming from those processes would be objectively valid. Like a cognitive system that must process perceptions using causal law, a faculty for deliberating on and freely choosing some acts must use practical reason. The a priori principle stemming from practical reason, namely the moral law itself, would be empirically real as objectively valid. There need not be any source of the law existing independent of the empirical moral agent because it would stem from her faculty of pure practical reason, but there is a validity to the law that is independent of the empirical moral agent.

Moral value illustrates the other way in which empirical reality would operate in morality, namely regarding properties of objects or objects themselves. If a transcendental condition for the existence of a moral agent is that there be some intrinsic value of something existing independent of any particular agent, then one might conclude that any empirical world in which moral agency can be actualized must include some entities with intrinsic value property (just as one might conclude that empirically real objects must have their own causal relations in any world that could include a being able to represent an objective experience). Here the empirical reality would be metaphysically independent of the empirical moral agent. In my next section I will get into more detail about realism regarding both the moral law and moral value.

Some features of experience would not even have a transcendental level. Kant uses the examples of colors as something that can be understood empirically but not at the transcendental level.[18] Colors are not objective but change with the subject and are clearly not independent of the subject, although related synthetic a priori properties of color in general like extension would have transcendental basis. Similarly in ethics some things would be only empirically ideal. In particular the value of optional ends chosen by empirical moral agents

---

[18] See KrV: A28–30/B44–45.

is only due to the specific individual's choice;[19] an example might be an agent adopting the end of pursuing one career rather than another, or seeking one flavor of ice cream when hungry.

This section has shown that the transcendental and empirical levels of analysis and the meaning of reality and ideality at each level in Kant's theoretical philosophy offer a coherent way to assess various claims about realism and idealism that carries over to his moral philosophy. The identification of the transcendental conditions for moral agency provides a characterization of realism or idealism at the transcendental level, while the actual existence of moral agents embodying those transcendental conditions form the empirical level.

II Using the Transcendental/Empirical Distinction

Two examples will have to suffice to show how this distinction can work in practice. The first example has to do with the status of the moral law. Suppose that a transcendental condition for moral agency is that there be a moral law that autonomously stems from the nature of the rational will rather than heteronomously from some other source of law, and that only moral agents are said to have this rational will. In that case the moral law would be transcendentally ideal but not transcendentally real. A transcendentally real moral law would be one which is an intrinsic part of reality but not tied to any particular kind of agent. Since non-Kantian moral theories do not offer transcendental analyses, it is anachronistic to include them here, but an example could be intuitionism in which good is seen simply as a real property of the universe. I would also label an ethical theory that placed the source of a moral law in God's mind, even simply in God's intellect, as a transcendentally real theory. Patrick Kain interprets Kant as a transcendental realist because he thinks that pure reason is somehow ultimately "in the nature of things" (Kain 2004, p. 303). These transcendental realists would also be empirical realists, holding that the moral law is valid independently of actual, particular moral agents.

Those who take Kant to be a transcendental idealist about the moral law could also hold to an empirical realism. Since the moral law is also not supposed to depend upon any particular empirical agents but is instead valid for all particular rational agents, it would be independent of any of the contingent features of an empirical moral agent and so be empirically real rather than

---

[19] See GMS: 427.

empirically ideal. Thus the moral law would be transcendentally ideal because it would depend upon the nature of the rational will in the very conception of the nature of moral agency but would be empirically real because not dependent upon the particular rational will of any particular moral agent. I think that this is actually a tidy way to resolve the dispute between realists and some idealists on the reality of the moral law: since it stems from pure practical reason, idealists and realists can insist that the moral law is transcendentally ideal and not independent of the very conception of a moral agent, but since it is independent of each particular moral agent, both can agree that the moral law is empirically real, that is, valid for all moral agents but not dependent upon contingent features they possess.

A second example concerns moral value. Kant holds that contingent ends depend only upon the particular faculty of desire of the actual subject.[20] Hence the value of contingent ends would have no transcendental status at all and would be empirically ideal. Objective value is more complicated. The most important objective value is the value of humanity. The value of humanity could conceivably have any of four statuses: transcendentally real or ideal or empirically real or ideal. A transcendentally real value of humanity would mean that the very morality requires that there be something that is of objective value independent of any characteristic of the transcendental moral agent at all. Those who hold that the value of humanity is independent of and prior to the categorical imperative could be transcendental realists about value if they understand value to be more than just a transcendental condition for morality but instead to be an independent fact about the nature of things in general. An alternative is to take the value of humanity to be independent of the categorical imperative but still only a transcendental condition for moral agency, in which case they would hold to a transcendental idealism about value. At the same time in both cases they would be empirical realists as well, holding that the value of actual human beings is independent of the empirical moral agent qua moral subject.[21] In contrast, those who hold that the value of humanity is

---

[20] See GMS: 427

[21] In theoretical philosophy Kant claims that a transcendental realism about space requires an empirical idealism because there would be no way for the empirical cognizer to know objects in themselves and hence to know that space is real. Cognizers could only represent space to themselves subjectively, and hence space would be empirically ideal. This same relation could hold in ethics if one stresses the epistemological question of access to value as does Oliver Sensen (2011, pp. 19–20). But if one abstracts from the epistemological point, one can say that the instantiation of the conditions of morality in nature would require an empirical realism for the value of humanity.

dependent on the categorical imperative or on pure practical reason are transcendental idealists about value because the value of humanity would depend upon the nature of the transcendental agent by being dependent on practical reason. These transcendental idealists about objective value could be empirical realists or empirical idealists. If one could allow for intrinsic value properties in Kant's ontology of nature, then an empirical realism works in which the value of humanity is a condition for there being moral agents, even though it is not a part of the nature of things as such, in the same way that causal relations among objects in nature are a condition for the transcendental cognizer but are not part of the nature of things as such. Those who, like me, think Kant has no room for value properties in nature and think that the value of humanity is a product of practical reason would deny this kind of metaphysical empirical reality and see absolute value as empirically real only in the sense of objective validity, where reason dictates that some entities must be treated in certain ways. There is a final option, namely, that the value of humanity has no transcendental ground at all but is merely a product of the contingent features of human nature, in which case it would be empirically ideal but neither transcendentally real or ideal.

These two examples, while sketchy, show how the distinction could work in practice. I think that using these two levels shows that in at least some cases disagreement between moral realists and moral idealists is based on the conflation of these two levels.

Applying this analysis to a few current approaches to the question of moral realism in Kant will show that they have shortcomings that can be improved by utilizing the transcendental/empirical distinction. I am not claiming to provide an exhaustive review of others' approaches but only to illustrate how some ambiguities can be resolved and some claims clarified using the distinction.

Jochen Bojanowski cites the definition of moral idealism that I provided in Rauscher (2002), "the belief that all of the moral characteristics of the world are dependent upon the human mind," and questions whether moral realism and what I call moral idealism (which he calls antirealism) are exhaustive. He rejects this dichotomy by distinguishing moral antirealism from what he labels moral idealism, which he defines to include the claim that practical reason is a cognitive faculty that knows the good but in some sense also produces it. His idealism holds "not that the good depends on the human mind but that its *existence* depends on self-affection in human cognizers" (Bojanowski 2012, p. 4). I understand his main point to be that he is rejecting a subjectivism that could result from construing the claim of dependence on the human mind to mean that moral facts have no other basis than the mere fact that a human mind happens to hold some belief or other about what is good. Bojanowski wants to retain the objectivity that comes with a conception of practical reason that transcends individual human agents. In this way practical reason defines what is good, but only when actual human or other finite rational agents utilize practical reason does that already identified good come into existence.

The ambiguity in his position is that the new conception "moral idealism" and the resulting assessment of practical reason do not specify the relation between actual moral agents and the nature of practical reason. Is practical reason something that is assessed utterly independently of its manifestation in actual agents? In that case, it would be on a different level from the existence claims and would not entail that realism/antirealism is a false dichotomy. Is practical reason something assessed at the same level as the existence of the good being dependent on the existence and practices of actual moral agents? In that case, it is on the same level, but even when practical reason is identified as the source of the definition of "good," both the existence *and the definition* of the good would still be dependent on the existence of moral agents who embody practical reason (assuming here that, as I had intended, by "human mind" is meant all similarly finite rational agents). This is because practical reason itself exists only if embodied in actual agents. (By analogy, phenomenal colors only exist because beings who see exist, and the kinds of colors these beings see depend upon the nature of the visual system in those agents – if beings who see did not exist, then the specification of the kinds of colors that could be seen would also not exist.) And in this latter case the mutual exclusivity of realism and antirealism would remain and Bojanowski's idealism would be subsumed under antirealism. Clearly Bojanowski does not intend this result.

In order to make Bojanowski's point clearer, a distinction must be made between the nature of practical reason with its accompanying moral law and thus defining of the good on the one hand and the realization of that practical reason in actual moral agents on the other hand. If one has this distinction in mind, then one can say that the transcendental nature of practical reason, considered in itself, is responsible for defining the good, making the good transcendentally ideal because dependent on the nature of practical reason. (It would be transcendentally real if it were independent of being defined by a cognitive faculty.) The good so defined would then be empirically real because it is defined independently of any particular empirical moral agent even though the existence of what is good would be empirically ideal because dependent on particular moral agents who utilize practical reason and thus, Bojanowski says, bring that good into existence. Hence, rather than denying that moral realism and moral antirealism are mutually exclusive, and then introducing a new, ambiguous third conception that Bojanowski calls "moral idealism," the dichotomy between moral realism and antirealism can be retained but applied at two different levels.

Another commentator whose work on moral realism illustrates the usefulness of the transcendental/empirical distinction is Allen Wood. I won't go into the complexities of his various claims about realism in Kant and his rejections of constructivism. I want to point only to one passage in which he makes a revealing claim about his own arguments:

> The argument draws no distinction between our having to take ourselves, from a practical standpoint, to be capable of judging according to objective reasons, and there actually being such reasons for us to judge according to. Analogously, and perhaps more controversially, it draws no distinction between taking ourselves (from a practical standpoint) to be capable of setting ends with objective worth and there really being objective worth for those ends to have. Still more controversially, it draws no distinction between our taking ourselves (from a practical standpoint) to be responding to moral requirements that are unconditionally obligatory and the actual existence of such categorical requirements. (Wood 1999, p. 381, note 30)[22]

This startling admission from someone who defends a realist interpretation of Kant's ethics seems to simply deny that there is a distinction between a mere assumption of validity and actual validity of various moral claims. Such an assertion examines moral realism on one level only: whether on the one hand the actual practical perspective that human beings have is the source of the moral reasons, values, and obligation or, on the other hand, whether there would be some independent standard outside of this actual perspective that humans have. It would put Kant's ethics in opposition to moral theories that see moral standards as entirely independent of practical reason. While this approach captures the essential distinction between Kant's and other, heteronomous ethical theories, and it accords with Kant's claim that acting under the idea of freedom is enough to make the moral law obligatory for us,[23] it does not do justice to a very important part of Kant's theory, namely, his careful investigation into the validity of morality. Kant was extremely concerned about whether human beings were justified in attributing moral standards to themselves and worried about whether the perceived moral standards were merely figments of our particular brain structure. Looking at realism at two levels can help to resolve this. It is clear that there is no phenomenal difference between having a practical perspective and having a valid practical perspective. But if one can assess the nature of morality at the transcendental level and

---

22 This position may be superseded by his later work.
23 See GMS: 448.

determine that it does have validity, that is, determine that the practical perspective is not merely a product of contingent human characteristics but is an objective transcendental condition for moral experience, then there is a difference in the actual moral agents not captured by the phenomena. Kant would be an empirical realist if the practical perspective is valid and an empirical idealist if not. Wood's abstracting from validity claims fails to capture this essential element of ethics for Kant.

The third and last example I will use is Patrick Kain. Kain is aware of the possibility of these two levels and comes closer than others to using it, although he does not emphasize or pursue it.[24] At one point he allows for the possibility of a "global constructivist antirealism" that takes moral claims to be transcendentally ideal rather than transcendentally real and would be similar to the restrictions imposed in theoretical philosophy to valid synthetic a priori judgments.[25] Morality would then, like space and time, be valid in a kind of empirical realism but dependent on the agent in a way similar to the transcendental dependence of space and time on the perceiver. This sort of approach is essentially the approach I take. Kain, however, rejects this approach because he interprets empirical realism to be limited to a theoretical empirical realism that insists on the universality of determinism and limits itself to beings who share the human forms of intuition of space and time. If the transcendental/empirical distinction is made within the confines of practical philosophy, it does not have those consequences. An empirical realism understood in practical philosophy is analogous to the empirical realism found in theoretical philosophy rather than subsumed under it; it is a further step to ask whether the requirements for empirical moral realism could be realized in the (theoretical) empirically real world of nature in space and time.[26] Regardless, the empirical reality of the practical can also be understood in terms of the validity of moral judgments which are understood as something different from theoretical judgments about ontology. Further, whatever transcendentally ideal elements of morality are found, they would apply not only to human beings but to any possible being

---

[24] Karl Ameriks (2013) uses the terms "empirical" and "transcendental" in his discussion of autonomy, but by "transcendental" he seems to have a metaphysical claim in mind that makes his use of the term quite different from mine.

[25] See Kain (2004, p. 261).

[26] That question of naturalism need not arise until specific elements of any moral empirical realism are identified that might conflict with the theoretical empirical realism, and even then interpretations that allow for naturalism are available. Setting out an interpretation of Kant's ethics that is compatible with a metaphysical but not a methodological naturalism is the second main thread of my book (Rauscher 2015).

who shares whatever those elements are based upon; for example, obligation under the categorical imperative would hold for any possible being with practical reason regardless of whether that being would share our forms of intuition of space and time. Kain rejects any transcendental idealism in ethics for other reasons, holding to what I would call a transcendental realism that takes the moral law to be based "in the nature of things" not limited to the human will (Kain 2004, p. 303). But if one accepts a transcendental idealism that bases moral validity on practical reason and thus justifies the validity of practical reason for empirical moral experience, one could be an empirical realist who holds that morality is part of the "nature of things" as objects in nature, namely empirically existing rational beings and whatever moral elements help to constitute their moral experience, because they embody practical reason from which morality stems.

These three examples are meant to show that using a two-level approach to the question of moral realism in Kant would help to clarify or improve some current approaches. Many complications arise when one asks the question whether Kant was a moral realist. Using the distinction between the transcendental and empirical levels of realism and idealism will help to pose that question in the correct way, one that is appropriate to the innovative philosophical approach taken in Kant's moral theory.

Literature

Kant

GMS   Grundlegung zur Metaphysik der Sitten, AA 4
KrV   Kritik der reinen Vernunft, AA 3 (B) and 4 (A)
MM II Moral Mrongovius II, AA 29

English translations are taken from the series *The Cambridge Edition of the Works of Immanuel Kant*, Cambridge University Press (1992 ff.).
All page and line numbers in parentheses refer to the so-called Akademie-Ausgabe (AA), i.e., to *Kant's gesammelte Schriften*, herausgegeben von der *Königlich Preußischen Akademie der Wissenschaften*, Berlin: Walter de Gruyter (1900 ff.).

Secondary Literature

Ameriks, Karl (2013): "Vindicating Autonomy: Kant, Sartre, and O'Neill." In: Oliver Sensen (ed.): *Kant on Moral Autonomy*. Cambridge: Cambridge University Press, pp. 53–70.

Bojanowski, Jochen (2012): "Is Kant a Moral Realist?" In: Dieter Heidemann (ed.): *Kant and Contemporary Moral Philosophy, Kant Yearbook*. Berlin/Boston: Walter de Gruyter, pp. 1–22.

Kain, Patrick (2004): "Self-legislation in Kant's Moral Philosophy." In: *Archiv für Geschichte der Philosophie* 86/3, pp. 257–306.

Rauscher, Frederick (2002): "Kant's Moral Anti-Realism." In: *Journal of the History of Philosophy* 40, pp. 477–499.

Rauscher, Frederick (2015): *Naturalism and Realism in Kant's Ethics*. Cambridge: Cambridge University Press.

Sayre-McCord, Geoffrey (1988): *Essays on Moral Realism*. Ithaca: Cornell University Press.

Sensen, Oliver (2011): *Kant on Human Dignity*. Cambridge: Cambridge University Press.

Stern, Robert (2011): *Understanding Moral Obligation: Kant, Hegel, Kierkegaard*. Cambridge: Cambridge University Press.

Street, Sharon (2010): "What Is Constructivism in Ethics and Metaethics?" In: *Philosophy Compass* 5, pp. 363–84.

Wood, Allen (1999): *Kant's Ethical Thought*. Cambridge: Cambridge University Press.

Melissa Zinkin
Kantian Constructivism, Respect, and Moral Depth

Abstract This paper defends a version of Kantian constructivism that focuses on the role of the feeling of respect for the moral law. For Kant, the moral worth of an action is constructed by the subject in a way analogous to the way the subject constructs objects of experience in the first *Critique*. Just as the formulations of the categorical imperative can be seen to be analogous to the categories of the understanding, so also can the feeling of respect be understood to be analogous to the a priori forms of intuition in the first *Critique*. By focusing on the role of the feeling of respect in constructing the moral worth of an action, Kantian constructivism can be defended against some of its critics. We can also see that for Kant the nature of moral worth requires understanding the moral law rather than knowledge of it.

* * *

> What justifies a conception of justice is not its being true to an order antecedent to and given to us, but its congruence with our deeper understanding of ourselves and our aspirations.
> – John Rawls, "Kantian Constructivism in Moral Theory," p. 519

In the second book of *Emile*, Rousseau argues, against Locke, that one should not reason with children. According to Rousseau, of all the faculties of man, reason is the one that develops with the most difficulty and the latest. He provides the following parody of a moral lesson to a child:

> Master: You must not do that.
> Child: And why must I not do it?
> Master: Because it is bad to do.
> Child: Bad to do! What is bad to do?
> Master: What you are forbidden to do.
> Child: What is bad about doing what I am forbidden to do?
> Master: You are punished for having disobeyed.
> Child: I shall fix it so that nothing is known about it.
> Master: You will be spied on.
> Child: I shall hide.
> Master: You will be questioned.
> Child: I shall lie.
> Master: You must not lie.

https://doi.org/10.1515/9783110574517-002

> Child: Why must I not lie?
> Master: Because it is bad to do, etc. [...]¹

Rousseau continues to say that, since children cannot grasp (*sentir*) the reason for duty,² when one tries to reason with them about what is the right thing to do, what results is that

> you teach (children) to be dissemblers, fakers, and liars in order to extort rewards or escape punishments. Finally by accustoming them always to cover a secret motive with an apparent motive, you yourselves give them the means of deceiving you ceaselessly, of depriving you of the knowledge of their true character, and of fobbing you and others off with vain words when the occasion serves. (Rousseau 1979, p. 91)

For Rousseau, children do not understand why they must do their duty because they do not yet have the faculty of reason. As a result, morality for them is like a mask that they can put on or take off. But what exactly is it that children are missing? What is it about the faculty of reason that enables those who possess it appropriately to grasp their duty and be moral such that they are not dissemblers or fakers?

I think that we can find in Kant an account of practical reason that shows how we are capable of grasping our duty through reason and hence how reason can be the source of morality. I will make my case by means of a discussion of Kant's metaethics, specifically, a defense of Kant as a metaethical constructivist. For Kant, the rightness of an action is something that is constructed by us from the activity of our own faculty of reason. I am able to grasp my duty and have a good will because I am the one who has constructed what it is that I ought to do. By "grasping my duty" I mean understanding the reason why some action is right for me to do. I will argue that for Kant the activity of the construction of moral value, in addition to being the practical activity of solving the problem of what I ought to do, as in Christine Korsgaard's account, is also that through which I understand why I ought to do what I ought to do.

Much of the contemporary debate over metaethics concerns whether moral philosophy should be taken to be a kind of knowledge. According to Korsgaard, what is wrong with moral realism is that it considers ethics to be a kind of

---

1 Rousseau (1979, p. 90).
2 "Connaître le bien et le mal, sentir la raison des devoirs de l'homme, n'est pas l'affaire d'un enfant."

applied knowledge.³ For her, morality cannot consist of facts we can know, but rather is what results from the practical activity of thinking about what one ought to do. Only in this way can morality be something we have to care about.⁴ This constructivist view of ethics is inspired by Korsgaard's interpretation of Kant. Korsgaard's version of constructivism has, however, recently been subject to much criticism. Critics have argued that Korsgaard does not rule out moral realism, and, moreover that she should not, since she cannot show that we can get morality simply from what is constitutive of rational agency. I will argue, however, that for Kant morality *is* a kind of cognition, albeit a kind different from the standard realist version, and that once we see this Kant's own constructivism can be defended against many of the realist criticisms that have been leveled against Korsgaard's version of constructivism. Once we see that for Kant rational agency requires a grasping, or understanding, of the moral law, then we will see how rational agency can indeed give us normativity.

My interpretation of Kant will focus on the role of the feeling of respect in his moral philosophy.⁵ Kant writes that respect is a feeling that is

> self-wrought by a rational concept and therefore specifically different from all feelings (received by influence), which come down to inclination or fear. What I recognize immediately as a law for myself I recognize with respect, which signifies merely the consciousness of the subordination of my will to law, without mediation of other influences on my sense. (GMS: 402)⁶

I will argue that, for Kant, the feeling of respect with which I recognize a law as a law for myself plays a role in the construction of the moral worth of an action. Moreover, I will argue that the feeling of respect involves a kind of knowledge of the moral law, namely an understanding of it, which is how I will interpret what Rousseau refers to as a "grasping" (*sentir*) of the reason for our duty. By focusing

---

3 See Korsgaard (2008b, p. 317).
4 Cf. Korsgaard (1996, pp. 13f.).
5 See Bagnoli (2013). Bagnoli also argues that "the feeling of respect plays a cognitive but non evidential role in the account of the cognitive and practical powers of reason" (Bagnoli 2013, p. 155). According to Bagnoli, "the 'basis of construction' is the subjective experience of respect for the legislative capacity itself. It is an emotional mode of practical knowledge of oneself as an agent" (Bagnoli 2013, p. 155). In what follows, I am in agreement with Bagnoli. I hope my paper contributes to Bagnoli's insights by showing how the feeling of respect can provide an argument against the threat of moral skepticism that Korsgaard thinks comes with moral realism. I also show how for Kant the self-understanding that is the result of the feeling of respect for the moral law is systematic.
6 For the list of abbreviations of Kant's works, see the "Literature" section of this paper.

on the feeling of respect, I think it is possible to provide a *Kantian* response to some of the criticisms of Korsgaard's version of Kantian constructivism.[7]

I therefore agree with recent commentators who have noted that what is wrong with moral realism from an antirealist, constructivist, perspective is not really that it considers morality to be a kind of knowledge rather than a practical activity, as Korsgaard argues. This is because it is possible for knowledge itself to be a practical activity. The problem, then, is not with taking morality to be a kind of knowledge, but with taking it to be a specific kind of knowledge, namely, knowledge of moral facts that are part of the "fabric of the world" and independent of us.[8] It is therefore possible for there to be a constructivist account of practical knowledge. My view is that once we consider moral cognition in terms of understanding rather than knowledge, we can see that Kant in fact has a constructivist account of practical cognition. I will argue that for Kant, the feeling of respect is that through which we understand the authority of the moral law and this understanding is the result of our systematically determining, or constructing, our will with regard to it. Moreover, I will argue, only if we construct our actions in this way can they have moral worth.

I will proceed as follows. In section 1, I will present a realist criticism of Korsgaard's Kantian constructivism. In section 2, I will give my own version of Kantian constructivism that differs from Korsgaard's and which can address the criticism discussed in section 1, namely that Korsgaard's constructivism does not rule out realism. In section 3, I will provide an account of the feeling of respect in Kant's moral philosophy and show the role it plays in the construction of morality. In section 4, I will then show how my version of Kantian constructivism can be also used to respond to the realist criticisms of constructivism that it cannot show that normativity is constitutive of agency.

1 Fitzpatrick's Critique of Korsgaard

Constructivism is the metaethical position that argues that moral values and moral norms are made – constructed – by human agents. This view has its origin in Rawls' interpretation of Kant, according to which moral truths are "constructions of reason" (Rawls 1980, p. 519). Constructivist moral theories

---

[7] See Bagnoli (2013, p. 155): "The 'basis of construction' is the subjective experience of respect for the self-legislative capacity itself. This moral feeling conveys our rational awareness of rational agency and shows our responsiveness to the demands of practical reason. It is an emotional mode of practical knowledge of oneself as an agent."
[8] See Bagnoli (2013), Engstrom (2013) and Bojanowski (2012).

are opposed to realist theories, which claim that there are moral truths independent of us that we can know or discover. However, as the use of the term "constructivist" implies, for the constructivist, the fact that morality is made, rather than discovered by us, does not mean that it is merely subjective or based on a whim. Rather, this construction occurs according to a plan, or, as in Rawls' account, from some "point of view that all can accept" (Rawls 1980, p. 519), and is therefore objective.

Today, when philosophers discuss Kantian constructivism, we usually have Korsgaard's version of constructivism in mind, which is based on her interpretation of Kant. According to Korsgaard, Kant is a moral constructivist because he sees moral value – what is right or good – as what is the result of a rational procedure. As Korsgaard puts it: "according to constructivism, normative concepts are not (in the first instance [...]) the names of objects or of facts [...] that we encounter in the world. They are the names of the solutions of problems (that is, practical problems faced by an agent), problems to which we give names to make them out as objects for practical thought" (Korsgaard 2008b, p. 322). According to Korsgaard, ethics is therefore not a kind of knowledge, but is rather the practical activity of solving practical problems. Indeed, this must be the case if ethics, which is supposed to tell us what we ought to do, is to be a guide for action. Solutions to practical problems, not the knowledge of moral facts, are what guide action.

For Korsgaard, morality is what solves the problem of what I ought to do. We solve this problem in a way that is compelling to us by constructing the solution from the ingredients of the problem itself. The constructivist asks: "is there some feature of the problem itself, or of the function named by the concept, that will show us the way to its solution?" (Korsgaard 2008b, p. 323). For example, what Kant saw as the problem of free action, namely, "how can I act according to a principle and still be free?", can be solved once we see that the principle that we act on is the principle that results from the use of our own reason. Here, the principle is not a fact about the world, but something that we construct as the answer to the problem of how it is possible to act with a free will. In the same way, the answer to the question of what I ought to do is one that I come up with myself by reflecting on the conditions of agency. According to Korsgaard, once we think about what are the conditions for rational agency, we will see that in order to be able to act, we must value something, and in order to be able to value something, we must value that which is the source of value, which is our humanity. For Korsgaard, then, once we understand what it is to be an agent, we will see that it requires that we value humanity as an end in itself. In addition, constructivism solves the problem of moral motivation, since if what is the right thing to do is my solution to a problem that is mine, then I will be motivated to do it. If, by contrast, what is the right thing to do is simply some fact that I can know, then it is still an open question of whether I will be motivated to perform this action.

The constructivist account of ethics that Korsgaard has argued for has, however, been subject to much criticism. William Fitzpatrick's paper "The Practical Turn in Ethical Theory: Korsgaard's Constructivism, Realism and the Nature of Normativity" pinpoints several flaws in Korsgaard's arguments. Central among them are the claims that Korsgaard does not have a convincing argument against realism and that she does not show that we can get normativity from the generic conditions of the exercise of agency.

According to Fitzpatrick, Korsgaard has done nothing to argue against the realist, who claims that "among a set of rival normative principles that equally solve a practical problem of agency, one principle is best if it has the virtue of being true" (Fitzpatrick 2005, p. 685). In fact, Fitzpatrick argues: "Korsgaard's idea of anchoring a practical principle to the will via its role in practical problem solving turns out to be entirely compatible with realism" (Fitzpatrick 2005, p. 685). Fitzpatrick notes that if the formula of humanity turned out to be a truth about the absolute value of humanity as an end in itself rather than a construction of reason, this could serve just as well as the solution to the problem of what the end of my actions must be. Indeed, its truth could make it the best solution to the problem. But, whereas Korsgaard argues that a principle can only have normative force for us if it is one that we ourselves construct, Fitzpatrick replies that if a principle is in fact true, then this can also give it a normative force. Certainly a principle that is constructed, but false, would have no genuine normative force. And, knowing that a practical principle is the right one can indeed motivate us to act on it. As Fitzpatrick notes: "the connection to agency [...] is no less clear and secure just because the principle is a realist truth instead of being constructed. A principle needn't be constructed from the will's procedures in order to be shown to have practical relevance for it" (Fitzpatrick 2005, p. 688). He continues to argue that, although ethics is no doubt practical, this does not mean that it is not also theoretical. It can be the "search for knowledge of a normative truth for the sake of the practical end of living well – and the theoretical aspect needn't pose any obstacle to meeting the demand for practical relevance" (Fitzpatrick 2005, p. 691). Whether or not Korsgaard can respond to Fitzpatrick, I think that Kant can. In what follows, I will present my own version of Kantian constructivism that can respond to the challenges that Fitzpatrick makes to Korsgaard's version of constructivism.

2 Kant's Constructivism

What distinguishes constructivism from realism is the idea that moral worth and moral norms are what result from the activity of practical reason and are not truths that exist independently of the subject. For the constructivist, something has moral worth because practical reasoners value it; we are the source of the value of the action. We do not value it because it already has some independent value. My own account of Kantian constructivism will emphasize that we are the source of the moral worth of an action because it is something that we construct, in the sense of *make*.[9] It therefore cannot be some truth independent of us that we discover, as the realist claims, since no moral value exists independently of our making it.

As Fitzpatrick points out, Korsgaard's description of constructivism, which makes morality the "solution to a problem" leaves it ambiguous how this solution comes into being. For example, in mathematics, although I can arrive at the solution to some problem through a mathematical procedure, it is arguable and indeed very plausible that the following of the procedure is not what makes the answer true. The answer is true because it is a fact of mathematics, and following the procedure has simply helped me to figure this out. Although I might *understand* why the solution is true through the following of the procedure, it is not the procedure that makes the solution true, nor is the procedure what must compel me to assent to its truth. What makes me say that the solution to a math problem is true is simply the fact that it is true. Similarly, Fitzpatrick would argue, although it is possible that I will be motivated to perform a certain action if it is the solution I have come up with to a problem that I, myself, have, this does not mean that I have constructed the moral value of the action. It could still be something independent of me. Nor does it mean that construction is the only source of motivation. According to Fitzpatrick, from Korsgaard's account, it is still possible that ethics is "a branch of knowledge, knowledge of the normative part of the world" (Korsgaard 1996, p. 37).

My account of Kantian constructivism avoids this criticism of Korsgaard by showing that constructivism is in fact incompatible with realism because it argues that what it means for the morality of an action to be constructed is not simply that the action is the solution to a problem, but also that it is something that we make in the sense of putting something new into the world. When I solve the practical problem of what to do, not only do I now

---

9 See Bagnoli (2013, p. 167), and Bojanowski (2012, p. 4).

gain the knowledge of what action I should perform, but I *make* my will into a good will. There is now an instance of rightness in the world where previously there was not.

In this way, Kant's practical philosophy is like his theoretical philosophy. Fredrick Rauscher has convincingly compared Kant's moral philosophy to his theoretical philosophy and argued that it is also transcendentally ideal. Rauscher argues that for Kant, moral norms, like the objectivity of experience in his theoretical philosophy, are mind-dependent, and hence ideal and not real. Therefore Kant should be taken to be a moral antirealist.[10] In addition, however, I think that a comparison to Kant's theoretical philosophy can also show that Kant is not simply a moral antirealist for whom morality is dependent on the subject, but also a constructivist, for whom morality is something that we *make*. [11] In the *Critique of Pure Reason*, Kant explicitly endorses the kind of constructivism I have in mind when he writes: "we can cognize a priori in things only what we ourselves have put into them" (KrV: Bxvii). Kant's point here is that we can cognize objects of experience a priori because we are the ones who have constructed them. Our own cognitive faculties are what produce a spatio-temporal ordering of representations according to a priori rules, and such an order would not be there were it not for our cognitive activity.

For Kant, the moral worth of an action is constructed by the subject in a way analogous to the way the subject constructs objects of experience in the first *Critique*. The way that I construct the moral worth of an action is by following the "formulae" (*Formeln*) (GMS: 436) of the moral law, the three versions of the categorical imperative. Just as, in Kant's first *Critique*, the concepts of our faculty of understanding – the categories – provide the a priori rule according to which we can synthesize representations and construct an object of thought, so, in Kant's moral philosophy, the formulae of the moral law, which is the law of our own reason, provide the a priori rules according to which we can construct a moral "object," that is, a right action and a will that has moral worth.

But this is not all. According to Kant's argument in the first *Critique*, when objects are thought by the categories alone, our knowledge is transcendent and goes beyond the bounds of experience. Therefore, in addition to the categories of the understanding, which provide the discursive condition for the construction of the objects of experience, another, sensible, component is

---

10 See Rauscher (2002, p. 485): "moral right depends for Kant in its entirety upon actual human consciousness of the categorical imperative, and is ideal and not real."
11 According to Bojanowski, Kant should be understood to be a moral idealist. He writes: "The idealism I want to ascribe to Kant holds not that the good depends on the human mind, but that its existence depends on self-affection in moral cognizers" (Bojanowski 2012, p.4).

required for experience to be possible. These are the a priori forms of intuition, space and time, which provide the sensible condition for the objects of our experience, and which are also the limiting conditions of our experience. Objects that do not appear to us in a spatial or temporal form are transcendent and cannot be objects of experience. Similarly, in Kant's moral philosophy, there is, I believe, a condition for the construction of morality analogous to that of sensibility in his theoretical philosophy. In addition to the formal condition – the formulae of the moral law – there is also the feeling of respect for the moral law, which is the limiting condition for the will. If I do not act from respect for the moral law, then I am following the CI procedure in a way that can be said to be "transcendent." A transcendent moral action is one that is willed just for the sake of its "rightness," or its conformity to what the moral law prescribes in general, without attending to how one's own will should be determined by the moral law in this particular instance. In this case my will is "objectively determined" by the moral law but not also "subjectively determined" (GMS: 400 f.) by it and the moral worth of my action can be said to be "empty" in a way analogous to the way concepts without intuition are empty in the first Critique. I have made my will conform with what is right for the sake of what is right, but still do not grasp why it is right. That is to say, I do not act with respect for the moral law.

When, in the *Critique of Practical Reason*, Kant writes that the moral law strikes down our self-conceit, he is indicating the limiting function of the feeling of respect. Our respect for the moral law is the recognition of its power to humiliate our self-conceit. Kant writes that the moral law

> strikes down self-conceit altogether, since all claims to esteem for oneself that precede accord (*Übereinstimmung*) with the moral law are null and quite unwarranted because certainty of a disposition in accord with this law is the first condition of any worth of a person [...] and any presumption prior to this is false and opposed to the law. (KpV: 73)

In other words, the feeling of respect for the moral law is the "certainty of a disposition in accord with this law." It is what limits our false esteem of ourselves that we have worth – even, and perhaps especially, when we are doing our duty – and ensures that such worth is only possible when our actions are performed in accord with the moral law, that is, with respect for the moral law.[12] Here the feeling of respect for the moral law is what distinguishes someone

---

[12] Ware argues that self-conceit is a kind of transcendental illusion. He writes that for Kant self-conceit is "the illusion of mistaking a maxim of satisfying the inclinations for an unconditional principle of the will" (Ware 2014, p. 736). Kant indeed writes that self-conceit is what occurs

from Rousseau's child, who could presumptuously claim esteem for himself when he does not do "what is bad to do," but without having the certainty of a disposition in accord with this law, that is, the feeling of respect.

Once we pay attention to the role the feeling of respect for the moral law plays in the construction of an action, we can see how a constructivist account of moral worth in Kant is in fact incompatible with a realist account of morality according to which what is right is a truth that is independent of us. For Kant, an action that is willed just for the sake of following a moral principle but without the feeling of respect – even if this principle is in fact true and something independent of us, as realists claim – cannot be an action that has moral worth. Such an action would be morally transcendent, or empty. It would be an action that is done just for rightness sake, but not one that produces a good will. It is therefore not an action we ought to do.

For Kant, the actions that we ought to perform are only those that are from respect for the moral law.[13] In other words, the feeling of respect for the moral law is part of what constitutes not only the goodness of the will but also the rightness of its action. What I ought to do is that action which is from the feeling of respect for the moral law. It is not that action of which I merely have knowledge that it is the right thing to do and for which I therefore ought to have respect. For Kant, respect is not simply that feeling that I have with regard to what I know is right. The feeling of respect is rather part of what constitutes the rightness of the action in the first place. Kant writes that "[r]espect is actually the representation of a worth that infringes on my self-love" (GMS: 401, note). Without the feeling of respect, we would not be conscious of the worth of the moral law in our action. If I do not feel respect for the moral law in performing my action then it is not one that, from a moral point of view, I ought to be performing. Here Kant's moral philosophy is different from his theoretical philosophy where there are two distinct faculties that constitute experience: understanding and sensibility. In Kant's moral philosophy, just one faculty is the source of morality; reason. The feeling of respect is not some moral sense distinct from reason, but is instead a feeling that is "self-wrought" from a

---

when self-love, without taking the moral law into account, "makes itself lawgiving and the unconditional practical principle" (KpV: 74), and this implies that actions done from self-conceit would not have the form of a moral action. We would lie, for example, and justify this with respect to self-love. I am arguing, however, that there is a form of self-conceit in which our actions can still have the external form of morality, but are not moral since the certainty of their rightness is prior to any determination by the moral law. I could simply be motivated by the self-conceit of my self-righteousness of doing what is "right" (see Zinkin 2006, p. 49).

13 Cf.: "*duty is the necessity of an action from respect for the law*" (GMS: 400).

concept of reason, the moral law. As such, respect is a part of the structure of our rational agency and of what is constitutive of morality.

Let us take as an example the giving of an apology. I can, for example, know that I have hurt you and that an apology is in order and is what I ought to do. But what morality requires is not simply giving an apology because I know I ought to – because it is the solution of the problem of what I ought to do – but rather the giving of an apology with the knowledge of *why* I have wronged you and thus of why the apology really is in order. That is, the action that is required is one that is from respect for the moral law through which I recognize the worth of the moral law as what infringes on my self-conceit. But if this is the case, then the moral worth of the action that is required is one that can only be constructed by me, as a result of my own rational activity, since part of the requirement is that it be from respect for the moral law.

By focusing on the role of the feeling of respect in Kant's account of morality, we can now see that morality is not a matter of knowledge of moral facts, as realists claim, but rather of what I will call the understanding of what is one's duty. That is, it is a matter of me determining my subject in such a way such that I perform an action in the right way – with an understanding of my duty. Here we can now say that for Kant morality is a kind of cognition. Rather than simply being the solution to a problem, as Korsgaard claims, morality involves an understanding of what I ought to do. Unlike knowledge, which is propositional, understanding concerns how the parts relate to a whole, and hence need not be propositional. And, whereas knowledge can be of isolated facts, understanding is of systems. Understanding, like a skill or techne, indicates a kind of mastery. To understand something is to be able to explain how it works or how it is done and to see how the parts are organized with respect to the whole.[14] This sense of understanding as a techne is, I think, behind Kant's constructivist statement in the first *Critique* cited earlier that "we cognize a priori in things only what we have ourselves put into them" (KrV: Bxiii). I think it also plays a role in his moral philosophy. For Kant, we have an understanding of why something is our duty because we have made it our duty through following the formulae of the categorical imperative. Through following the CI procedure (systematically, for all three formulae, as will become clear in what follows) we gain a respect for the moral law – which indicates our understanding of its authority for us. And, understanding why an action is our duty

---

14 See Zagzebski (2001, pp. 240 f.).

is part of what makes it what we ought to do.[15] If I do not understand why I ought to apologize, then I ought not to. Or else I will be like Rousseau's child who uses "vain words when the occasion serves."

By seeing morality as a kind of understanding rather than knowledge, we can respond to Fitzpatrick's criticism of Korsgaard by saying that, even though, in mathematics, the *truth* of the solution to a problem might not depend on the construction procedure by which I arrive at it, but can be independent of it, nevertheless, in the case of moral action, the *understanding* of the rightness of the action is indeed dependent on the procedure by which I arrive at its rightness. And it is in the *understanding* of why an action is the one I ought to perform that its moral worth, as well as its normativity for me, consists, rather than in any independent moral truth. We can then say that for Kant the norm that is the result of a construction procedure is not simply the solution to a moral problem that we have, but is also a norm that – through the construction procedure – we come to understand as normative for us.[16]

3 Respect

I will now give a more detailed account of the subjective determination of the will through the feeling of respect for the moral law that shows the role it plays for Kant in constructing morality. Once we are clear about the role of respect in Kant's moral philosophy we can see how morality is indeed constitutive of rational agency. Kant can therefore respond to Fitzpatrick's second criticism of Korsgaard that one cannot get normativity simply from rational agency. I will argue that for Kant rational agency includes not just the requirement that in order to act we need a reason in the sense of an end that

---

[15] See Engstrom: "Also contained in that self-consciousness (of practical knowledge) is the understanding that the power of agency belonging to the self that figures in such self-knowledge lies in the efficacy of its capacity for practical knowledge, so that it is through judging that they should φ that persons choose to φ and thereby φ. Persons, then, as practical knowers, necessarily understand their agency as the efficacy of a capacity for such rational self-knowledge [...]" (Engstrom 2013, p. 147).

[16] See Bojanowski: "Genuine practical cognition is not only the cognition of a given object as good. Instead, the existence of the object needs to be brought about by the cognition itself. Practical cognition therefore must precede the given normative facts that obtain in the world. In order to issue an action, it must, in contrast to theoretical knowledge, be the source of an emotion; the feeling of 'respect for the moral law'" (Bojanowski 2012, p. 13).

is a good worth pursuing, as in Korsgaard's account,[17] but also that we need a reason in the sense of an explanation that we can grasp. We need to understand why, in the scheme of things, our action is significant and is worth performing. This would not be an explanation from the third-person theoretical perspective,[18] but would rather be a first-person explanation to ourselves through which we understand the reason why we ought to perform an action. It is by understanding our purpose in acting that we constitute our identity in the sense of integrity that Korsgaard herself describes.[19] On my view, practical reason is the source of our integrity because it is what systematically orders our maxims according to their value in a way that we can understand the reason why an action ought to be performed. Because it orders our maxims according to a fundamental principle, it is also the source of the depth of our identity – an identity in which our motives of action are systematically integrated into our self with respect to a practical principle – without which we would merely have the superficial morality of children.[20]

Respect plays a role in the construction of the moral worth of an action because it is that through which we understand the authority of the moral law. In the *Groundwork*, Kant explains the role of respect as follows. He writes:

> [...] *duty is the necessity of an action from respect for law.* For an object as the effect of my proposed action I can indeed have *inclination*, but *never respect*, just because it is merely an effect and never an activity of a will [...] Only what is connected with my will merely as a ground and never as an effect, what does not serve my inclination but outweighs it or at least excludes it altogether from calculations in making a choice – hence the mere law itself – can be an object of respect and so a command. Now an action from duty is to put aside entirely the influence of inclination and with it every object of the will; hence there is left for the will nothing that could determine it except objectively the *law* and subjectively *pure respect* for this practical law, and so the maxim of complying with such a law even if it infringes upon all my inclinations. (GMS: 400 f.)

---

17 Or at least on Fitzpatrick's construal of it (see Fitzpatrick 2005, p. 662). Korsgaard's own view, especially her account of practical identity is more complex than Fitzpatrick allows. See Korsgaard (1996, pp. 100–103). The aim of my paper is not to argue against Korsgaard, but to show how Kant himself could respond to criticisms of Korsgaard's version of Kantian constructivism.
18 See Korsgaard (1996, p. 16).
19 See Korsgaard (1996, p. 102).
20 This is not to say that the systematic unity of the self is not part of Korsgaard's account, but rather that she does not make it as central as I do. Korsgaard writes: "In fact deliberative action by its very nature imposes constitutional order on the soul. When you deliberate about what to do and then do it, what you are doing is organizing your appetite, reason and spirit, into the unified system that can be attributed to you as a person. Deliberative action pulls the parts of the soul together into a unified system" (Korsgaard 2008a, p. 119).

To act from respect for the moral law is not simply to know what is the right thing to do – for my will to be "objectively determined" by the law – but also for me to understand why what is objectively the right thing to do is what *I* ought to do, that is, for my will to be subjectively determined by the law. To act from respect for the moral law is therefore to incorporate the moral law into my own subjective will. For example, I could help someone in need because I know it is "the right thing to do." This would be for my will to be objectively determined by the law.[21] But it is only when I ask myself the further question "why have I chosen to do what is the right thing to do?" that my will can be subjectively determined by the law. Here I do not simply adopt an end. Rather, I introspect in order to understand why I have chosen to do this "right" action. I seek to explain this action to myself. Such introspection produces understanding. After reflecting on my motive of action I might come to see that the reason I wanted to do what was the right thing to do is from self-love and the desire for honor. Here, along with a deeper understanding of the structure of my motivations I feel the humiliation that accompanies such self-knowledge of my self-love. But I also now recognize the worth of the moral law as what infringes on my self-love. It is this recognition of the worth of the moral law in subjectively determining my will that gives the will its moral worth. But to recognize the moral law as a law for myself is to understand why it must be the law for my willing – because it is the law of my own reason.

Respect for the moral law is thus the understanding of its authority such that I have a reason to put aside the influence of the inclinations and act for the sake of the law alone.[22] Here respect is indeed a kind of intuition – that of the authoritativeness of the moral law as the law of my own will. But, it should be noted, just as in Kant's first *Critique* in which something can only be an object of intuition because it is structured through forms of intuition that are subjective and a priori, so in Kant's moral philosophy, we can only grasp the authoritativeness of the moral law because we ourselves have thought through our motives for action with regard to it and come to an understanding of its rightness *for us*. It is in this way that the feeling of respect is "self-wrought." Just as the a priori forms of intuition are the subjective condition for the construction of

---

[21] Here the feeling of respect functions similarly to that of conscience. See Schmidt/Schönecker (2015).

[22] See Bagnoli (2013, p. 178): "the experience of respect establishes the special kind of efficacy that is peculiar to practical subjects insofar as they are autonomous. Respect conveys practical knowledge as knowledge of oneself as a practical subject and in this function it can produce a motive. Second, respect works as a deliberative constraint that regulates self-love and self-interest. It thus accounts for the general practice of self-government."

particular spatial and temporal forms, so our respect for the moral law is the subjective condition for the construction of the normativity and the moral worth of my action.

There are therefore two ways in which an action can be done for the sake of the moral law, only one of which has moral worth. One is for the will to only be objectively determined by the moral law. This would be to obey the law without regard for how it relates to my inclinations. It is to do what is right just because one knows that it is right. Someone who acts in this way has a superficial relation to what is right and can be said to act in a morally "empty" way. Like Rousseau's child, such a form of morality is "fake." The action is transcendent and empty of moral worth. This is not because one acts for a motive other than that of the moral law. It is rather because, in following the moral law, one has not engaged in any "calculations in making a choice" and hence has not come to understand how the moral law is authoritative for their own particular set of inclinations. This view of moral worth is consistent with moral realism, for which what is right is something that is part of the "fabric of the world" and distinct from us. Here we can see why, for Korsgaard, such a moral view can lead to moral skepticism. Korsgaard writes that "the moral skeptic is someone who thinks that the explanation of moral concepts will be one that does not support the claims that morality makes on us. He thinks that once we see what is really behind morality, we won't care about it any more" (Korsgaard 1996, p. 13). If morality is just acting for the sake of the moral law, it is possible that morality is just a superficial mask behind which hides an empty shell, or the thoughts of a child. It is not something that is deeply lodged in us.

The other way to act for the sake of the moral law is for the will to be both objectively determined by the law and subjectively determined by respect for the moral law. In this case, I construct an action that has moral worth since I subjectively determine my will by excluding my inclinations from my calculations in making a choice. I sort through my motives and grasp the one that is most fundamental; the moral law. I help someone in need because I understand that to do so is to be in accord with my own reason and not simply because, as Rousseau's child might say: "it is my duty." In this way I am the source of the normativity of my action, since what I ought to do is what results from this procedure of introspection.

Here it should be emphasized that an action is not something distinct from the way in which it is performed. Rather, the respect for the law with which I act is part of my action. It is not the case that there is an action, such as not enslaving someone and then, in addition to this, my performing the action from respect for the moral law. For Kant, acting from respect for the law is what constitutes – or constructs – the action as the action that it is, namely, one that has moral worth. An action done without respect for the moral law and one done with respect for the moral law are two distinct actions. This is analogous to Kant's theoretical philosophy in which the mere concept of a substance is not the same thing as a substance as a possible object of experience. The former can be the concept of a soul. The latter cannot be. A concept of what is right is not itself right. What is right is our making our will conform to the concept.[23]

I have argued that it is, in part, through respect for the moral law that we construct the moral worth of an action. The feeling of respect gives an action its moral worth because it is that through which we understand, or "grasp" the authoritativeness of the moral law with regard to our maxims of action and hence "make" our own subjective will a good will. Without the feeling of respect, there would be nothing of real moral value in the world. Rather there

---

[23] Here one can give a response to realist critics of Korsgaard who argue that the rightness of, for example, not treating someone like a slave, is not constructed through the activity of willing according to the categorical imperative, as Korsgaard claims, but rather that the rightness is there all along as a fact about humanity, and it is this fact that is the source of the rightness of the action. In Watkins/Fitzpatrick (2002, p. 361) the authors argue that moral realism provides a more natural and direct way to think about moral worth. They write: "What is wrong about enslaving someone, for example, seems to be something straightforwardly and simply about her, given what she is – the dignity that belongs to her as a rational being. To cash out the wrongness of such an action and its normative force for me in a way that requires a detour through a story about what I have to do in order to exercise my will at all seems like a move in precisely the wrong direction. It does not seem true to ordinary moral experience, which certainly does not represent other people's value and its significance for us as deriving from commitments bound up with the exercise of our own wills under certain generic constraints inherent to the nature of willing. The phenomenology, for what it is worth, is that other people, as rational agents, simply matter, and that this makes it inappropriate for us to treat them as if they did not, apart from any commitments that might arise generally through the exercise of our own wills." According to Watkins and Fitzpatrick, constructivist accounts thus give us a counter-intuitive and roundabout way of arguing for the rightness or wrongness of an action. But their argument against constructivism assumes that what is at issue is the worth of actions considered in abstraction from the will that performs them, that is, with the wrongness of enslavement, rather than with the worth of the will that enslaves someone. Yet Kant is not concerned with the worth of moral facts as such, but rather with the worth of a good will. For Kant, a story about the exercise of the will is thus not a detour around the wrongness of the action, but is instead what focuses on that in which the morality of the action consists, namely, the will. On my interpretation of Kant, even if it is a fact about us that we have a dignity in virtue of our rational nature, what gives our action moral worth is that we act from respect for the moral law which instructs us about this fact, that is, that we refrain from enslaving someone for the right reasons. For Kant, what we ought to do is not simply not enslave someone, but not enslave them for the right reasons, that is, from respect for the moral law.

would only be a superficial moral value, or morality in name only. Just as, without the a priori forms of intuition in the first *Critique*, we would only have concepts that are "empty."

I therefore think that Kant has the feeling of respect in mind as what is "analogous" to intuition when, at the conclusion of his discussion of the three formulae of the categorical imperative, he notes that the dissimilarity between them is "indeed subjectively rather than objectively practical, namely to bring an idea of reason closer to intuition (according to a certain analogy) and thereby to feeling" (GMS: 436). What I take Kant to mean here is that it is by using all three different formulae one can come to a deeper understanding of the moral law such that we grasp its authoritativeness for us and act from respect for it. Kant continues in this passage to say:

> For all maxims have 1) a form [...] 2) a matter [...] (and) 3) a complete determination of all maxims by means of that formula, namely that all maxims from one's own lawgiving are to harmonize with a possible kingdom of ends as with a kingdom of nature. A progression takes place here, as through the categories of the unity of the form of the will (its universality), the plurality of the matter (of objects, i.e., of ends), and the *allness* or totality of the system of these. But one does better always to proceed in moral *appraisal* (*Beurteilung*) by the strict method and put at its basis the universal formula of the categorical imperative: act in accordance with a maxim that can at the same time make itself a universal law. If, however, one wants to provide access for the moral law, it is very useful to bring one and the same action under the three concepts mentioned above and thereby, as far as possible bring it closer to intuition. (GMS: 436 f.)

Here we see Kant describing a progression through which we integrate the moral law into our subjective will. Kant writes that if one simply wants to appraise one's action for its morality, one does best "to proceed by the strict method and put at its basis the universal formula of the categorical imperative." This would be to objectively determine one's will by the moral law. If, however, one wants to go deeper, and "also to provide access for the moral law," and to bring the moral law "closer to intuition," Kant writes that it is useful "to bring one and the same action under the three concepts mentioned above," that is, to fit it into the system of the three formulae of the moral law.[24]

Bringing one and the same action under the systematic unity of the three formulae of the categorical imperative provides access to the moral law and brings it closer to intuition because it is through this activity that one is able

---

[24] See here Schönecker/Wood (2015, p. 174). They write that the formula of the realm of ends is here effectively the formula of autonomy, which is "stronger than the FUL and the FH, for this formula not only tells us which maxims can be thought or willed but also which maxims ought to be binding on us."

most completely to determine one's will subjectively, that is, to make the moral law our sole incentive of action, and hence act from respect for the moral law. When we do this, and hence bring the moral law closer to intuition, we understand our duty.[25] We do what practical reason requires of us in order to be moral, and what children, who do not have the faculty of reason cannot do. This understanding of our duty is what it means to act from respect for the moral law, it is also what gives our action moral worth.

The moral worth of an action is therefore what is constructed by us through the use of our own reason in deciding what to do. Here, I think that the answer to the question "why be moral?" does not just concern what can be called the motivational question of "what do I gain from this action?" (to which Korsgaard replies: "your humanity"), but also the "understanding" or teleological question of "what is the significance of this action?" to which the answer is that it fits in with who I consider myself to be (what Rawls means by its "congruence with our deeper understanding of ourselves and our aspirations," and Korsgaard means by our "integrity"). Here I am arguing that the systematizing function of the faculty of reason (which pertains to reason in both its theoretical and practical use) and not just its ends setting function is the fundamental source of the moral worth of an action. This systematizing function plays a role in morality, as we have seen, in "leading the same action" through all three formulae of the moral law so as to bring it closer to intuition. And the systematic ordering of our own ends (as well as of our ends with others) is required by the Kingdom of Ends formulation of the categorical imperative. When Kant describes the Kingdom of Ends, he does not just refer to a systematic union of various rational beings, but also to a whole "of the ends of his own that each may set for himself" (GMS: 433). That is to say that Kant considers that there ought to be a systematic unity of ends for each individual. In fact, in the *Metaphysics of Morals* Kant writes that ethics can be defined as the system of the *ends* of pure practical reason, that is, ends that are also duties,[26] which are one's own perfection and the happiness of others. Ethics therefore consists in systematically ordering

---

[25] Or "insight." In the *Jäsche Logic*, Kant puts insight as the second highest degree of cognition. He writes: "to cognize something through reason, or to have insight into it (*perspicere*)" (JL: 65). This point we reach in few things, and our cognitions become fewer and fewer the more we wish to perfect them as to content. In the *Critique of Pure Reason*, Kant writes: "When Gallileo rolled balls of weight chosen by himself down an inclined plane, or when Torricelli made the air bear a weight [...] or when Stahl [...] a light dawned on all those who study nature. They comprehended that reason has insight only into what it itself produces according to its own design [...]" (KrV: Bxii f.). For a fascinating discussion of the concept of insight in Kant, see Hebbeler (2015).
[26] See TL: 381.

our maxims with regard to these ends, and it is through being systematically organized that they gain their moral worth.[27]

In order to unify systematically our ends we must understand our actions with regard to their organizing principle. To order our ends systematically, we must place limitations on those ends that are not our duties and, indeed, strike down those of our motives whose ends are self-love and self-conceit. Such ordering is done with regard to that principle of reason with respect to which a systematic order is possible and for which it is the goal; the moral law.

4 Systematicity and Moral Agency

Once we see that reason has a systematizing role in Kant's moral philosophy that enables us to understand what our overall purpose is in acting, I think we can show how Kant can answer critics of constructivism, such as Fitzpatrick, who say that one cannot get morality simply from rational agency. According to Fitzpatrick, Korsgaard is wrong to say that we must adopt the formula of humanity as practically necessary in order to solve the practical problem of agency,[28] and that we must have a normative conception of what there is a reason to do in order to act at all. Fitzpatrick argues that it is not necessary that we value humanity in order to have a reason to act. But Kant himself has resources to respond to Fitzpatrick who focuses on Korsgaard's use of Kant's formula of humanity. Kant can say that in order to be a rational agent, one must have some ordering principle according to which one chooses one's actions. But there is only one principle that can order our reasons for action and that is the principle of practical reason itself, the moral law. Because it is what orders our ends, we are also committed to that principle by which we think through which of our ends is most "congruent with our deeper understanding of ourself" and create a systematic unity of our own ends. This commitment is what results from the procedure of acting from respect for the moral law, by which we strike down those of our ends that are from self-conceit and which cannot fit in with a rational system of ends. In other words, to act from reasons is to participate in a systematic structuring of reasons, whose principle is the moral law.[29]

---

27 See also TL: 216 and Sensen's paper in this volume.
28 See Fitzpatrick (2005, p. 681).
29 See Ferrero (2009).

Similarly, as a final point, I think that David Enoch's criticism of Korsgaard's view that normativity is constitutive of agency can be addressed by the Kantian constructivism I have presented in this paper. Enoch argues that even if the norm of self-constitution is constitutive of agency, we still need a reason to be an agent in the first place. According to Enoch, it is possible to be a schmagent, that is, someone who acts but does not have any stake in his or her action – "a nonagent who is very similar to agents but who lacks the aim (constitutive of agency but not of schmagency) of self-constitution" (Enoch 2006, p. 179). Indeed, why can't we just be aimless slackers?[30] Enoch's point is that the normativity of acting is something that is in addition to action and hence requires an additional justification than simply being what is derived from agency, since it is possible to be a schmagent and simply not care about any norms for acting.

I think Kant's answer to this objection would be just to agree that such schmagents, or slackers, are a different kind of person than agents and non-slackers, just as children are different from adults. They are people who do not or cannot make use of what Kant calls the faculty of practical reason. As a result, not only do they not have any ends in acting, but, moreover, they do not care about any ends they could have, since they have no feeling of respect for any norms. I hope to have shown that, for Kant, the faculty of practical reason is not only constitutive of the moral worth of an action but also, as that faculty from which the feeling of respect is self-wrought, it is what is constitutive of our caring about an action such that what is normative for us is a deep part of ourselves.

Literature

Kant

GMS Grundlegung zur Metaphysik der Sitten, AA 4
JL   Jäsche Logik, AA 9
KpV Kritik der praktischen Vernunft, AA 5
KrV Kritik der reinen Vernunft, AA 3 (B) und 4 (A)
TL   Metaphysische Anfangsgründe der Tugendlehre, AA 6

---

30 See Milgram (2012). I would like to thank the members of the conference on Kant's Moral Realism and Antirealism in Siegen, especially Elke Schmidt, as well as members of the philosophy department at National Taiwan University, for their helpful comments.

English translations are taken from the series *The Cambridge Edition of the Works of Immanuel Kant*, Cambridge University Press (1992 ff.), except for the *Logic*, edited and translated by Robert S. Hartman and Wolfgang Schwartz, New York: Dover (1988).

All page and line numbers in parentheses refer to the so-called Akademie-Ausgabe (AA), i.e., to *Kant's gesammelte Schriften*, herausgegeben von der *Königlich Preußischen Akademie der Wissenschaften*, Berlin: Walter de Gruyter (1900 ff.).

Secondary Literature

Bagnoli, Carla (2013): "Constructivism about Practical Knowledge." In: Carla Bagnoli (ed.): *Constructivism in Ethics*. Cambridge: Cambridge University Press, pp. 135–182.

Bojanowski, Jochen (2012): "Is Kant a Moral Realist?" In: *Kant Yearbook* 4, pp. 1–22.

Engstrom, Stephen (2013): "Constructivism about Practical Knowledge." In: Carla Bagnoli (ed.): *Constructivism in Ethics*. Cambridge: Cambridge University Press, pp. 133–152.

Enoch, David (2006): "Agency Schmagency: Why Normativity Won't Come From What is Constitutive of Action." In: *Philosophical Review* 115/2, pp. 169–198.

Ferrero, Luca (2009): "Constitutivism and the Inescapability of Agency." In: *Oxford Studies in Metaethics* 4, pp. 303–333.

FitzPatrick, William J. (2005): "The Practical Turn in Ethical Theory: Korsgaard's Constructivism, Realism, and the Nature of Normativity." In: *Ethics* 115/4, pp. 651–691.

Hebbeler, James (2015): "Kant on Necessity, Insight, and *A Priori* Knowledge." In: *Archiv für Geschichte der Philosophie* 97, pp. 34–65.

Korsgaard, Christine M. (1996): *The Sources of Normativity*. Cambridge: Cambridge University Press.

Korsgaard, Christine M. (2008a): "Self-Constitution in the Ethics of Plato and Kant." In: Christine M. Korsgaard: *The Constitution of Agency. Essays on Practical Reason and Moral Psychology*. Oxford: Oxford University Press, pp. 100–126.

Korsgaard, Christine M. (2008b): "Realism and Constructivism in Twentieth Century Moral Philosophy." In: Christine M. Korsgaard: *The Constitution of Agency. Essays on Practical Reason and Moral Psychology*. Oxford: Oxford University Press, pp. 302–326.

Milgram, Elijah (2012): "Practical Reason and the Structure of Actions." In: Edward N. Zalta (ed.): *The Stanford Encyclopedia of Philosophy* (on the web).

Rauscher, Frederick (2002): "Kant's Moral Anti-Realism." In: *Journal of the History of Philosophy* 40/4, pp. 477–499.

Rawls, John (1980): "Kantian Constructivism in Moral Theory." In: *The Journal of Philosophy* 77/9, pp. 515–572.

Rousseau, Jean-Jacques (1979): *Emile or On Education*. Translated by Allan Bloom. New York: Basic Books.

Schmidt, Elke Elisabeth/Schönecker, Dieter (2014): "Kants Philosophie des Gewissens – Skizze für eine kommentarische Interpretation." In: Mario Egger (ed.): *Neue Wege zum Verständnis von Kants Transzendental- und Moralphilosophie*. Berlin/Boston: Walter de Gruyter, pp. 279–312.

Schönecker, Dieter/Wood, Allen (2015): *Immanuel Kant's Groundwork for the Metaphysics of Morals. A Commentary*. Cambridge: Harvard University Press.

Ware, Owen (2014): "Kant on Moral Sensibility and Moral Motivation." In: *Journal of the History of Philosophy* 52/4, pp. 727–746.
Watkins, Eric/FitzPatrick, William J. (2002): "O'Neill and Korsgaard on the Construction of Normativity." In: *The Journal of Value Inquiry* 36/2, pp. 349–367.
Zagzebski, Linda (2001): "Recovering Understanding." In: Matthias Steup (ed.): *Knowledge, Truth and Duty: Essays on Epistemic Responsibility and Virtue*. Oxford: Oxford University Press, pp. 235–250.
Zinkin, Melissa (2006): "Respect for the Law and the Use of Dynamical Terms in Kant's Theory of Moral Motivation." In: *Archiv für Geschichte der Philosophie* 88/1, pp. 31–53.

Realist Interpretations of Kant

Christoph Horn
Kant's Theory of Historical Progress: A Case of Realism or Antirealism?

Abstract The debate on the ontological foundations of Kant's philosophy is usually focused on his theoretical and practical philosophy. Does Kant believe that there is an external world which pre-exists our constitution of spatio-temporal beings, as he describes it in the first *Critique?* Or is he an idealist concerning external reality? And does Kant think that we should assume the independent existence of moral values? Or do we ourselves ultimately create them? Whereas both scholarly discussions are complex and far from having an unambiguous solution, the question of realism and antirealism is rarely raised on the basis of his philosophy of history, although it is a promising approach. In this contribution, I defend the thesis that Kant, while he seems to introduce his theory of history in the sense of a mere projection, quite clearly develops the idea of an "objective progress." Seen from this perspective, his philosophy of history can also help us better understand his putative antirealism in the theoretical and practical realm.

* * *

When the question arises if Kant's overall philosophical position is best described in terms of realism or antirealism, we usually look to the *Critique of Pure Reason* to provide an answer.[1] In this context, one central issue is to decide whether the idea of Kantian transcendental idealism actually involves a realism with regard to spatio-temporal objects, according to which the objects of our experience exist independently 'out there' in the world. Or is it rather the case that, given Kant's view of the matter, we are so intrinsically involved in the constitution of the spatio-temporal objects of experience that it would be false to say that such objects exist independently of us? Different aspects of Kant's theoretical approach (and different claims made by him) seem to point in opposite directions. Thus, while the basic model emphasizing the two sources of receptivity and spontaneity or again the 'refutation of idealism' as presented in the first *Critique* suggest a realist position, the theory of space and time as 'pure forms of intuition,' the theory of categories, or the thesis that things in

---

1 See, for example, the important contribution by Chiba (2012) who also provides details about the relevant literature on the subject.

themselves lie entirely beyond the limits of experience, all seem to support an antirealist position.

Since the 1980's there has also been a very similar debate regarding Kant's practical philosophy. The discussion here has focused on whether Kant's moral philosophy is essentially based on a kind of 'rational constructivism,' as some members of Rawls' school prominently claimed.[2] In his *Dewey Lectures* John Rawls himself described his own constructivist approach in passing as 'Kantian' and expressly interpreted Kant as a 'constructivist.'[3] The point of these constructivist approaches lies in the claim that while the phenomenon of morality cannot be regarded as independent of the standpoint of practical agents, this does not imply that morality is merely an arbitrary or subjective projection on our part. For morality can be defended as a 'rational construction' (as suggested by the title of Onora O'Neill's book *Constructions of Reason* of 1989), and the Kantian realm of ends can be interpreted in this sense as something that we ourselves create.[4] If these readings were correct, then the central concern of Kant's moral thought would not be to provide an absolute rational grounding of ethics. Instead, Kant would primarily be concerned with emphasizing the idea of autonomy as self-legislation: we must then regard morality both as a human creation and as something that obligates us in the strictest sense. Whether constructivism, if it should prove to be correct, actually implies a form of antirealism or should, on the contrary, be described as a 'procedural realism' is, however, another question.[5] But in either case moral reason is not conceived here in 'substantialist' terms. Yet this discussion has also been succeeded in more recent years by a lively debate regarding the meta-ethical foundations of Kant's moral philosophy, and specifically regarding the realist or antirealist character of this philosophy.

Now the questions raised by the philosophy of history will allow us to consider Kant's philosophical position in a further fresh and independent manner. Kant defends a surprisingly ambitious idea of the historical 'progress of mankind', although it is not immediately clear whether he regards this idea, from a meta-theoretical perspective, as a kind of construction or even projection, or whether he understands it in terms of a substantialist conception of reason. In what follows I am principally concerned with clarifying the character of Kant's philosophy of history in some detail. It will become plausible,

---

[2] For a critique of the antirealist perspective of the Rawls School see Kain (2004, 2006a and 2006b).
[3] See Rawls (1980).
[4] See Korsgaard (1996).
[5] In this regard see Korsgaard (1996, p. 35).

I think, that Kant actually emphasizes the substantive content of his idea of history so strongly that in this regard (and perhaps more generally) we must recognize that Kant does indeed endorse a substantial conception of reason.

I

Kant's philosophy of history has always presented considerable difficulties of interpretation for its readers. When we look at the relevant texts[6] we certainly receive the impression that Kant seriously wants to defend a relatively unambiguous position in relation to the philosophy of history; and at the very least he seems throughout to endorse the basic thought that the course of history exhibits a specific logic that is bound up with the development of human capacities and with the idea of political progress; and he always holds that some kind of cosmopolitan social and political order stands at the end of history. On the other hand, this position does not seem to sit particularly well with Kant's other philosophical convictions either in the context of his theoretical or of his practical philosophy. For Kant makes concessions to certain positions (usually regarded as quite un-Kantian) which involve a 'metaphysical dogmatism,' such as a Stoic conception of natural teleology, an Aristotelian essentialism, a perfectionism in relation to the human species, and a providential theology. He also repeatedly speaks of 'nature' as if human history unfolded under its guidance or even in an 'automatic' or 'mechanical' manner. These are all claims which seem to threaten Kant's central idea of moral autonomy.

How are these challenging questions to be resolved? On the one hand, there are two things which clearly indicate the fundamental seriousness of Kant's concern with the philosophy of history: in the first place, the most important basic theses which were developed in his earliest contribution to the philosophy, namely the *Idea for a Universal History from a Cosmopolitan Point of View* of

---

[6] The most important texts in this regard are the following: *Idea for a Universal History from a Cosmopolitan Point of View* of 1784, *What is Enlightenment?* of 1784, *Critique of the Power of Judgement* (§§ 83–84) of 1792, *On the Common Saying* of 1793, *Perpetual Peace: A Philosophical Sketch* of 1793, the *Anthropology* of 1798, and *The Contest of Faculties* (section II) of 1798. There are also a number of relevant shorter writings and lecture courses such as the *Friedländler Anthropology* (FA: 465–728). These texts have been presented and furnished with a careful analytical commentary in the edition by Frank and Zanetti (1996, pp. 1080–1355).

1794, are repeated by Kant in their essential aspects later on as well.⁷ And in the second place, the *Idea for a Universal History* itself was certainly not the result of some passing mood or sudden whim on Kant's part. On the contrary, there was a fairly compelling reason for its composition: Kant clearly felt it was necessary to clarify his own position publicly on the subject of the philosophy of history.⁸ It should also be noted that in certain respects his essay is expressly directed against Herder's book *Ideas towards a Philosophy of History* which came out in the same year.⁹ It seems obvious, therefore, that his *Idea for a Universal History* represented something like a manifesto of his own considered position.

To what extent might it be true that Kant's position on the philosophy of history falls back into a form of metaphysical dogmatism? Which precise status does he ascribe to our reason that is, as he believes, committed to interpreting history as necessary and progressive development? Is it not rather our construction based on certain rational representations that cannot claim any reality independently of ourselves?

In his *Idea for Universal History*, a text which appeared three years after the first edition of the *Critique of Pure Reason* and one year before the *Groundwork for the Metaphysics of Morals*, Kant develops a philosophy of history which can be summarized as follows: Every '*Gattung*' or kind of living being (in modern terms: every biological species) is programmed by nature to fully realize and unfold the distinctive capacities of the individuals that make it up. Humanity is no exception in this regard. Yet there is an important difference here. For the individuals of every non-human species unfold their potentialities and predispositions ontogenetically (to put this in biological terms), i.e., within the course of their own individual lifespan, whereas this is impossible as far as the individual human being is concerned. Thus, the human species occupies a special position inasmuch as its development unfolds over much more extended periods of time, so that human beings can only expect the full realization of their capacities in a more indirect way through the development of the species as a whole (i.e., phylogenetically). Thus, while non-human animals as a rule develop and exercise their capacities fully in the course and context of their individual

---

7 In *On the Common Saying* and in *The Contest of Faculties* it is quite true that a 'moral progress' of humanity is also explicitly discussed alongside the notion of political progress; but this difference from the earlier writings should not, I think, be overemphasized.
8 The *Gothaische Gelehrte Zeitung* had featured a report concerning Kant's thoughts on the philosophy of history and Kant felt obliged to respond directly. This is what prompted him to publish his essay in the *Berlinische Monatsschrift*.
9 The fact that Kant specifically composed two reviews of the book also shows how seriously he took Herder's work in this regard.

lives, human individuals will only be fully able to develop the typical capacities which human beings possess at some later historical point of time (though only, of course, for those individuals who will exist at that time). And here a political dimension enters this picture of a natural-historical development of humanity, for Kant is convinced that all this will only come about once the relations between human beings have become entirely subject to principles of right. It is only then that the complete development of human capacities can be attained. But this in turn will involve a cosmopolitan social and political order where the rule of right prevails completely, an order which in Kant's eyes marks the endpoint of the whole historical process. He tells us that "a universal cosmopolitan condition" alone will constitute "the womb wherein all the original capacities of the human race can develop" (IaG: 28.34–36).[10] And Kant will also later endorse this view that only a universal cosmopolitan condition of this kind will facilitate the complete development of our human powers and capacities.[11] It is true that Kant's theoretical position sounds slightly different in his essay *On the Common Saying*, but here too it is the destructive experience of countless wars which is finally supposed to lead to the establishment of a "cosmopolitan constitution" (ÜG: 310f.), even if he has little to say about the full development of our natural human capacities in this connection.

The theory as briefly outlined on the basis of the *Idea for a Universal History* initially looks rather un-Kantian, as we have observed, and in any case is remarkable enough in its own right.[12] Yet there is no doubt that Kant expressly defends such a theory. But how precisely is it to be understood? Let us turn once again to the problem of realism and antirealism: does Kant's philosophy of history imply a form of metaphysical realism, and therefore a regression to dogmatic metaphysics and a typically 'extravagant employment of reason' (an objection he typically raises against dogmatic positions)? So soon after the appearance of the first *Critique* this hardly seems likely, especially since Kant himself also takes this opportunity to accuse Herder's *Ideas towards a Philosophy of History* of dogmatism, and must therefore believe that his own position is

---

[10] For the list of abbreviations of Kant's works, see the "Literature" section of this paper.
[11] See KU: 432.
[12] Thus we might ask why Kant does not accept the idea that certain individuals, such as Plato, Leonardo da Vinci or Goethe, might once already or might today succeed in fully developing their talents and capacities, and concede that others in the future might well not succeed in doing so. What exactly can good political conditions or circumstances contribute to the perfecting of a given individual, and what exactly is impeded by the lack of such conditions and circumstances?

immune to such charges.¹³ But how could we possibly decide, with the conceptual means of a critical philosophy, whether nature is actually pursuing the realization of a specific end with human beings, and if so what it is? And how would Kant respond if he were asked how precisely he arrived at his suggestion that the course of human history is to be interpreted in natural-historical terms? Eckhart Förster has formulated the situation in which Kant's theory has placed him in the following aporetic form: on the one hand, the idea of a plan which stands behind history and somehow guides it cannot be an *a priori* concept; for we require empirical data and specific evidence either to verify or to falsify such a claim.¹⁴ On the other hand, the concept in question cannot be based on experience either; for no historical material, however rich and detailed it may be, would be able to substantiate or to refute the notion of something like a fundamental plan for human history. What is more, Kant claims that we are talking here about a *hidden* plan which eludes our ordinary experience, even though it is supposed to be somehow accessible to philosophical reflection.¹⁵ The things which are meant to support the idea, according to Kant, are actually therefore by no means obvious.

What theoretical status can Kant legitimately assign to any attempt to offer a philosophy of history within the framework of his transcendental idealism? In the *Idea for a Universal History* Kant responds to the question as to how the philosopher must address the problem of history as follows:

> Since the philosopher cannot presume any individual purpose among human beings in their great drama, there is no other expedient for him except to try to see if he can discover a natural purpose in this idiotic course of things human. In keeping with this purpose, it might be possible to have a history with a definite natural plan for creatures who have no plan of their own. (IaG: 18.5–11)

The text assumes an inescapable need on the part of reason to find a meaning for the seemingly meaningless or 'idiotic' course of human history. Just before these remarks Kant emphasizes that history certainly appears to the observer as if "everything in the large [is]¹⁶ woven together from folly, childish vanity, even from childish malice and destructiveness" (IaG: 18). As the passage we have just cited from the introductory remarks to the *Idea for a Universal History*

---

13 Kant writes specifically with regard to Herder: "This too is still metaphysics, and indeed even very dogmatic metaphysics, even though our author, in accordance with the general fashion, affects to reject metaphysics" (RH: 54.8–10).
14 See Förster (2009, p. 194).
15 See IaG: 17.23.
16 All insertions in square brackets by the author.

clearly indicates, for the philosopher there is no other 'expedient' (which is precisely what the word *Auskunft* signifies here) than to appeal to the notion of a hidden law-like plan of nature. Kant describes his theoretical intention in this essay as that of "finding a clue [*Leitfaden*] to such a history" (IaG: 18). In this connection he draws a parallel between this quest and that pursued by Kepler and Newton in the history of astronomy, suggesting that some individual will arise in the future and prove similarly successful in interpreting human history in terms of a natural history when the laws governing its course have been identified.

Kant understands his own contribution in the *Idea for a Universal History* as that of furnishing an initial sketch which only needs to be realized in detail in the future, when a "philosophical mind (which would have to be well-versed in history) could essay" (IaG: 30.32) the task in question. This remark does not imply that his own sketch is merely tentative in character, for while Kant regards it as incomplete, he certainly does not consider it as just one possible perspective amongst others. The nine theses which make up the *Idea for a Universal History* make very emphatic claims taken individually, and especially taken as a totality. It is difficult to see where Kant derives the following five elements from, and how precisely he could justify them: (a) he begins by claiming that all the natural potentialities of a species are predisposed to unfold and develop. But while in other species all these potentialities unfold within the lifespan of each individual, human beings occupy a distinctive position since humanity can only achieve the full development of its capacities as a 'kind' or species rather than simply as individuals.[17] This is also why, for Kant, human history can be interpreted as natural history; (b) nature does nothing in vain; there is no potentiality or endowment we can find in nature which is without some end or purpose. Nature therefore obeys a principle of economy in endowing all natural species solely with the minimum that is required for them to maintain and preserve their life;[18] (c) nature wishes to give human beings the impression that they have accomplished whatever they have achieved in history on their own account, although nature itself is decisively active in the background here (through what we might call the principle of the invisible hand); (d) nature works in the course of history through the principle of "unsociable sociability," i.e., through the fact that while human beings have a propensity to seek out the company and proximity of others, they also have a propensity to isolate themselves from human community on account of "vainglory, lust for power,

---

17 See IaG: 18.
18 See IaG: 19.

and avarice" (IaG: 21.8), that is, on account of their egocentricity. According to Kant, this creates a permanent situation of conflict and social rivalry which is also intended by nature in this very form ("she wills discord," IaG: 21.31) in order to promote the development of civilization; (e) since "the development of our natural capacities" ultimately works to the good, this suggests "the ordering of a wise Creator" rather than "the hand of an evil spirit" (IaG: 22.2).

All these points (a-e) are so unexpected coming from the author of the *Critique of Pure Reason* that I should like to spell them out as follows: in his philosophy of history Kant presents (a) an essentialistic perfectionism in the spirit of Aristotle, although, as we have pointed out, for Kant it is principally the development of the species which represents the perfectionist dimension rather than, in contrast to Aristotle, that of the individual; (b) a (rather Stoic-looking) teleology of nature together with a principle of parsimony which postulates that nature always pursues its ends by the most economical of means; (c) an invisible hand principle which maintains that nature is active behind the back of human beings, even though it simultaneously allows us the impression that we have achieved everything on our own account; (d) a principle of antagonism according to which nature keeps human beings in a sort of constant productive unrest on account of selfish individual impulses and turbulent social changes ("unsociable sociability");[19] (e) a fairly explicit theological interpretation of the whole process of nature. How is it possible for Kant to risk setting out these theses on the logic behind the course of history, theses which interpret the latter in perfectionist, natural-teleological and theological terms? Are we not inevitably dealing here with assumptions that practical philosophy is compelled to make for the sake of realizing its normative ideals? And if so, then the theoretical status of Kant's philosophy of history would basically amount to that of a projection (if perhaps a useful and unavoidable one).

II

The assumption that Kant's historical perspective results simply from a practical interest in the realizability of moral-political norms actually proves on closer inspection to be false. On the contrary, Kant believes that human beings could

---

[19] This theme of 'unsocial sociability' which features in the *Idea for a Universal History*, namely the notion of social antagonism as a principle of progress, is also found in the third *Critique* (KU: 432) and in the *Anthropologie* (Anthro: 331). For the theoretical background to all of this see Ferguson (2012).

hardly accomplish anything that would actually fulfil such norms; it looks rather as though he puts his trust in a developmental logic which he is prepared to describe as a kind of 'mechanism' or 'automatism.'[20] And it would be completely wrong to assume that Kant's interest in history was primarily a practical rather than theoretical one.[21] And it is equally wrong to claim that the author of the *Critique of Pure Reason* leaves no room to discuss any concept that goes beyond the limits of experience, such as that of the *telos* of nature or the *telos* of history.[22] Kant believes, on the contrary, that reason itself does possess a means of going beyond experience which is nonetheless legitimate, namely the concept of an 'idea.' 'Ideas,' for Kant, are pure concepts of reason which allow us, within certain limits, to go beyond the employment of reason that is limited to experience. The decisive point here is that such concepts furnish merely regulative rather than constitutive principles of knowledge.[23] Ideas enable us to describe a systematic and coherent unity and regularity in a field of reality which usually presents itself to us in manifold and disorganized ways. Whether this approach is to be understood in a realist or an antirealist fashion is not easy to say *prima facie*. Kant suggests a quasi antirealist conception of ideas when he describes the perspective on the world which is produced by an idea as a *focus imaginarius*.[24] Here an idea is presented as a heuristic principle which can fruitfully be employed in our investigation of nature or history, as the following text indicates:

> Now in order to remain strictly within its own boundaries, physics abstracts entirely from the question of whether the ends of nature are intentional or unintentional; for that would be meddling in someone else's business (namely, in that of metaphysics). It is enough that there are objects that are explicable only in accordance with natural laws that we can think only under the idea of ends as a principle, and which are even internally cognizable, as far as their internal form is concerned, only in this way. In order to avoid even the least suspicion of wanting to mix into our cognitive grounds something that does not belong in physics at all, namely a supernatural cause, in teleology we certainly talk about nature as if the purposiveness in it were intentional, but at the same time ascribe this intention to nature, i.e., to matter, by which we would indicate (since there can be no misunderstanding

---

20 See Horn (2014, pp. 256–279).
21 See, for example, Yovel (1980, p. 6): "Kant was interested in history primarily as a moral task rather than as a cognitive object." This view has rightly been contested by Kleingeld (1995), who argues that Kant's engagement with the concept of history is as much theoretically as it is practically oriented.
22 For an overview of the whole question of teleology and its significance in Kant's work, see Guyer (2009) and Frank/Zanetti (1996, vol. 3).
23 See, for example, KrV: A671/B699.
24 See KrV: A644/B672.

here, because no intention in the strict sense of the term can be attributed to any lifeless matter) that this term signifies here only a principle of the reflecting, not of the determining power of judgement [...]. (KU: 382)

The teleological perspective which may be employed for understanding something in the context of physics, for example, belongs to 'reflecting judgement' rather than 'determining judgement,' and is not therefore a legitimate result of speculative reflection; on the contrary, it is merely 'ascribed' to nature. And in the same context Kant goes on to mention several other notions which also play a role in the *Idea for a Universal History*, such as the 'wisdom,' the 'economy,' the 'forethought,' and the 'beneficence' of nature.[25] In other words, Kant thinks that reason cannot avoid regarding a given whole like the field of physics or human history as a totality whose parts must purposively be related to each other and to the whole; yet reason does not grasp this totality by recourse to any metaphysical insight but solely by means of heuristic insight. This approach certainly sounds antirealist in character. However, there is an important passage in first *Critique*, from the chapter on the *Architectonic* in the *Doctrine of Method*, which sounds as if it involves a more emphatic or substantial conception of reason:

> In accordance with reason's legislative prescriptions, our diverse modes of knowledge must not be permitted to be a mere rhapsody, but must form a system. Only so can they further the essential ends of reason. By a system I understand the unity of the manifold modes of knowledge under one idea. (KrV: A832/B860)

Kant here explains in general terms why, amongst other things, he also introduces a teleological perspective with regard to nature and history. There can be no area of knowledge where the results make up a rhapsody rather than constituting a system. A mere manifold of items and forms of knowledge without inner systematic connection – in other words, without a teleological or purposive-grounded unity – would run counter to the systematizing interests of reason. As this passage shows (and particularly the immediate continuation of these remarks which we have not cited here), Kant holds that this approach is

---

[25] "Hence in teleology, insofar as it is connected to physics, we speak quite rightly of the wisdom, the economy, the forethought, and the beneficence of nature, without thereby making it into an intelligent being (since that would be absurd); but also without daring to set over it, as its architect, another intelligent being, because this would be presumptuous; rather, such talk is only meant to designate a kind of causality in nature, in accordance with an analogy with our own causality in the technical use of reason, in order to keep before us the rule in accordance with which research into certain products of nature must be conducted" (KU: 383).

not just compatible with the Critical Philosophy but specifically required by it. Kant describes the perspective of such systematizing unity precisely as an 'idea.' And he then proceeds to clarify this point as follows:

> The idea requires for its realisation a *schema*, that is, a constituent manifold and an order of its parts, both of which must be determined a priori from the principle defined by its end. The schema, which is not devised in accordance with an idea, that is, in terms of the ultimate aim of reason, but empirically in accordance with purposes that are contingently occasioned (the number of which cannot be foreseen) yields *technical* unity; whereas the schema which originates from an idea (in which reason propounds the ends a priori, and does not wait for them to be empirically given) serves as the basis of *architectonic* unity. Now that which we call science, the schema of which must contain the outline (*monogramma*) and the division of the whole into parts, in conformity with the idea, that is, a priori, and in so doing must distinguish it with certainty and according to principles from all other wholes, is not formed in technical fashion, in view of the similarity of its manifold constituents or of the contingent use of our knowledge *in concreto* for all sorts of optional external ends, but in architectonic fashion, in view of the affinity of its parts and of their derivation from a single supreme and inner end, through which the whole is first made possible. (KrV: A833f./B861f.)

In the quoted text, Kant distinguishes between an 'idea' and a 'schema': the idea is the principle which establishes unity, while the schema involves the aspect of execution or application in relation to the manifold. An empirically based schema furnishes a 'technical' unity, whereas a reason based one furnishes an 'architectonic' unity. And it is the latter which makes science possible in the first place: the unity through which a given manifold is ordered in relation to a highest end.

In his essay *The Idea for a Universal History* Kant clearly alludes both to the idea which allows us to understand history and to the schema which serves this idea. The idea tells us that what nature intends for individuals of every species is the complete and distinctive realization of their capacities; the schema arises from the circumstance that this can only be conceived, in the case of human beings, as a long and difficult supra-individual process. Kant therefore claims that human reason cannot live with the thought that there is something as simply chaotic and disorganized as human history seems to be (insofar as it is interpreted in merely empirical terms). On the contrary, Kant argues that "this idea may still serve as a guiding thread for presenting as a system, at least in broad outlines, what would otherwise be a planless conglomeration of human actions" (IaG: 29.14–16).

How precisely are we to understand this claim? It seems clear that this approach is just as susceptible to an antirealist or constructivist interpretation as it is to a substantialist-metaphysical one. In the debate regarding the realism or antirealism of Kant's theoretical and practical philosophy there seems to be no advantageous standpoint which we could exploit in order to interpret Kant's philosophy of history. And since the philosophy of history, generally speaking, addresses an issue with regard to which there is surely already considerable scepticism – namely the notion that the course of history might exhibit some purposive sense of direction – Kant's observations on the real content of such a notion clearly indicate what he means by the concept of an 'idea' and how substantial his conception of reason and the knowledge it is capable of yielding actually is. In the next section therefore we shall examine Kant's claims and conclusions in the light of the following question: does he regard the 'idea' of history that we have discussed merely as a useful and expedient assumption, or does he see it as a substantial kind of knowledge?

III

As with the debate over the realism or antirealism of Kant's theoretical and practical philosophy, we must now also consider both these possibilities (a and b) specifically in relation to his philosophy of history.

(a): *Antirealist readings:* there are some good reasons for interpreting Kant's general philosophical position as antirealist in character. Thus in his philosophy of history too that which appears as a purposive process and as a purposiveness of nature in general would have to be interpreted merely as a deliberate construction on our part. Strictly speaking, the idea of historical progress seems not to correspond to anything in reality; on the contrary, the notion of the course of history as somehow governed by nature seems to arise simply from our own structuring perspective on the history of humanity. And it is indeed striking that Kant is hardly interested in the interpretation of events from the past,[26] and is only really interested in the present and the future.[27] One possible line of interpretation would be to endorse what could be called the *deliberate perspective reading*. According to this view the perspective adopted in relation to political-historical reality would be a deliberately or intentionally constructed one; it would help Kant to *produce* precisely what is allegedly *diagnosed* by means of it. The fact that his essay is described as an *Idea for a Universal History* which is composed *from a Cosmopolitan Point of View*, i.e., with the specific

---

26 With the rare exception of a few remarks in Thesis IX of the *Idea for a Universal History*, IaG: 29.16 – 37.
27 As Weyand already pointed out: "Kant's philosophy of history basically reveals only a prospective rather than a retrospective perspective on history" (Weyand 1963, p. 8).

intention of promoting a cosmopolitan ideal, would then imply that the text was merely meant to suggest or encourage the thought that there might be some such purposive development in history.

But this interpretation is certainly mistaken. For Kant thinks that there in fact is such a development, and this perspective is not based on some deliberate construction on our part. Thus in his essay *On the Common Saying* Kant clearly says there is considerable "evidence" for the moral progress of humanity (ÜG: 310.4), and in the essay on *The End of All Things* he also speaks quite explicitly of "evidence drawn from experience" (ED: 332.18). Nonetheless, it does not seem possible simply to exclude an antirealist reading when we consider a passage from a late text such as the *Anthropology from a Pragmatic Point of View*. For here it appears clear that we merely "feel ourselves" to be determined by nature to pursue and achieve human progress, although this is not actually the case:

> The character of the species, as it is known from the experience of all ages and by all peoples, is this: taken collectively (the human race as one whole), it is a multitude of persons, existing successively and side by side, who *cannot do without* being together peacefully, and yet *cannot avoid* constantly being objectionable to one another. Consequently, they feel destined by nature to [develop], through mutual compulsion under laws that come from themselves, into a cosmopolitan society (cosmopolitanism) that is constantly threatened by disunion but generally progresses toward a coalition. In itself it is an unattainable idea but not a constitutive principle (the principle of anticipating lasting peace amid the most vigorous actions and reactions of human beings). Rather, is only a regulative principle: to pursue this diligently as the destiny of the human race, not without grounded supposition of a natural tendency toward it. (Anthro: 331.16–30)

One should note that here too the human vocation to promote moral and political progress does not proceed without what Kant calls a "well-grounded supposition." Although this seems a weaker claim, it is still obviously an affirmative one. This passage clearly takes up the notion of the progressive development of humanity as species which was defended in the *Idea for a Universal History*, a development that is still grounded in the social antagonism of human individuals. In addition, this text also makes the distinction between regulative and constitutive principles quite explicit, something which was not the case in the *Idea for a Universal History*.

This suggests the case for a more defensive version of the antirealist interpretation than that associated with the deliberate 'constructionist' reading. We could describe this weaker version as a reading that *emphasizes our own perspective in the present*. This reading would claim that Kant identifies the basis of historical progress simply as something that is rooted in the specific historical awareness of progress that is entertained by his contemporaries. It is a characteristic feature of this specific historical consciousness that it experiences its own time and its own civilization as a reflective result of an extended history (or also interprets it as a regression in comparison with an earlier more enlightened past). Other significant factors in this moral and political self-understanding on the part of his contemporaries would include the extremely rapid development of modern scientific knowledge and its technological applications, along with the ongoing exploration and increasing awareness of the world as a whole. That considerations of this kind certainly play an important role in Kant's thought is clearly revealed, for example, by a passage in *On the Common Saying:*

> For, that what has not succeeded up to now will therefore never succeed does not even justify abandoning a pragmatic or technical purpose (for example, that of flights with aerostatic balloons), still less a moral purpose that, if only it is not demonstratively impossible to effect it, becomes a duty. (ÜG: 309f.)

Even fantastical-sounding technological aims – like flights by balloon – may one day prove to be feasible, as recent history of technology (the Montgolfière hot air balloons) reveals. And we must be even more prepared to uphold a moral aim or intention, even if its realization has not successfully been achieved. Kant even says that it is a duty for us to do so, as long as we are unable to demonstrate its impossibility. Kant continues as follows:

> Besides, a good deal of evidence can be put forward to show that in our age, as compared with all previous ages, the human race as a whole has actually made considerable moral progress (short-term checks can prove nothing to the contrary), and that the outcry about its incessantly increasing depravity comes from the very fact that when it reaches a higher level of morality it sees farther ahead, and its judgment about what one is as compared with what one ought to be, hence our self-reproach, becomes all the more severe the more levels of morality we have already climbed during the whole of the course of the world that we have become acquainted with.

In this passage Kant draws an explicit parallel between the technical and moral progress of humanity. But the text also shows that Kant's own view of such developments clearly implies that we are not simply dealing here with an *awareness* of progress on the part of his contemporaries but with real and genuine progress. It is precisely in societies that have actually made such progress that the lament over the "increasing depravity" of the present arises – an unjustified feeling of decline, therefore, which in truth reveals precisely the progress which has already been achieved. According to Kant, this too is the sign of a positive development, for it is in morally more progressive times that we apply stricter standards upon ourselves and others. We receive the definite impression, therefore, that Kant is indeed thinking of an actual unfolding of reason in human history. This process is of course closely connected with the awareness or consciousness of actual living human beings at a particular point of time, but certainly cannot be reduced to this. And in terms of a widely shared perspective at the beginning of our new century Kant does not seem to be entirely unjustified in taking this view: if we consider the course of history between Kant's time and the present, we too would probably be inclined to identify a fundamental tendency towards the world-wide diffusion of democracy, human rights, education, a gradual process of 'enlightenment,' and scientific and technological progress, as well as a movement towards the institutionalization of legal principles in the context of international political relations.

Yet this particular reading is also certainly indefensible: it fails to take seriously either the concept of 'idea' which is developed in the chapter on the *Architectonic* in the first *Critique* or the emphatic cognitive claim which is developed in the *Idea for a Universal History*. The fact that Kant believes that the claim of historical progress depends on genuine insight or knowledge finds its clearest expression in his remarks on the French Revolution in *The Contest of Faculties*. There Kant emphatically tells us that "the proposition that the human race has always been progressively improving and will continue to develop in the same way is not just a well-meant saying to be recommended for practical purposes. Whatever unbelievers may say, it is tenable within the most strictly theoretical context" (SF: 88.34–7). The antirealist view is also undermined by what Kant says in the first *Critique* in the chapter on *The Final Purpose of the Natural Dialectic of Human Reason*, where he claims that an idea, in this case the idea of God, creates altogether new views on the unity of the world.[28] In the third *Critique* too Kant formulates an explicit moral proof of the existence of God on the basis of the concept of the Highest Good: God must exist in order to guarantee the final end of human morality.[29] If Kant's argument were really to be understood in an antirealist sense, the 'final end' is precisely not what it would yield. And then again it is also possible to raise objections to the notion of a 'constructive' subject in this connection: what subject would we be talking about as a constituent factor here, and precisely what kind of activity would such a 'construction' represent? It is quite possible in general to understand what social or even individual 'constructions' might signify, but what precisely are we to understand by a rational construction

---

28 KrV: A686f./B714f.: "Such a principle opens out to our reason, as applied in the field of experience, altogether new views as to how the things of the world may be connected according to teleological laws, and so enables it to arrive at their greatest systematic unity."
29 See KU: § 87, especially 450. For a reconstruction of this argument in the context of the philosophy of history see Yovel (1980, pp. 104f.).

which is pursued by our own reason (a reason that is not conceived in natural terms)?

(b): *The metaphysical-substantial interpretation:* according to a second interpretation of his position the quasi-realist character of Kant's conception of an 'idea' could be dissolved if we recognize the substantial cognitive value of the latter, while emphasizing at the same time that this arises in the essentially indirect manner of a 'rational idea.' From this point of view, there is nothing dubious or illegitimate about an insight which is derived by reference to an idea. But the cognitive process involved here would not be speculative or metaphysical, but merely indirect and defensive in character. As far as Kant's philosophy of history is concerned this reading (b) seems to be clearly preferable. Kant regards his insights concerning the course of history, according to all the textual evidence, as matters of objective knowledge. An important interpretative point here is to recognize – as modern interpreters confronted with the precarious theoretical foundations of Kant's philosophy of history – that we take care not to confuse the question regarding *its plausibility for us* with the question regarding *its plausibility for Kant*. As we have pointed out, the various elements of his theory appear to be framed in an extremely ambitious, dogmatic, speculative and 'substantial' fashion. Regarding Kant's theory of history, we are perhaps confronted with the most far-reaching and at the same time most implausible construction of an 'idea' to be found anywhere in Kant's work. And this raises the question why Kant should open himself to the difficulties which arise from such a theory precisely by accepting its substantial truth. There must have been very strong considerations that led him to espouse a theory of history which is as hard to defend as this one.

But we must also recognize that in one important respect Kant is claiming less than one might believe. Thus, he has no intention of suggesting that absolutely every event in the world forms part of a teleological meaning in history which is oriented towards the end we have identified. Nor does he defend a linear development in the course of history, and it is easy to show that he acknowledges the presence of events which run counter to the overall historical process, namely those things which do not prove conducive to this process even indirectly.[30] This implies that there must also be events that are 'indifferent' in character, that indeed the majority of events may be of this character. In other words, Kant does not assume that we can decipher every historical event and

---

30 In *On the Common Saying* (309 f.), Kant speaks of certain "checks" and admits that the historical process is "*interrupted* from time to time." And his remarks in *The Conflict of Faculties* (SF: 78) also clearly indicate that he regards the failure of the French Revolution as perfectly possible.

every feature or circumstance of natural history as a contribution to the progress we may anticipate or hope for.

Kant is certainly no historical determinist. He merely thinks that the whole of history is subject to a guiding principle, that of 'nature,' and can itself be understood as an effect and product of this same nature. For Kant this principle is the unfolding of species-relative capacities, something which might be compared to Darwin's principles of ever-increasing adaptation to the environment and those of mutation and selection.[31] These principles do not have to be understood in a determinist sense. It is enough for them to furnish the impetus for a development the detailed and precise course of which remains indeterminate. It is quite clear, on the other hand, that he never formulates the strong kind of philosophy of history which assumes, for example, the existence of meaningfully organized stages, periods and epochs or attempts to identify the precise laws which govern the course of history. Thus, Kant never bends historical data in order to fit them into some rigid schema, nor does he ever try to predict anything or present himself as a kind of historical prophet. What he says is merely that nature behaves as an independent agent which invisibly or imperceptibly insinuates itself, as it were, into the realm of free human action in order to realize a 'plan' or 'final end.' The history of humanity will develop, according to Kant, towards a rationally based international order of peace which in the distant future will eventually embrace all human beings. What we are talking about here is a tendency which underlies the course of history, rather than a process which is determined by natural laws. The cosmopolitan end point is inscribed in the logic of human history as an unfolding process although the path that leads there or the moment of time in which it is attained is not determined in advance. This thesis regarding a meaningful history of human development is therefore entirely compatible with the contingent character of the factual events and circumstances of political history; what is important about the thesis is simply that the effect of the covertly operating principle can be read off from the historical facts in general.

Nonetheless, Kant often introduces non-deterministic considerations of a natural-teleological kind which are supposed to support a specific historical teleology. According to this view nature realizes its program in the course of

---

[31] A comparison with Darwin's theory of evolution could also show how it is possible to defend the thesis of a stable and dominant natural tendency without thereby endorsing a determinist position. This theory is also indifferent with regard to causal determinism, for it is compatible either with a theory of physical determinism or with a theory of indeterminacy with regard to the natural world. Even so, the differences between the positions of Kant and Darwin are of course enormous. For further discussion of this issue see Horn (2011, pp. 113–115).

human history. Reflections of this kind are particularly evident in the *Groundwork for the Metaphysics of Morals* (394–396) and in § 83 of the third *Critique*.[32] Kant's argument in the *Groundwork* is based on rejecting the notion that happiness is the only ultimate end of human nature. Kant undertakes to refute this view in the following way: the natural capacities and potentialities of every living being are constituted in such a way that they are adapted in the optimal manner to the pursuit and realization of its ends. Let us assume then that happiness constituted the natural end of the human being. In that case we should be able to find the evidence for this in the natural capacities and predispositions of human beings. Yet in actual fact human beings are to a considerable degree guided and determined by practical reason. If the final end of human beings did consist in the pursuit and realization of happiness, then the human possession of reason would prove to be a dysfunctional element of our natural character and potential. For a stronger repertoire of immediate instinctual capacities would surely lead us much more reliably and effectively to the required end. On the contrary, however, the "true vocation" which reveals itself in the natural capacities of the human being who possesses practical reason lies precisely in bringing forth "a will that is good in itself." The decisive point here is that nature has endowed us with practical reason. Reason does not merely lend itself to a purely theoretical employment but can also exercise "an influence on the will," as Kant puts it. A good will, as he goes on to explain, need not "be the sole and complete good, but it must still be the highest good and condition of every other, even of all demands for happiness" (GMS: 396). In the third *Critique* Kant sees particular natural phenomena above all, such as the presence of vermin or mosquitoes as purposive in the sense that they can exert a positive influence on human behaviour.[33] The entire process of nature is viewed by Kant in these anthropocentric terms. It is in this sense that the philosophy of history is already prepared for in the context of natural history.

It seems to me that Kant's philosophy of history in particular provides an important argument in favour of a realist and substantialist reading of his conception of reason. For, in this area we see Kant – more clearly here than in

---

[32] For an interpretation of this latter passage see Horn (2006).
[33] "Thus one could say, e.g., that the vermin that plague humans in their clothes, hair, or bedding, are, in accordance with a wise dispensation of nature, an incentive for cleanliness, which is in itself already an important means for the preservation of health. Or the mosquitoes or other stinging insects which make the wilds of America so trying for the savages are so many goads to spur these primitive people to drain the swamps and let light into the thick, airless forests and thereby as well as by the cultivation of the soil to make their abode more salubrious" (KU: 379.22–31).

relation to other less precarious questions – as someone who has to spell out the real substantive content of his claims. And on the basis of this textual evidence there can be no doubt that he actually does so here, that he undertakes to offer his readers objective cognitive insights, even if they are not ones which are acquired by means of speculative methods. It would be false to take the indirect character of Kant's approach, based as it is on his concept of 'ideas,' as evidence for an antirealist position. Quite the reverse holds true.

Literature

Kant

Anthro   Anthropologie in pragmatischer Hinsicht, AA 7
ED   Das Ende aller Dinge, AA 8
FA   Friedländer Anthropologie, AA 25
GMS   Grundlegung zur Metaphysik der Sitten, AA 4
IaG   Idee zu einer allgemeinen Geschichte in weltbürgerlicher Absicht, AA 8
KrV   Kritik der reinen Vernunft, AA 3 (B) und 4 (A)
KU   Kritik der Urteilskraft, AA 5
RH   Rezension Herder, AA 8
SF   Streit der Fakultäten, AA 7
ÜG   Über den Gemeinspruch: Das mag in der Theorie richtig sein, taugt aber nicht für die Praxis, AA 8

English translations are taken from the series *The Cambridge Edition of the Works of Immanuel Kant*, Cambridge University Press (1992 ff.), except for the *Idea for a Universal History from a Cosmopolitan Point of View*, translated by Lewis White Beck, in: Immanuel Kant: *On History*, New York: Macmillan Publishing Co. (1958).
All page and line numbers in parentheses refer to the so-called Akademie-Ausgabe (AA), i.e., to *Kant's gesammelte Schriften*, herausgegeben von der *Königlich Preußischen Akademie der Wissenschaften*, Berlin: Walter de Gruyter (1900 ff.).

Secondary Literature

Ameriks, Karl (2009): "The Purposive Development of Human Capacities." In: Amélie Oksenberg Rorty/James Schmidt (eds.): *Kant's Idea for a Universal History with a Cosmopolitan Aim*. Cambridge: Cambridge University Press, pp. 46–67.
Ameriks, Karl (2011): "Das Schicksal von Kants Rezensionen zu Herders Ideen." In: Otfried Höffe (ed.): *Immanuel Kant, Schriften zur Geschichtsphilosophie*. Berlin/New York: Walter de Gruyter, pp. 119–136.

Chiba, Kiyoshi (2012): *Kants Ontologie der raumzeitlichen Wirklichkeit. Versuch einer anti-realistischen Deutung der Kritik der reinen Vernunft.* Berlin: Walter de Gruyter.
Ferguson, Michaele (2012): "Unsocial Sociability: Perpetual Antagonism in Kant's Political Thought." In: Elisabeth Ellis (ed.): *Kant's Political Theory. Interpretations and Applications.* Pennsylvania: State University Press, pp. 150–169.
Förster, Eckart (2009): "The Hidden Plan of Nature." In: Amélie Oksenberg Rorty/James Schmidt (eds.): *Kant's Idea for a Universal History with a Cosmopolitan Aim.* Cambridge: Cambridge University Press, pp. 187–199.
Frank, Manfred/Zanetti, Véronique (1996*): Immanuel Kant: Schriften zur Ästhetik und Naturphilosophie. Text und Kommentar.* Frankfurt a. M.: Suhrkamp.
Guyer, Paul (2009): "The Crooked Timber of Mankind." In: Amélie Oksenberg Rorty/James Schmidt (eds.): *Kant's Idea for a Universal History with a Cosmopolitan Aim. A Critical Guide.* Cambridge: Cambridge University Press, pp. 129–149.
Horn, Christoph (2006): "Kant on Ends in Nature and in Human Agency: The Teleological Argument (GMS 394–6)." In: Christoph Horn/Dieter Schönecker (eds.): *Groundworks for the Metaphysics of Morals. New Essays.* Berlin/New York: Walter de Gruyter, pp. 45–71.
Horn, Christoph (2008): "Kant und die Stoiker." In: Barbara Neymeyr/Jochen Schmidt/Bernhard Zimmermann (eds.): *Stoizismus in der europäischen Philosophie, Literatur, Kunst und Politik.* Berlin: Walter de Gruyter, pp. 1081–1103.
Horn, Christoph (2011): "Das Interesse der Philosophie an der Menschheitsgeschichte. Aufklärung und Weltbürgertum." In: Otfried Höffe (ed.): *Immanuel Kant, Schriften zur Geschichtsphilosophie.* Berlin: Walter de Gruyter, pp. 103–118.
Horn, Christoph (2014): *Nichtideale Normativität. Ein neuer Blick auf Kants politische Philosophie.* Berlin: Suhrkamp.
Kain, Patrick (2004): "Self-Legislation in Kant's Moral Philosophy." In: *Archiv für Geschichte der Philosophie* 86, pp. 257–306.
Kain, Patrick (2006a): "Constructivism, Intrinsic Normativity and the Motivational Analysis Argument." In: Heiner Klemme/Manfred Kühn/Dieter Schönecker (eds.): *Moralische Motivation. Kant und die Alternative* (Kant-Forschungen 16). Hamburg: Meiner, pp. 59–78.
Kain, Patrick (2006b): "Realism and Anti-realism in Kant's Second Critique." In: *Philosophy Compass* 1, pp. 449–465.
Kleingeld, Pauline (1995): *Fortschritt und Vernunft. Zur Geschichtsphilosophie Kants.* Würzburg: Königshausen und Neumann.
Korsgaard, Christine M. (1996): *Creating the Kingdom of Ends.* Cambridge/New York: Cambridge University Press.
O'Neill, Onora (1989*): Constructions of Reason. Explorations of Kant's Practical Philosophy.* Cambridge: Cambridge University Press.
Rawls, John (1980): "Kantian Constructivism in Moral Theory." In: *Journal of Philosophy* 77, pp. 512–577.
Sommer, Andreas Urs (2006): *Sinnstiftung durch Geschichte? Zur Genese der spekulativ-universalistischen Geschichtsphilosophie zwischen Pierre Bayle und Immanuel Kant.* Basel: Schwabe Verlag.
Weyand, Klaus (1963): *Kants Geschichtsphilosophie. Ihre Entwicklung und ihr Verhältnis zur Aufklärung.* Köln: Kölner Universitäts-Verlag.

Wolff, Michael (2013): "Kant über Freiheit und Determinismus." In: Werner Euler/Burkhard Tuschling (eds.): *Kants 'Metaphysik der Sitten' in der Diskussion*. Berlin: Duncker & Humblot, pp. 27–42.

Yovel, Yirmiyahu (1980): *Kant and the Philosophy of History*. Princeton: Princeton University Press.

Patrick Kain
Dignity and the Paradox of Method

Abstract In this paper, I advocate a value realist interpretation of Kant's ethics by examining, in some detail, both Kant's discussion of the grounding of the moral law in *Groundwork* II and his discussion of the "paradox of method" in the *Critique of Practical Reason*. On a plausible reading of both the *Groundwork* and second *Critique*, Kant maintains that human beings, and more generally, rational beings, have dignity or inner worth. We cognize through the moral law that our existence and inner value is the objective ground of the law and that we are the "subject[s] of the moral law." This dignity of rational beings is fundamental and irreducible. This qualifies as a distinctive kind of value realism.

* * *

> But suppose there were something *the existence of which in itself* has an absolute worth, something which, *as an end in itself* could be a ground of determinate laws; then in it, and in it alone, would lie the ground of a possible categorical imperative, that is of a practical law.
> (GMS: 428.3 – 6)[1]

In the *Groundwork*, Kant insists that the "ground of a possible categorical imperative, that is of a practical law" could only lie in the existence of something of absolute worth – in particular, the existence of "the human being and in general of every rational being" (GMS: 428.5 – 7). This suggests that, according to Kant, "goodness is fundamental," as Paton insisted (Paton 1947, pp. 5, 45, 116, 177).[2] Allen Wood has recently suggested that "[p]erhaps the most fundamental proposition in Kant's entire ethical theory is that rational nature is the supreme value and the ground of whatever value anything else might possess" (Wood 1999, p. 121). Bolder yet, Wood has recently insisted that even "the principle of morality itself [...] is grounded on an objective end- humanity as an end in itself." "Kantian ethics rests on a single fundamental value – the dignity or absolute worth of rational nature" (Wood 2008, pp. 59, 94). This

---

[1] For the list of abbreviations of Kant's works, see the "Literature" section of this paper.
[2] While Paton says value is fundamental in Kant, he also suggests Kant is an idealist about value (Paton 1947, p. 110; 1944, p. 24; 1942; 1927).

position implies, among other things, some robust metaphysical assertions. It alleges that rational beings, e.g., human beings, *really* have dignity: our dignity is not dependent upon anyone's acts or anyone's attitudes toward us. And it alleges that this dignity is metaphysically *fundamental:* it is not metaphysically reducible to some other element or feature of the theory.[3]

Of course, assertions of "Kantian value realism" run against the grain of much work done on Kant's ethics and in Kantian ethics. We have been told, time and again, that, in the words of C. D. Broad: "for Kant the notion of duty or obligation and the notions of right and wrong are fundamental" (Broad 1930, p. 116) and the concept of the good is not. An insistence upon the "priority of the right," as Rawls called it, is widely considered to be central to Kant's theory and a hallmark of deontological, as opposed to teleological, value-based moral theories (Rawls 1971, § 6, note 16; cf. Rawls 2000, pp. 156, 226 – 232).[4] On this more familiar approach, there is a deep distinction between the right and the good, and, according to Kant, the right must be more fundamental. "Nothing can have a worth other than that which the law determines for it" (GMS: 436.1–2). Indeed, the "priority of the right" and a rejection of value realism appear, to many interpreters, to lie at the heart of what Kant called his "paradox of method":

> […] the concept of good and evil must not be determined before the moral law (for which, as it would seem, this concept would have to be made the basis) but only (as it was done

---

[3] Following a common usage in contemporary philosophy, I consider "realism" in a particular domain as the thesis that claims within that domain, literally construed, are either true or false, and that at least some of them are in fact true and knowable. Since literal construals of fundamental moral claims do not have them depend on people's beliefs, actions (or "constructive activity"), or attitudes, *moral realism*, in this strict sense, maintains that (some) fundamental moral claims are true independently of people's beliefs, actions, activities, attitudes and conventions (Sayre-McCord 1988, p. 22). While moral realism, so understood, includes some knowledge requirement, it does *not* specifically require a Moorean "intuitionist" epistemology. I have argued elsewhere for a moral realist interpretation of Kant's conception of self-legislation (see Kain 2004).

By "value realism" I mean the thesis that some fundamental value claims are true, independently of anyone's beliefs, actions, activities, attitudes, or conventions regarding them, and are known, and that some of these value claims are not purely derivative or reducible to some non-value claims. For other value realist interpretations of Kant's ethics, see Langton (2007), Rosen (2012), Stern (2012 and 2013), and Guyer (2000).

[4] For one helpful discussion of Rawls on this point, see Reath (2003).

here) after it and by means of it. [...] the moral law first determines and makes possible the concept of the good, insofar as it deserves this name absolutely. (KpV: 62.36–63.4, 64.3–5)[5]

Kant's emphasis on the priority of the moral law in this passage seems, to many, to imply that goodness is derivative, rather than fundamental, precluding Kantian value realism.[6]

In this chapter, I will advocate a value realist interpretation of Kant's ethics by examining, in some detail, both Kant's discussion of the grounding of the moral law in *Groundwork* II and his discussion of the "paradox of method" in the *Critique of Practical Reason*. I will propose a unified interpretation of these texts, which manifests a distinctive kind of value realism.

The Value of Humanity in the *Groundwork*

In the middle of *Groundwork* II, Kant considers: "something the existence of which in itself has an absolute worth, something which, as an end in itself could be a ground of determinate laws" (GMS: 428.3–5). But the expository and systematic roles of this invocation of absolute worth and grounding are

---

[5] It is easy to misstate or misunderstand the alleged "priority of the right" in Kant. In the wake of Sidgwick or Broad, we may mistakenly assume it insists upon the priority of notions of duty, obligation, and imperatives, to notions of goodness and value. In this classic passage, however, Kant mentions the priority (in some sense) of "the [moral] law," but not of duty, obligation or imperatives per se. Kant also frequently invokes the idea of a divine will or holy will to emphasize the point that obligation and duty, and more generally, imperatives, are the manifestations to us finite beings of something more fundamental: "objective laws (of the good)" (GMS: 414.1–2). In response to Paton, Beck acknowledged that value is more fundamental than obligation for Kant, but insisted *principle* is most fundamental (Beck 1960, p. 128).

[6] On some influential interpretations, the moral law or rational principle is fundamental and value is derivative or reducible, which precludes Kantian value realism (Sensen 2011, Johnson 2007). On some other influential accounts, acts of rational volition are fundamental and such acts ground both the moral law and value, which precludes Kantian moral realism altogether. Schneewind writes, for example: "Goodness and value [...] are always explained in terms of rational willing. They cannot themselves be used as final explanations of what it is rational to will"(Schneewind 1996, p. 286). Korsgaard makes a similar claim about the value of objectively good ends, which she later extends to all value (Korsgaard 1983, pp. 182f.). Korsgaard has prominently contended that "for Kant acts of valuing are the source of all value – all legitimate normative claims – not the other way around. Obligation does not arise from value: rather, obligation and value arise together from acts of legislative will" (Korsgaard 2005, p. 95). I argue against this latter interpretation, and on behalf of a moral realist interpretation of self-legislation in Kain (2004).

not immediately obvious. Kant's primary goal in the *Groundwork* is to search for and establish the supreme principle of morality,[7] yet he has by this point in the text already formulated the categorical imperative in the "Formula of Universal Law," which makes no explicit mention of value, and the "deduction" of the categorical imperative is planned for *Groundwork* III (and will not focus very explicitly on "value"). So, why does Kant consider this "grounding" issue here? And what is he suggesting here about how "absolute worth" "grounds" the moral law? I contend that, in the context of his expository strategy in *Groundwork* II, Kant intends to articulate the putative "connection" between rational beings and the moral law (if there is one), and to prepare the way for the introduction of the Formula of Autonomy.[8] One of Kant's important systematic claims here is that the absolute worth of each rational being must be the *objective ground of the moral law* (if there is such a law).

Kant opens *Groundwork* II by insisting that,

> unless we want to deny the concept of morality any truth and any relation to some possible object, we cannot dispute that its law is so extensive in its import that it must hold not only for human beings but for all *rational beings as such*, not merely under contingent conditions and with exceptions but with *absolute necessity* [...]. (GMS: 408)

Empirical observation of human behavior, or even of human inclinations cannot establish the validity of such a moral law or give us insight into the nature of its validity. "Because moral laws are to hold for every rational being as such," it is important "to derive them from the universal concept of a rational being as such" (GMS: 412). Kant explains that rational beings have "the capacity to act *in accordance with the representation* of laws, that is in accordance with principles [...]" (GMS: 412) and he proceeds to note a distinction between a holy will, "a capacity to choose *only that* which reason independently of inclination cognizes as practically necessary, that is, as good" and a finite, unholy will, "not *in itself* completely in conformity with reason" (GMS: 412f.), but commanded by reason, in the form of imperatives. Kant contends that the moral law must appear to finite, unholy wills as a categorical imperative, and that the categorical imperative can be formulated as the Formula of Universal Law: "act only in accordance with that maxim through which you can at the same time will that it become universal law" (GMS: 421).

---

[7] GMS: 392.

[8] In many ways, the central question in this section, and several parts of my answer, resemble those of Guyer (1995).

After deriving this formulation of the categorical imperative and examining the moral status of a few particular maxims in light of it, Kant revisits some of the opening themes of section II, suggesting that there is more to be said about how the categorical imperative is grounded in reason, about how the categorical imperative is "connected" to the idea of a rational being.[9] "Duty is to be a practical unconditional necessity of action and it must therefore hold for all rational beings (to which alone an imperative can apply at all)." The supreme principle of morality must be valid a priori, "even though every propensity, inclination, and natural tendency of ours were against it" (GMS: 425). "If there is [a necessary law *for all rational beings*][10], then it must already be connected (completely a priori) with the concept of the will of a rational being as such" (GMS: 426). Kant is clear that he does not intend to fully establish the law (and, by implication, this actual connection) until the third section of the *Groundwork*, but he proceeds to clarify the nature of the putative connection nonetheless. Reflection upon this crucial "connection" is what leads Kant to his "postulate" that "rational nature exists as an end in itself" and possesses an absolute worth that "grounds" the objective practical law; this allows him to articulate his second major formulation of the categorical imperative, the "Formula of Humanity" (GMS: 428f.). At the outset, Kant hints that the connection being sought between the law and the will must be a "relation of a will to itself insofar as it determines itself only by reason" (GMS: 427.14).

Somewhat abruptly, Kant introduces the concept of an "*objective ground*" of a will's self-determination, an *end* (GMS: 427.22).[11] He implies, without immediate

---

9 Indeed, on some approaches, it is puzzling that, after introducing the Formula of Universal Law as a suitable formula of the categorical imperative and indicating that a good will can be sufficiently motivated by its recognition of how a maxim fares under this formula, Kant does not proceed directly to the "deduction" of the moral law in *Groundwork* III, or at least go directly to the discussion of autonomy later in *Groundwork* II. Why is any additional condition necessary (see Reath 2013b; but for a different approach see also Reath 2013a)?
10 All insertions in square brackets by the author.
11 Kant insists, but does not explain here, that a will must have an "objective ground of its determination," an end, and he implies that the Formula of Universal Law is not itself such an end or objective ground, nor does it reveal what such an objective ground could be. It may be a bit confusing that Kant proceeds to suggest that, apparently in addition to this, an "objective ground" of the law is necessary. (Similar concern may seem to arise when Kant proceeds to insist that obligation must be self-legislated.) But Kant intends these claims, and subsequent reflections in *Groundwork* II, to be complementary claims about the unconditionally valid moral law. Kant need not claim, as a psychological matter, that each morally worthy action must involve explicit representations of universalizability, and of ends-in-themselves or absolute worth, and autonomy and a kingdom of ends. We may have some of these ideas before our eyes without thinking any of them in their abstract form (GMS: 403f.). Philosophically, there is no

explanation, that a consideration of objective grounds or ends can shed additional light on the putative connection between rational beings and the moral law. Kant distinguishes two kinds of objective grounds or ends: subjective ends and objective ends.[12] For one thing, an agent may represent something she can bring about – perhaps some artifact she can make or a state of affairs she might bring about – and that represented possible object informs, guides or governs her action of promoting, effecting, or realizing that object. Such ends "to be effected" can be linked to the inclinations, desires and incentives of the agent, and they are classified as "relative" or "material" or "subjective" ends, with only relative value. While such subjective ends can "ground" hypothetical imperatives, they cannot ground principles valid for all rational beings. So, subjective ends cannot be the "objective ground" of a law.[13] But, there could be a different sort of end or objective ground of action, an objective end, which might be the (objective) ground of a law. "Suppose there were something the *existence of which in itself* has an absolute worth, something which as *an end in itself* could be a ground of determinate laws" (GMS: 428.3–6); if there were something like that, it would *ground* the practical law.

One noteworthy feature of the kind of end Kant has in mind here is that it is an *existent end*; its *existence*, as opposed to its consideration as a not-yet-existent possible effect, is important to its conception as an end (and its primary role as a ground). Its existence and worth appears to be logically prior to the actions or principles it grounds. It may inform, guide, or govern action, not primarily in the way that an "end to be effected" does, but by, for example, grounding limits on what other ends (and ends to be effected) may be chosen, and on what means in pursuit of those ends might be legitimate (GMS: 428, 431). In addition, Kant's supposition is that this end is an end whose existence "has an absolute worth."

---

formal bar upon reflection and analysis uncovering and articulating some necessary conditions, perhaps implicit, of an already stated sufficient condition (Allison 2011, p. 206, note 4).

12 When he speaks of grounds here, Kant is, at least in part, concerned with potential grounds of action (*Bewegungsgründe*) or "motives" for a rational being, with the range of elements that may inform, guide, or govern an agent's action, by way of their representation. Kant seems to use "*Bewegungsgründe*" to cover both the mental act or psychological state of having an end or intention, and its content or object (the end).

13 Often, Kant's general descriptions of "ends" tend to focus upon ends "to be effected," not existent end-in-themselves, but these descriptions can certainly include "obligatory ends" and thus are not restricted to "subjective ends" (Rel: 6, TL: 381, 385). At this point in *Groundwork* II, Kant does not explicitly consider objective or obligatory ends-to-be-effected, though the idea of a good will and the idea of a possible kingdom of ends will enter the discussion a bit later. Allison argues that obligatory ends cannot ground the moral law (in the relevant way) since they are grounded in the law (Allison 2011, p. 208).

> These, therefore, are not merely subjective ends, the existence of which as an effect of our action has a worth *for us*, but rather *objective ends*, that is, beings the existence of which is in itself an end, and indeed one such that no other end, to which they would serve *merely* as a means, can be put in its place [...]. (GMS: 428.25–29)

If there were such a thing, it could be "the ground of a possible categorical imperative" (GMS: 428.4–5).

The concept of *grounding* principles is central to this part of the text,[14] but what sort of grounding is involved here? The discussion of grounding that leads up to the introduction of the Formula of Humanity culminates in a cluster of several grounding claims.[15] While some of the claims included here concern epistemic grounds, I contend that the central grounding claim is metaphysical, not merely epistemic or psychological.

> If then, there is to be a supreme practical principle and, with respect to the human will, a categorical imperative, it must be one such that, from the representation of what is necessarily an end for everyone because it is an *end in itself*, it constitutes an *objective* principle of the will and thus can serve as a universal practical law. (GMS: 428.34–429.2)

Abstracting from Kant's preferred candidate for a moment ("rational nature exists as an end-in-itself"), we can observe that he consistently identifies the ground in an indicative statement, rather than in an imperative, in a statement about something being an end-in-itself or being of absolute value: "because it is an end in itself," it is necessarily an end for everyone, and this, in turn, allows it to constitute the supreme practical principle. Of course, Kant often emphasizes that the moral law must be valid for all rational beings, even for those not subject to imperatives (on account of their holy wills), so we already have some reason to expect that a non-imperatival representation of the moral law may be more fundamental than imperatival formulations of it.[16] More than this, however, it is striking that Kant's statement of the *ground* of the law is an indicative statement about *the absolute worth or existence as an end-in-itself of an existent being or beings,* not a statement about or a description (or prescription) of action. The ground is a (putative) metaphysical fact, expressed in an indicative statement about existence. "The ground of this [supreme practical] principle is: *rational nature exists as an end in itself*" (GMS:

---

14 Cf. GMS: 427.32–429.8, 431.10, also 438.7.
15 Cf. GMS: 429.2–8 and 429, note.
16 See GMS: 412–414. While Kant often asserts a necessary connection between imperatives and claims of goodness, it is significant that Kant often suggests that the claims of existent goodness are more basic.

429.2–3). Some existent beings of absolute value could be a sufficient (objective) ground for a rational being, for any rational being, to will and act in some determinate way.

If there *is* an objective end, and it is cognized by a rational being, it grounds her grasp of and action upon an unconditional law. If a rational being represents an objective end, she may infer that some action is called for and she may proceed to action on the basis of this representation. But the objective grounding relation is not primarily an epistemic or psychological relation. Kant doesn't claim that we must first represent this objective end in order to determine what needs to be done (indeed, he suggested that we can often determine what needs to be done via the Formula of Universal Law). Nor does Kant claim that this representation is necessary to provide our motivation, as if we are impotent in the absence of such a representation. We might grasp and even act upon such a law without explicitly representing the objective end to ourselves. Rather, his point is that the law's validity depends upon there being such an objective end, and it being the case that the objective end could objectively ground the cognition and action of a *perfectly* rational being and ground an imperative for an imperfectly rational being. This is a metaphysical, and not merely epistemic or psychological relation. This alleged metaphysical fact would ground the appropriate action (and ground an imperative for the appropriate action, supposing it is contingent whether the action is carried out or not).

Of course, there are several other "grounding" relations also mentioned here, some of which are epistemic. Kant is supposing here, as he does throughout *Groundwork* II, that there is a valid moral law, in order to articulate how such a law would be grounded in the existence of something (and "connected" to the nature of a rational being). The grounds for this supposition are explored in *Groundwork* III. Kant also indicates that there are "rational grounds" (*Vernunftgründe*) for his metaphysical grounding claim, epistemic grounds which he does not elaborate here, and he pledges that "the grounds" (GMS: 429.6, 429, note) for some of these claims will be found in *Groundwork* III.[17] Kant is not claiming here that he proves: first that every rational being has absolute worth or exists as an end-in-itself, in order to then infer that every rational being must represent rational nature (or his own existence) in this way, from which he can then also infer that there is a categorical imperative. (Nor is he here promising such an argumentative strategy for *Groundwork* III.)

---

17 The nature and strategy of *Groundwork* III is beyond the scope of this chapter. I am largely sympathetic with the treatment of Schönecker (2006). For a promising recent discussion of the place of value claims in *Groundwork* III, see also Stern (2010, pp. 471f.; 2013, pp. 33f.).

Rather, he is provisionally postulating that every rational being has absolute worth or exists as an end-in-itself, and claiming that this putative fact would be the needed metaphysical ground of any practical law.[18] Further discussion of the epistemic and metaphysical grounds for some of these claims is deferred to *Groundwork* III. In any event, this multiplicity of grounding relations helps to bring into relief the crucial metaphysical grounding relation that Kant is positing here.

Of course, Kant does propose a particular candidate for this grounding role: "the human being and in general every rational being *exists* as an end in itself" and has "absolute worth" (GMS: 428.7–8).[19] Kant briefly considers some alternative candidates, and eliminates them fairly quickly: objects of our inclinations, our inclinations themselves, and non-rational creatures have a relative or conditional worth, not absolute worth.[20] Without much explanation, Kant asserts: "rational beings are called *persons* because their nature already marks them out as an end in itself [...]" (GMS: 428.21–23). From the representation of it, "of what is necessarily an end for everyone because it is an end in itself," an objective principle of the will can be composed.[21] Kant then articulates the formula for such a principle – in terms of its ground –, i.e., his second major

---

18 Some commentators suggest that GMS: 429.3–7 contains a crucial argument against egoistic moral skepticism, an argument from recognizing the value of my own existence to recognizing the value of every rational being. But it is neither clear that Kant intends such an argument, nor how it would go, based on the text. Kant does imply that we have valid rational grounds for representing our existence as an end-in-itself. But, as Stern (2013) points out, the contrast Kant draws here between how the human being represents his existence and how other rational beings represent it may be concerned instead with questions about whether the moral law applies to *all rational beings* (including non-human rational beings, such as God) and requires everyone to treat *us* as ends-in-themselves, a topic Kant considers elsewhere. (On this point, Stern cites MAM: 114 f. I would add KpV: 87.27–30 and 131.20–23, which are even more explicit [briefly discussed below].) For a similar point, see Kerstein (2006, pp. 210 f.).
19 As we will see below, there is some controversy about what exactly Kant has in mind by "humanity" or "the human being" and "rational nature" in this context.
20 This seems to be an argument by elimination, rather than a single, linear "regress" argument, and even by Kant's own lights it is not clear that it is exhaustive of all potential candidates: here he does not explicitly consider objects with "fancy price" (GMS: 435) or objects of wonder, for example. For discussion of this elimination argument, see Timmermann (2006), Kerstein (2006), and Martin (2006).
21 Indeed, on one reading of GMS: 429.7–9, Kant claims that the existence of rational beings as an end-in-itself *is* the objective principle (the "*es*" in 429.7 may refer to the "*Dasein*"), and is the "highest practical ground" from which the laws of the will must be able to be derived. Kant may be suggesting that this is what the Formula of Humanity, which he is in the process of deriving, is intended to express.

formulation of the categorical imperative, the Formula of Humanity: "So act that you use humanity whether in your own person or in the person of any other, always at the same time as an end, never merely as a means" (GMS: 429.10 – 12).

A bit later in *Groundwork* II, Kant reflects back on this formula of the categorical imperative and elaborates upon how "the rational being itself" is uniquely suited to be an existent end-in-itself that grounds an unconditional law, if there is one.

> Now this end can be nothing other than the subject of all possible ends itself, because this subject is also the subject of a possible absolutely good will; for, such a will cannot without contradiction be subordinated to any other object. [...] the subject of ends, that is, the rational being itself, must be made the ground (*Grund*) of all maxims of actions, never merely as a means but as the supreme limiting condition in the use of all means, that is, always at the same time as an end. (GMS: 437.30 – 438.7)

Earlier Kant eliminated other candidates because they were not plausibly of "objective value" or "ends-in-themselves" (GMS: 428). Here Kant makes more explicit a stronger reason for excluding the other candidates that he had mentioned earlier: the end-in-itself (or the objective ground of a law) must *be* "the subject of a possible absolutely good will" because such a possible absolutely good will "cannot be subordinated (*nachgesetzt*) to any other object."[22] If something other than a rational being were the existent end-in-itself that grounded the moral law, then every rational being, including an absolutely good will, would be subordinated to or constrained by that other thing. Perhaps as importantly (for present purposes), the sought for "connection" between a rational being and some end-in-itself *other* than a rational being, would seem to be at best conditional and mediated, dependent upon some "interest." But the relation of a rational being to itself, and perhaps to other rational beings, could be direct and immediate. If there is an unconditional law for all rational beings, it seems that a rational being itself could be its ground in a way nothing

---

[22] Kerstein considers this as a supplement to Kant's earlier argument from elimination. In part, Kant is appealing to a substantive claim of ordinary moral cognition articulated at the beginning of *Groundwork* I: the only thing that can be considered good without qualification is a good will (GMS: 393.5 – 7). He is not claiming that this implies that the realized good will itself must be the sought for end-in-itself (rather: the "subject of a possible absolutely good will" and the "subject of all possible ends" is the end-in-itself), but the end-in-itself certainly cannot be some completely distinct object (or kind of object) with which the good will would conflict, or to which it would be subordinate (Kerstein 2006, pp. 212 – 218). Kerstein notes that one cannot have a good will without having "humanity" (which is correct), but he doesn't emphasize the important teleological connection between these characteristics of a rational being (see below).

else could. This claim, that the *ground* of the moral law is the existence and worth of the rational beings to whom the law applies, reveals something important about the sought after "connection" between the will and the law. As Kant had intimated, the requisite connection would be a "relation of a will to itself insofar as it determines itself only by reason" (GMS: 427.14).

By explicitly focusing on the absolute worth of humanity as an end-in-itself, the Formula of Humanity is supposed to reveal something about the ground of the moral law that was not explicit in the Formula of Universal Law. Without qualifying or retracting his derivation of the Formula of Universal Law, Kant implies that the absolute worth of humanity is supposed to be the metaphysical ground of this formula, and every genuine formula, of the moral law. This intended lesson is confirmed by Kant's subsequent observations in *Groundwork* II about the Formula of Autonomy, which "follows" from the previous two formulae.[23] What the Formula of Humanity contributes to this third formula is attention to the rational agent itself, and to every rational agent, as the ground and "object" of an unconditional law.

> [I]f there is a categorical imperative (i.e., a law for every will of a rational being) it can only command that everything be done from the maxim of one's will as a will that could at the same time have as its object itself as giving universal law; for only then is the practical principle, and the imperative that the will obeys, unconditional, since it can have no interest as its basis. (GMS: 432.18–24)

If rational beings not only represent (or cognize) and declare laws, but rational beings are themselves the *ground* of the moral law, it is fitting to claim that rational beings *legislate* these laws and that nothing else can ground or legislate any other unconditional laws to them or for them. The Formula of Autonomy makes explicit the unconditional validity of the moral law because it indicates that unconditional lawgiving cannot depend upon any "interest" by invoking

---

23 Kant contends that these two formulae (along with the third) "are at bottom only so many formulae of the very same law," (GMS: 436, cf. 437) that they are derivable from the concept of a rational being, and that each of the first two may be derived from the other and they together lead to the third (GMS: 437f.). As an interpretive matter, it is clear that Kant considers the formulae to be inter-derivable and extensionally equivalent. My interpretation aims to be consistent with this contention, without requiring it. Kant's grounding claim is that the worth of rational beings grounds the moral law, in each of its authentic formulations, not that the Formula of Humanity grounds the Formula of Universal Law, whatever that might mean. The orders of presentation and of derivation are not necessarily indicative of metaphysical grounding relations or metaphysical dependence relations, contra Formosa (2013).

"the idea of the will of every rational being as a *will giving universal law*" (GMS: 431 f.).

> The practical necessity of acting in accordance with this principle, that is, duty, does not rest at all on feelings, impulses, and inclinations but merely on the relation of rational beings to one another, in which the will of a rational being must always be regarded as at the same time *lawgiving*, since otherwise it could not be thought as an *end in itself*. Reason accordingly refers every maxim of the will as giving universal law to every other will and also to every action toward itself, and does so not for the sake of any other practical motive (*Bewegungsgrund*) or any future advantage but from the idea of the *dignity* of a rational being, who obeys no law other than that which he himself at the same time gives. (GMS: 434.20 – 30)

I have argued elsewhere that the legislation, and the self-legislation, of the moral law is not a sovereign or discretionary act. Kant is not saying that "ends-in-themselves" get to create moral laws (perhaps whatever laws they please, subject perhaps to a few procedural requirements) or to give laws their fundamental authority by willing them. Rather, the content and authority of the unconditional law to which rational beings are subject is and must be grounded in the nature of those very rational beings.[24] But what could it mean to say that the moral law is grounded in the nature of the rational will, but not grounded *by* its acts? Kant's account of rational beings as the objective end of the moral law helps to explicate this "connection" of the law to rational beings. The absolute worth or dignity of rational beings, their own nature as end-in-itself, metaphysically grounds the moral law, and it is the articulation of this point that gives rise to the claim that the moral law is self-legislated by rational beings.

The "dignity (*Würde*) of a rational being" (GMS: 434.29) is a kind of worth or value (*Werth*), distinct from price (*Preis*).

> What is related to general human inclinations and needs has a *market price*; that which, even without presupposing a need, conforms with a certain taste, that is, with a delight in the mere purposeless play of our mental powers, has a *fancy price*; but that which constitutes the condition under which alone something can be an end in itself has not merely a relative worth, that is, a price, but an inner worth, that is, *dignity*. (GMS: 434.35 – 435.4)

Whereas price depends upon a relation – a particular relation to inclinations, need, or taste – dignity (of the sort described here) is an *inner* worth, a worth not dependent upon its bearer's relation to something distinct from itself. This

---

24 See Kain (2004).

inner worth, Kant insists, "constitutes the condition under which alone something can be an end in itself" and it grounds the moral law.[25]

There is some controversy about what exactly Kant intends to designate as the bearer of this dignity or absolute worth. Sometimes, Kant insists "morality, and humanity insofar as it is capable of morality, is that which alone has dignity" (GMS: 435.7–9). Then he proceeds to claim "fidelity in promises and benevolence from basic principles (not from instinct) have an inner worth" (GMS: 435.11–12). And sometimes, Kant suggests dignity belongs to a "rational being, who obeys no law other than that which he at the same time gives" (GMS: 434.29–30). The opening lines of *Groundwork* I insist that the good will is the only thing that is good without limitation or absolutely good.[26] So which is it: does dignity belong to every rational being capable of morality or does dignity belong to a good will (and its acts)?[27] I believe the answer is: both. As Sensen has helpfully explained: "Kant has a two-fold conception of

---

25 Some commentators emphasize Kant's claims that dignity is something which its bearer *has*; but the same surface grammar applies to the relation (or relational property) of price. More important, I think, is Kant's repeated emphasis upon dignity as inner worth (GMS: 435.4, 435.12, 454.37; cf. TL: 435.2, 436.10). In many other contexts Kant uses "dignity" to refer to an elevation of one thing in relation to another (as Sensen exhaustively catalogues) in terms of value, such as the elevation of an officeholder to ordinary citizens. In this context, however, Kant emphasizes that "dignity" refers to a kind of inner worth. While it still implies a comparison with or elevation above things of mere price (if there are any), this inner worth does not presuppose there is anything with price (or anything distinct at all). As Sensen concedes, "inner" implies something that can be judged in "isolation, i.e., independently of any relations that may hold" (Sensen 2011, p. 185); but this means that inner worth is not merely elevation. Moreover, even if Sensen were right that dignity always involves elevation and that dignity is distinct from inner worth (which would be the intrinsic basis of its elevation?), inner worth remains intrinsic to its bearer and available for grounding the law.
26 Cf. GMS: 393.
27 Some commentators suggest that Kant isolates a particular feature or disposition or *capacity* or activity of rational beings, rather than the individual rational beings, as the bearer of dignity or the end-in-itself. Kant's seemingly abstract references to "rational nature" and his various uses of "humanity" and "person" in the *Groundwork* create some confusion, but, as Timmermann argues, there are good textual reasons for taking Kant to refer to individual rational beings as ends-in-themselves. He repeatedly says that it is rational beings or human beings that are ends-in-themselves, and his occasional use of "rational nature" is best taken as an equivalent stylistic variant signifying individual creatures (Timmermann 2006, pp. 71f.).

Commentators also disagree about whether the crucial feature of rational beings, in virtue of which they have dignity, is a general capacity for choice, a specific capacity for moral choice, or a committed choice of moral goodness (a good will). One source of this disagreement is Kant's terminology in the *Religion*, where he distinguishes between animality, humanity, and personality as our predispositions (*Anlagen*) to good (Rel: 26–28).

dignity. The capacity for morality is one's initial dignity, while actually being morally good is the fully realized form of one's dignity" (Sensen 2011, p. 168).

The basic idea is teleological and perfectionist: "Everyone has an initial dignity in having certain capacities (e.g., reason, freedom). But only if one makes a proper use of one's capacities does one fully realize one's initial dignity" (Sensen 2011, p. 163).[28] "The human being and in general every rational being exists as an end in itself," an existent being "with absolute worth" and an existent "objective end." It is not just that Kant predicates inner worth or dignity both of rational beings capable of morality and of good wills, he explicitly ties them together teleologically, on multiple occasions. The true and highest purpose and vocation (*Bestimmung*) of practical reason is to produce a will good in itself.[29] Such a good will is the only good without qualification. Both "morality" and "humanity insofar as it is capable of morality, is that which alone has dignity" (GMS: 435.7–9).[30]

In short, in *Groundwork* II, Kant contends that all rational beings (capable of morality) have inner worth, which is not dependent upon anyone's acts or mental acts; and this dignity is properly recognized as the ground of the moral law.[31] This is a distinctive kind of value realism. Part of Kant's distinctive position consists in his claim that only the inner worth or dignity of rational beings can be the ground of the moral law.[32] This value appears fundamental,

---

[28] I agree that Kant exemplifies this feature of what Sensen calls the "traditional paradigm"; I also agree that Kant exemplifies a particular version of perfectionism and that he gives priority to duties, rather than rights (see Sensen 2011, chapter 4). I am not convinced by Sensen's other contentions that, according to Kant and many other "traditional" theorists, dignity is "not a value" (Sensen 2011, p. 162), and that for Kant in particular, value claims can be reduced to claims about imperatives (Sensen 2011, pp. 32–35, 100–104, 190); but I cannot settle these issues here.
[29] Cf. GMS: 396, 434.34.
[30] Thus, to be clear, I take it that "initial dignity" belongs to rational beings with (and in virtue of) the capacity for morality, not to beings merely with (or in virtue of) a general capacity for choice or general "freedom" itself, pace Wood (2008, p. 88) and Guyer (2000), for example.
[31] The bearer of dignity is a rational being. Initial dignity is completely independent of anyone's mental acts or attitudes. The bearer of realized dignity, a good will, must include certain acts and attitudes, but the dignity does not depend upon anyone's acts or attitudes toward the bearer.
[32] Bacin has recently suggested that Kant, like others such as Pufendorf, invokes dignity in a "subordinate justificatory role," as a motivational "shorthand" for the derivation of some specific obligations, but does not invoke a "new metaethical thesis" such as "dignity as a ground of morality" (Bacin 2015, pp. 104f., 103). I agree that Kant appeals to human dignity and "humanity as an end in itself" to derive particular duties; that is indeed central to the derivation

not reducible to something else. I do not contend that Kant first proves that rational beings have dignity, that is, inner worth, and then derives the Formula of Humanity (or some other formula) from that. Kant's argument at this point of the *Groundwork* is conditional: if there is a moral law for rational beings, there is an objective end that grounds it, and this must be the rational being itself. The dignity of human beings, and the claim that this dignity is itself the ground of the moral law, is presented as a discovery or postulate rather than a premise. Indeed, this discovery is presented as a crucial step to Kant's claims about self-legislation and autonomy that are generally agreed (somehow or other) to be a crucial and distinctive element of Kant's moral philosophy.

The Paradox of Method in the second *Critique*

According to *Groundwork* II, the inner worth or dignity of rational beings is the objective ground of the moral law. Yet, as we noted at the outset of this chapter, many readers suppose that all forms of value realism are ruled out by Kant's contention, in the *Critique of Practical Reason*, that *the rational will*, or pure practical reason, and its *law*, must be the basis of "the concept of the good."

> If the concept of the good is not to be derived from an antecedent practical law but, instead, is to serve as its basis, it can only be the concept of something whose existence [as an effect possible through freedom] promises pleasure and thus determines the causality of the subject, that is the faculty of desire, to produce it. (KpV: 58.10–14; cf. 62–64, quoted above)

Taken at face value, this admittedly "paradoxical" assertion may seem incompatible with the account, just articulated, of the absolute worth of rational beings as the objective ground of the moral law. One of Kant's central claims is that the moral law cannot be grounded in the goodness of a possible object to be produced. The question is what Kant's claims, or his arguments for them, imply about whether the inner worth or dignity of rational beings can ground the moral law. I will argue that Kant's paradox of method does not preclude this claim, and that it, and the second *Critique* as a whole, shed further light on Kant's distinctive form of value realism.[33]

---

of duties from the Formula of Humanity (GMS: 429 f.). But I have argued that Kant does insist that the absolute value of rational beings is a ground of the moral law.

33 For previous treatments of the paradox of method sympathetic with some kind of Kantian value realism, see Ameriks (1996 and 2003, p. 270) and Guyer (2000, chapter 4).

The first thing to note is that, despite some appearances, Kant's "paradox of method" is not driven by a *definition* of goodness that precludes value realism.[34] In the second *Critique* in particular, Kant is concerned with proper "philosophic procedure" and "method," which he takes to require that controversial issues are not prematurely decided with loaded expositions or definitions (KpV: 9, note). Kant begins the chapter in question with several semantic observations, however. Ordinary language, he claims, recognizes a distinction between "the agreeable" and "the good"; and, he suggests that predications of goodness involve some reference to a subject's faculty of desire. By a "good" object of practical reason is "understood a necessary object of the faculty of desire" and ordinary language "requires that good and evil always be appraised (*beurtheilt*) by reason" rather than mere feeling (KpV: 58). These semantic points are intended to prepare the way for, but do not, by themselves, settle the substantive issues, and certainly not by definition.

Second, Kant is determined to highlight what he calls questions of "method"; the paradox is a "paradox of method." At least initially, the focus is on method and on epistemological, rather than ontological, issues. Kant acknowledges that it *seems* that we should begin our moral investigations with the concept of a good object "as an effect (*einer möglichen Wirkung*) possible through freedom," an object "to be made actual (*wirklich*)" (KpV: 57.18–25, cf. 60.19), not with a principle or law of the will. In general, principles and laws are judgments, containing concepts, so it is hard to see how we could begin with a principle.[35] The *Critique of Pure Reason* quite properly considered the central concepts of speculative reason (not to mention sensibility) before deducing its principles.[36] And it may seem that this is the method to follow when considering the will, too. The will or faculty of desire is "a being's faculty to be by means of its representations the cause of the actuality of the objects of these representations"; (KpV: 9, note) this implies that "every volition must have an object" (KpV: 34) and this object must bear some relation to the will. We also often appraise the objects we desire and intend to produce. Indeed, it may *seem*

---

[34] Unfortunately, Beck mistakenly rendered *bestimmen* (determine) as "define" (Beck 1956, pp. 65f., translating KpV: 63.4 and 64.4), and was followed by many, including Rawls (2000, p. 227) and Schneewind (1998, p. 512). In Kant's German, *bestimmen* can indicate either epistemic determination or metaphysical determination, not to mention often suggesting teleological destiny or vocation. A similar issue arises with the interpretation of GMS: 436.1.
[35] See KpV: 19.
[36] See KpV: 16. Kant consistently talks about the order of precedence between the *principle* or law of the will and the *concept* of the good, and contrasts this order with the first *Critique*'s examination of concepts before principles (KpV: 16.30–31, 42, 45f., 90f.).

that the only concept we can form of goodness is that of "goodness *for*" something or someone, where we must presuppose some kind of "interest" which directly or indirectly grounds the validity or bindingness of the good thing, or good act, for the agent.[37] Kant's paradoxical methodological contention is that, all of this to the contrary, we should not assume that *this* is the right place to begin our inquiry: it begs the central question to assume that we must begin with the concept of a good object to be produced. Kant argues that, if we begin with such a concept, "it can be only the concept of something whose existence promises pleasure" (KpV: 58), which can only be judged by experience and in relation to the contingent and variable feeling of individual subjects. This would assume that the will can have only "empirical determining grounds," grounds which could never suffice for a necessary moral law valid for all rational beings.

Indeed, Kant insists that, at this point in the second *Critique*, he has already identified a *formal* principle, a "rational principle [...] already thought as in itself the determining ground of the will without regard to possible objects of the faculty of desire" (KpV: 62.10–12). This formal principle appears to us finite rational beings as a categorical imperative and "prescribes to maxims only their lawful form without regard to an object" (KpV: 63.31–32).[38] This formal principle can, and only a formal principle can, determine the will "a priori and immediately" (KpV: 64.13–14). With respect to the epistemic order of principles and concepts, Kant has also already contended that this formal principle "first discloses to us the concept of freedom" (KpV: 30, cf. 16); the moral law is the "*ratio cognoscendi* of freedom," which is "the *ratio essendi* of the moral law" (KpV: 4, note).[39] Here Kant is emphasizing the importance of

---

[37] This was one of the central contentions of Kant's "astute" critic, Pistorius, whose review of the *Groundwork* Kant aimed to rebut in the second *Critique* (KpV: 9, note).

[38] Kant seems to have something like the Formula of Universal Law or the Formula of Autonomy (and a "lawgiving of its own") at the front of his mind throughout the first half of the second *Critique*, with little allusion to Formula of Humanity. But later in the second *Critique*, explicit emphasis is placed on persons as ends in themselves (e. g., KpV: 87, 110, 131 f., 162). In the relevant sense, of course, the Formula of Humanity is also a formal principle.

[39] This is part of Kant's "great reversal," in which he abandons *Groundwork* III's strategy to establish freedom and then deduce the moral law from it (Ameriks 2003). While this point about the disclosure of the concept of freedom is distinct from (and prior to) the point about the concept of goodness in the paradox of method, it helpfully reminds us of the initially methodological and epistemological points Kant has in mind when he emphasizes the priority of a principle (the moral law) over a determinate concept (such as the concept of goodness), when he says, for example, that "it is the moral law that first determines and makes possible the concept of the good, insofar as it deserves this name absolutely" (KpV: 64.3–5).

identifying the supreme principle of morality before specifying some good to be produced; he insists his rivals mistakenly search first for an object of pleasure or desire.[40]

Kant's point is not merely methodological or epistemic, however. Kant draws two important substantive conclusions about goodness from these observations. First: there can be something *absolutely good* if, and only if, there is a formal principle; and only *actions or persons* can be absolutely good. Kant draws this lesson twice: it is actions and rational agents, rather than mere things or objects to make actual, that should be called good absolutely.[41] Second, Kant notes that, if he is right, questions about which *objects* will be intended and produced by agents whose wills are determined by this principle can only be properly addressed after this principle is "established and justified," so he defers many of these questions until the *Dialectic* section of the book (where he considers what he calls "the highest good," the object of pure practical reason, KpV: 64.27–34).[42] Part of the metaphysical point is that neither the value of people's state of happiness or unhappiness nor the value of the effects of actions is fundamental. The "goodness" of a possible object to be produced cannot ground the moral law, because it lacks the requisite immediacy to the will, and the universality and necessity characteristic of the moral law (which it would allegedly ground).[43]

Part of what Kant recognizes may seem "paradoxical," or absurd, or obscure, is the thesis that the *value of actions or persons* can be prior to and separable from the value of the ends which actions (or people) produce or intend to produce, that the value of persons or actions can be a ground of action

---

40 See KpV: 64.9–15.
41 See KpV: 60.19–25, 62.15–18. As Paton noted, a purported "definition" of goodness in terms of the object of a rational will does not easily capture Kant's own central examples: the immediate goodness of good action and the absolute goodness of a good will (Paton 1944, pp. 6, 14, 24; 1947, pp. 27, 103f., 110f., 201). This seems to be further reason to think Kant's observation about the relation between goodness and a rational will is not a real definition of goodness. Johnson contends that the good will and humanity can be considered necessary objects of a rational will, so they are compatible with "the official Kantian theory of value" (Johnson 2007). Even if something like this is right, it suggests that we are working with a criterion of goodness or a nominal definition rather than a real definition.
42 We can determine which actions and agents are good by judging them according to (one or another formulation of) the formal moral law (and later, we can also judge which material ends or objects are good). This all suggests that Kant is not thinking of actions or persons or a good will as possible objects to be produced.
43 Kant explicitly targets rival approaches as unsatisfactory accounts of the "*Grunde eines Gesetzes*" (KpV: 64.10).

(*Bewegungsgrund*) independently of desired ends to be effected.⁴⁴ Yet, he insists, if there is a moral law, this must be the case. The capacity of the will to be determined by a formal principle (*immediately by reason*, without regard for a possible object of desire) is revealed to us by our immediate consciousness of that very law.⁴⁵ This capacity is our "personality"; it is our vocation to a "higher end" and gives us our worth (KpV: 61, 66, 162); this is the key to all (absolute) goodness. Again, the point that Kant is most insistent upon in this chapter is that the "goodness" of a possible object to be produced cannot ground the moral law. To emphasize this point, Kant contrasts the goodness of the "realized dignity" (as Sensen might put it) of a good will that always conforms to the law, with that of some pleasant result. Kant also affirms, in the midst of this very discussion, that the basis of our worth is that we *have* reason for a higher purpose, our capacity and vocation for moral goodness.⁴⁶ Kant thereby reasserts his two-fold teleological conception of the dignity of rational beings. These claims are allegedly revealed by reason, rather than mere feeling, they are allegedly necessary, and they represent an immediate relation of any rational being to itself. Thus, Kant's objections, in his discussion of the "Paradox of Method," to grounding the moral law in an object to be produced do not rule out his own claims about the inner worth of rational beings. These remarks within the "paradox of method" seem to harmonize with the *Groundwork's* contention that the worth of a person can be the metaphysical ground of the moral law.

Of course, in the second *Critique* and this chapter of it in particular, Kant does not discuss at great length the worth or dignity of human beings, or its role as an objective ground. The *Critique of Practical Reason* has a specific critical focus and it presumes that one is already familiar with the *Groundwork*. But, in fact, in the second *Critique* Kant does invoke the worth of humanity several times – and with great emphasis.⁴⁷ Indeed, the culmination of his analysis of "respect for the moral law" is his insistence that the *origin* (*Ursprung*) of duty is *our personality*, so that a person is "subject to his own personality [...]" (KpV: 86.34–87.12).⁴⁸

---

44 Cf. GMS: 439.4–7.
45 See KpV: 29 f.
46 See KpV: 61.32–62.7.
47 See KpV: 87, 110, 131 f., 152, 162
48 Here, and elsewhere, the English phrase "subjected to" (*unterworfen*) can be misleading when found in proximity to Kant's claims about being the "subject of the moral law" (*das Subject des moralisches Gesetzes*), as if being the "subject of the moral law" is simply being

> [...] on this origin are based many expressions that indicate the worth of objects according to moral ideas. [...] [a rational being] is to be used never merely as a means but as at the same time an end. We rightly attribute this condition even to the divine will with respect to the rational beings in the world as its creatures, in as much as it rests on their *personality*, by which alone they are ends in themselves. (KpV: 87.13–30)

Similar to his contention in the *Groundwork* that we rational beings are "the subject of all ends" and, thus, the "legislators" of the moral law (GMS: 431, 437 f.), Kant insists that rational beings are not just under the moral law, but rather are "the *subject[s] of the moral law*": "humanity in our person must, accordingly, be *holy* to ourselves: for he [the human being] is the *subject of the moral law* and so of that which is holy in itself" (KpV: 131.24–25, cf. KpV: 87.20).[49] "This idea of personality, awaken[s] respect by setting before our eyes the sublimity of our nature (in its vocation) [...]" (KpV: 87.31–32).

There is much that needs to be unpacked here and in Kant's "Conclusion" to the second *Critique:*

> Two things fill the mind with ever new and increasing admiration and reverence, the more often and more steadily one reflects on them: *the starry heavens above me and the moral law within me.* [...] The second begins from my invisible self, my personality, and presents me in a world which has true infinity ... [It] infinitely raises my worth as an *intelligence* by my personality, in which the moral law reveals to me a life independent of animality and even of the whole sensible world [...]. (KpV: 161 f.)

Kant alleges deep connections between "the moral law within me," its "beginning from my invisible self, my personality," what the law "reveals to me," and "my worth as an intelligence by my personality."[50] These connections are attributed to reason, rather than mere feeling (though they are reflected in feelings such as reverence and respect); they represent an immediate relation of any rational being to itself; and Kant emphasizes that they extend universally, so that even God's actions are somehow conditioned by our worth. Again, in his discussion of the "Paradox of Method," Kant's objections to grounding the moral law in an object to be produced do not conflict with his own claims that the inner worth of rational beings is the objective ground of the moral law.

---

someone subject *to* it. Kant's point is that the subjects of the law are those for whom the law indicates respect (even from God!); they are ends-in-themselves that ground the law.

49 In both of these passages, Kant boldly insists that our worth conditions even the divine will to treat us as ends never as mere means.

50 As Reath has suggested, for Kant, and for Rawls's Kant, "it is difficult to keep the notions of law and value apart in the end" (Reath 2003, p. 148). Which notion is most fundamental, and in which respects, is a question deserving further attention.

Consistent with his methodological claims in the "paradox of method" that we must begin with a principle, Kant does not begin his philosophical account with a cognition of our inner worth (and "vocation" for a good will) in order to derive the moral law and principle of action from that recognition as its ground.[51] Such an approach would involve starting with some warranted cognition of some aspect of *ourselves*, with a self-cognition of our value which would determine our action immediately and in a way valid for all rational beings.[52] Kant insists that our empirical-phenomenal self-cognition is certainly unsuitable for such a role: it is empirical and not a priori, it is not sufficiently universal, it can reveal only material determining grounds such as my needs and desires, and so it cannot ground the moral law. Of course, Kant also denies, especially after the "great reversal," that I can have a determinate theoretical cognition of myself, as a thing-in-itself with freedom, for example.[53] We cannot *begin* with a substantive self-cognition that would determine us to action immediately and in a way valid for all rational beings because we don't seem to have any such cognition of ourself. After his "great reversal," Kant maintains that it is only "the fact of reason," our awareness of the moral law (in the form of a categorical imperative), that reveals our positive freedom, and reveals our dignity to us. Yet *what* this awareness of the moral law reveals to us is a cognition of our "proper self" (GMS: 457, 461) which can determine the will immediately and a priori; it reveals our "personality" which is the origin of duty (KpV: 86). It reveals that we are each "subjected to [our] own personality"; it is "the humanity in [our] person which is holy to us [...]" and "by virtue of the autonomy of [our] freedom, [we] are the subject of the moral law, which is holy" (KpV: 87).[54] Through the fact of reason we discover our inner worth, which is the objective ground of the moral law.[55]

---

51 In a way, of course, Kant does sometimes "begin" his reflections on common rational cognition this way, as in the opening lines of *Groundwork* I, for example (GMS: 393).
52 As Sensen puts it: "How could one know that one has this property?" (Sensen 2011, p. 93)
53 See e. g., KpV: 42.
54 "For, it is our reason itself which by means of the supreme and unconditional practical law cognizes itself and the being that is conscious of this law (our own person) as belonging to the pure world of understanding and even determines the way in which, as such, it can be active" (KpV: 105).
55 Sensen argues against Kantian value realism because he thinks Kant's epistemology is incompatible with knowledge of others' dignity (Sensen 2011). I contend Kant holds that we do not have immediate cognitive access to *others'* freedom or inner worth; as in our own case, this must depend on the "fact of reason." Yet, Kant does not seem especially concerned with skepticism about *others* freedom or dignity, in particular. If there is a moral law, we have good reason to think that it applies to us, which is good reason to take it to apply to

Conclusion

On a plausible reading of both the *Groundwork* and second *Critique*, Kant maintains that human beings, and more generally, rational beings, have dignity or inner worth. We cognize through the moral law that our existence and inner value is the objective ground of the law and that we are the "subject of the moral law." This dignity of rational beings is quite fundamental and irreducible. This qualifies as a distinctive kind of value realism.[56]

Literature

Kant

GMS Grundlegung zur Metaphysik der Sitten, AA 4
KpV Kritik der praktischen Vernunft, AA 5
MAM Mutmaßlicher Anfang der Menschengeschichte, AA 8
Rel Die Religion innerhalb der Grenzen der bloßen Vernunft, AA 6
TL Metaphysische Anfangsgründe der Tugendlehre, AA 6

With the exception of occasional minor modifications, quotations from Kant are taken from the series *The Cambridge Edition of the Works of Immanuel Kant*, Cambridge University Press (1992 ff.).

All page and line numbers in parentheses refer to the so-called Akademie-Ausgabe (AA), i.e., to *Kant's gesammelte Schriften*, herausgegeben von der *Königlich Preußischen Akademie der Wissenschaften*, Berlin: Walter de Gruyter (1900 ff.).

Secondary Literature

Allison, Henry E. (2011): *Kant's Groundwork for the Metaphysics of Morals: A Commentary*. Oxford: Oxford University Press.
Ameriks, Karl (1996): "On Schneewind and Kant's Method in Ethics." In: *Ideas y Valores* 102, pp. 28–53.

---

what appear to be other rational beings, as well as ourselves; and to imply that we have obligations *to* such other rational beings – in virtue of their dignity. For a discussion of how Kant thinks we cognize which creatures have freedom (and dignity) and can obligate us, see Kain (2009).

56 I am grateful to the editors and to seminar participants and audiences in Pelotas, Siegen, and Vienna, for thoughtful comments on earlier versions of this paper.

Ameriks, Karl (2003): *Interpreting Kant's Critiques*. Oxford: Oxford University Press.
Bacin, Stefano (2015): "Kant's idea of human dignity: Between tradition and originality." In: *Kant-Studien* 106, pp. 97–106.
Beck, Lewis White (trans.) (1956): *Immanuel Kant: Critique of Practical Reason*. New York: MacMillan.
Beck, Lewis White (1960): *A Commentary on Kant's Critique of Practical Reason*. Chicago: University of Chicago Press.
Broad, Charlie D. (1930): *Five Types of Ethical Theory*. London: Routledge and Kegan Paul.
Formosa, Paul (2013): "Is Kant a Moral Constructivist or a Moral Realist?" In: *European Journal of Philosophy* 21, pp. 170–196.
Guyer, Paul (1995): "The Possibility of the Categorical Imperative." In: *Philosophical Review* 104, pp. 353–385.
Guyer, Paul (2000): *Kant on Freedom, Law, and Happiness*. Cambridge: Cambridge University Press.
Johnson, Robert N. (2007): "Value and Autonomy in Kantian Ethics." In: *Oxford Studies in Metaethics* 2, pp. 133–148.
Kain, Patrick (2004): "Self-Legislation in Kant's Moral Philosophy." In: *Archiv für Geschichte der Philosophie* 86, pp. 257–306.
Kain, Patrick (2009): "Kant's defense of human moral status." In: *Journal of the History of Philosophy* 47, pp. 59–101.
Kerstein, Samuel (2006): "Deriving the Formula of Humanity." In: Christoph Horn/Dieter Schönecker (eds.): *Groundwork for the Metaphysics of Morals*. Berlin/Boston: Walter de Gruyter, pp. 200–221.
Korsgaard, Christine M. (1983): "Two Distinctions in Goodness." In: *Philosophical Review* 92, pp. 169–195.
Korsgaard, Christine M. (2005): "Fellow Creatures: Kantian Ethics and Our Duties to Animals." In: Grethe B. Peterson (ed.): *The Tanner Lectures on Human Values* 25. Salt Lake City: Utah University Press, pp. 77–110.
Langton, Rae (2007): "Objective and unconditioned value." In: *The Philosophical Review* 116, pp. 157–185.
Martin, Adrienne (2006): "How to Argue for the Value of Humanity." In: *Pacific Philosophical Quarterly* 87, pp. 96–125.
Paton, Herbert J. (1927): *The Good Will: A Study in the Coherence Theory of Goodness*. London: George Allen & Unwin.
Paton, Herbert J. (1942): "The Alleged Independence of Goodness." In: Paul A. Schilpp (ed.): *The Philosophy of G. E. Moore*. Evanston: Northwestern University Press, pp. 113–134.
Paton, Herbert J. (1944–45): "Kant's Idea of the Good." In: *The Proceedings of the Aristotelian Society* 45, pp. ii-xxv.
Paton, Herbert J. (1947): *The Categorical Imperative: A Study in Kant's Moral Philosophy*. London: Hutchinson.
Rawls, John (1971): *A Theory of Justice*. Cambridge: Harvard University Press.
Rawls, John (2000): *Lectures on the History of Moral Philosophy*. Cambridge: Harvard University Press.
Reath, Andrews (2003): "Value and Law in Kant's Moral Theory." In: *Ethics* 114, pp. 127–155.

Reath, Andrews (2013a): "Formal Approaches to Kant's Formula of Humanity." In: Mark Timmons/Sorin Baiasu (eds.): *Kant on Practical Justification: Interpretative Essays.* New York: Oxford University Press, pp. 201–228.

Reath, Andrews (2013b): "The ground of practical laws." In: Stefano Bacin/Alfredo Ferrarin/Claudio La Rocca/Margit Ruffing (eds.): *Kant und die Philosophie in weltbürgerlicher Absicht: Akten Des XI. Internationalen Kant-Kongresses.* Berlin/Boston: Walter de Gruyter.

Rosen, Michael (2012): *Dignity: Its History and Meaning.* Cambridge, Mass.: Harvard University Press.

Sayre-McCord, Geoffrey (1988): "The Many Moral Realisms." In: Geoffrey Sayre-McCord (ed.): *Essays on Moral Realism.* Ithaca: Cornell University Press, pp. 1–23.

Schneewind, J. B. (1996): "Kant and Stoic Ethics." In: Stephen Engstrom/Jennifer Whiting (eds.): *Aristotle, Kant, and the Stoics: Rethinking Happiness and Duty.* Cambridge: Cambridge University Press, pp. 285–301.

Schneewind, J. B. (1998): *The Invention of Autonomy: A History of Modern Moral Philosophy.* Cambridge: Cambridge University Press.

Schönecker, Dieter (2006): "How is a categorical imperative possible? Kant's deduction of the moral law in *Groundwork* III." In: Christoph Horn/Dieter Schönecker (eds.): *Kant's Groundwork for the Metaphysics of Morals. New Interpretations.* Berlin/Boston: Walter de Gruyter.

Sensen, Oliver (2011): *Kant on Human Dignity.* Berlin/Boston: Walter de Gruyter.

Stern, Robert (2010): "Moral Skepticism and Agency: Kant and Korsgaard." In: *Ratio* 23, pp. 453–474.

Stern, Robert (2012): *Understanding Moral Obligation: Kant, Hegel, Kierkegaard.* Cambridge: Cambridge University Press.

Stern, Robert (2013): "Moral Skepticism, Constructivism, and the Value of Humanity." In: Carla Bagnoli (ed.): *Constructivism in Ethics.* Cambridge: Cambridge University Press.

Timmermann, Jens (2006): "Value without Regress: Kant's 'Formula of Humanity' revisited." In: *European Journal of Philosophy* 14, pp. 69–93.

Wood, Allen W. (1999): *Kant's Ethical Thought.* Cambridge: Cambridge University Press.

Wood, Allen W. (2008): *Kantian Ethics.* Cambridge: Cambridge University Press.

Lara Ostaric
Practical Cognition, Reflective Judgment, and the Realism of Kant's Moral *Glaube*

Abstract Kant's notion of moral *Glaube*, i.e., a rational assent to the existence of objects of the Ideas of God and the soul's immortality, can be approached from both an antirealist and a realist perspective. According to the former, moral *Glaube* is speculative reason's "presupposition" (*Voraussetzung*) (KpV: 122.20) of the objects of these Ideas either in order to avoid its own inner contradictions or to help one maintain one's moral disposition. It is antirealist in spirit because the assumptions that reason makes may have nothing to do with how things are in reality. According to the latter, moral *Glaube* is an assent that takes for its ground reason's determination of a real and given object. This determination, given the limitation of our discursive understanding, is not theoretical and, hence, cannot result in theoretical cognition of this object. Instead, Kant calls it "practical cognition" (*das praktische reine Vernunfterkenntnis*) (KU: 470.8–9). In this essay, I argue that if we pay closer attention to Kant's neglected notion of "practical cognition" and of reflective judgment in the third *Critique*, additional evidence becomes available for why Kant should be understood as a realist with respect to moral *Glaube* and why the antirealist interpretations do not adequately capture Kant's view. I identify two forms of realism with respect to Kant's notion of moral *Glaube*, "rational necessitation realism" (RNR) and "moral image realism" (MIR). The former emphasizes rational necessity of a normative, not merely prudential, sort and knowledge-like quality of moral *Glaube*. The latter, while consistent with the former, emphasizes the coherence between the conditions of objective reality that must be met by the claims of theoretical reason (science) and those of the practical.

* * *

Introduction

Kant's notion of moral *Glaube*,[1] i.e., a rational assent to the existence of objects of the Ideas of God and soul's immortality, can be approached from both an

---

[1] In the first *Critique* and his lectures on logic, Kant distinguishes several types of *Glaube*. While I discuss some of them briefly below in the essay, my main concern remains moral *Glaube*.

https://doi.org/10.1515/9783110574517-005

antirealist and a realist perspective. According to the former, moral *Glaube* is speculative reason's "presupposition" (*Voraussetzung*) (KpV: 122.20)[2] of the objects of these Ideas either in order to avoid its own inner contradictions, or to help one maintain one's moral disposition. It is antirealist in spirit because the assumptions that reason makes may have nothing to do with how things are in reality. According to the latter, moral *Glaube* is an assent that takes for its ground reason's determination of a real and given object. This determination, given the limitation of our discursive understanding, is not theoretical and, hence, cannot result in theoretical cognition of this object. Instead, Kant calls it: "practical cognition" (*praktische reine Vernunfterkenntnis*) (KU: 470.8–9). The former conception of *Glaube* is more widely discussed in Kant literature while the latter, to my knowledge, has received little attention thus far. The matter is more complicated because Kant's writings seem to offer textual support for both views.

In this essay, I identify two forms of antirealism regarding Kant's notion of moral *Glaube*. One form of antirealism is pragmatic in nature because it takes the representations of moral *Glaube* as necessary illusions aimed at directing our will in a way that would be conducive to preserving the unity of our reason. The other form of antirealism is psychological because it approaches the representations of moral *Glaube* as necessary for answering the subject's psychological needs required for maintaining its own will directed towards the good, for example, the need to feel that our actions have bearing on moral outcomes. However, I argue that if we pay closer attention to Kant's neglected notion of "practical cognition" and of reflective judgment in the third *Critique*, additional evidence becomes available for why Kant should be understood as a realist with respect to moral *Glaube* and why the antirealist interpretations do not adequately capture Kant's view. I identify two forms of realism with respect to Kant's notion of moral *Glaube*, "rational necessitation realism" (RNR) and "moral image realism" (MIR). The former emphasizes rational necessity of a normative, not merely prudential sort and knowledge-like quality of moral *Glaube*. The latter, while consistent with the former, emphasizes the coherence between the conditions of objective reality that must be met by the claims of theoretical reason (science) and those of the practical.

In this essay, I proceed as follows: Part one summarizes Kant's arguments for moral *Glaube* that support the antirealist approach; part two analyzes the shift in

---

Because Kant's notion of "Glaube" is technical, denoting a form of rational assent with specific criteria of what constitutes its proper justification, I leave the term in the original German because neither "faith," nor "belief" would be an entirely adequate translation into English.
2 For the list of abbreviations of Kant's works, see the "Literature" section of this paper.

Kant's approach to moral *Glaube* from the Canon of the first *Critique* to the concluding paragraphs of the third *Critique*, that is, from moral *Glaube* as having a "degree" of truth to moral *Glaube* being as true as knowledge, but from a "practical point of view"; part three discusses Kant's notion of "practical cognition"; part four is centered on identifying the arguments in favor of the "rational necessitation realism" (RNR); part five discusses the role of reflective judgment for Kant's moral *Glaube* with a special focus on identifying the arguments for "moral image realism" (MIR). In section six, I offer some concluding remarks.

1 The Antirealist Arguments of Kant's Moral *Glaube*

Kant, acknowledging both our rational and sentient nature, conceives of the Idea of the highest good as consisting of two heterogeneous elements: virtue and happiness distributed in proportion to morality.[3] The relation between the two is not contingent because the former is a condition of the latter. But the necessity of their relation cannot be analytic: by pursuing happiness one will not as a consequence become virtuous and by acting virtuously one will not consequently become happy. The connection between the two concepts is an a priori synthesis for which Kant must provide a transcendental deduction, i.e., a proof of its objective reality. After the Canon of the first *Critique*, one can identify two distinct arguments for the objective reality of the Idea of the highest good.[4] The first argument is the "argument from the truth of the moral law" (TML) and the second argument is the "argument from human psychology" (AHP). Both arguments could be understood from an antirealist perspective: the former in a pragmatic and the latter in a psychological sense. Below I address each in turn.

---

[3] See KpV: 110.10–35.
[4] In the Canon of the first *Critique*, the Idea of the highest good still serves as an "incentive" (*Triebfeder*) (KrV: A813/B841) for acknowledging the moral law as binding for us. It is only after his confrontation with Christian Garve's review of his first *Critique* and Garve's translation of Cicero's treaties *On Duties* that Kant develops the concept of moral duty in the first section of his *Groundwork* and the feeling of respect for the moral law in the second *Critique*. Moral duty and the feeling of respect for the moral law no longer need any external incentives but, rather, are grounded in the autonomy of the subject. For a more detailed discussion of Garve's influence on the development of Kant's ethical theory see Förster (1992, pp. 172–177).

1.1 An Antirealist Reading of Kant's Argument for the Highest Good "from the Truth of the Moral Law" (TML)

Kant's "argument from the truth of the moral law" (TML) runs as follows:

> [S]ince the promotion [*Beförderung*] of the highest good [...] is an a priori necessary object of our will and inseparably bound up with the moral law, the impossibility of the first must also prove the falsity of the second. If, therefore, the highest good is impossible in accordance with practical rules, then the moral law, which commands us to promote it, must be fantastic and directed to empty imaginary ends and must therefore in itself be false. (KpV: 114.1–9)[5]

According to Kant, we do not have a moral duty to realize the highest good. We only have a duty to fulfill the moral law. Thus, the highest good is not the object of our will. The immediate object of our will is the fulfillment of the moral law, or the realization of the moral good in the world. But "the *promotion* [*Beförderung*] of the highest good [...] is an a priori necessary object of our will and inseparably bound up with the moral law" (KpV: 114.2; my emphasis). Thus, although we do not have an obligation to realize the *ideal* of the highest good, we have an obligation to strive towards this ideal the best way we can.[6]

One of the necessary conditions for the realization of the highest good is "the complete conformity of dispositions with the moral law," or "holiness" (KpV: 122.9–10). Since the latter is impossible for a human being, but required

---

[5] For a similar version of Kant's argument for the highest good see also KpV: 125. Traces of TML survive also in the third *Critique* (see KU: 471, note). – All insertions in square brackets by the author.

[6] Adams is critical of TML. He contends that if the assumption of God's existence and the soul's immortality is justified only as a necessary condition for *realizing* the moral *ideal* commanded by the moral law, and only approximation of the highest good can be the content of any reasonable morality, then the assumption of the existence of the conditions of the highest good is no longer justified (see Adams 1979, p. 123). In Ostaric (2010, p. 25), I endorsed Adams (1979) without acknowledging that Kant indeed is ambiguous on this issue, suggesting at places, such as in the passage cited above, that the object of the will is to "promote" and not to realize the highest good. But even if we take Kant to mean that the former and not the latter is the object of the will, Willaschek contends that if for Kant the object of the will is to work towards realizing the highest good, then it is sufficient to hope to realize the highest good and it is not necessary to believe that the necessary conditions for its realization are given (see Willaschek 2010, p. 181, note). However, on a more charitable reading of Kant's claim we can take him to mean that "striving towards" and "promoting" the highest good presupposes a sense of progress, which, unlike the realization of the moral ideal, can and should be the content of any reasonable morality. This progress, however, is also impossible to conceive by relying merely on the laws of nature and instead requires the postulation of the necessary conditions for the highest good.

as practically necessary by the moral law we need to assume an endless progress towards the completion of this conformity. Because this endless progress is possible only "on the presupposition of the *existence* and personality of the same rational being continuing *endlessly*," we are justified in assuming the soul's immortality. Kant calls this assumption the postulate of the immortality of the soul.[7] Furthermore, the highest good demands a necessary connection between happiness and morality. But the realm of nature is entirely independent from our realm of freedom and hence there is nothing in nature that would guarantee to us happiness proportionate to morality. Therefore, "the highest good in the world is possible only insofar as a supreme cause of nature having a causality in keeping with the moral disposition is assumed" (KpV: 125.14–16). The latter is Kant's postulate of the existence of God.

Kant's notion of moral *Glaube*, or a "pure practical rational belief" (KpV: 144) is a taking-to-be-true (*Fürwahrhalten*, KpV: 142.2.), or an assent to the postulates from a "need of pure reason" (KpV: 142.4). Kant uses the word "need" (*Bedürfniß*) in this context to distinguish the rational necessitation presupposed by moral *Glaube* from the one that is presupposed by moral duty: "It is well to note here that this moral necessity is subjective, that is, a need, and not objective, that is, itself a duty; for there can be no duty to assume the existence of anything (since this concerns only the theoretical use of reason)" (KpV: 125.31–34). The rational necessitation presupposed by moral *Glaube* is not "objective" because the assumption of God's existence and the soul's immortality is not commanded by the moral law, i.e., it is not the case that these postulates are categorical imperatives of some sort. But on the antirealist reading, the "subjective" aspect of rational necessitation is understood pragmatically. That is to say that the taking-to-be-true (*Fürwahrhalten*) of *Glaube* is understood as a subject entertaining a representation of the objective reality of God and the soul, as if these representations were real, and for the sake of directing one's will in a certain way.[8] This interpretation of Kant's moral *Glaube* is antirealist in spirit

---

[7] By a "postulate" Kant understands "a *theoretical* proposition, though one not demonstrable as such, insofar as it is attached inseparably to an a priori unconditionally valid *practical* law" (KpV: 122.22–25). The assent is then the assent of theoretical reason (assenting to the truth of a theoretical proposition) necessitated by the need of practical reason.

[8] Gardner (2011) identifies this interpretation in Kant's early critic Friedrich Karl Forberg (1770–1848) and also later in Hans Vaihinger (1852–1933). Gardner rightly comments that these interpretations are "reconstructive" because "the theological postulates are intended by Kant to ground hope, not merely to express it" (Gardner 2011, p. 193). I take him to mean by this that for Kant hypothetically entertaining God's existence and soul's immortality in hope that this may in fact be true is not sufficient for moral *Glaube*. Instead, moral *Glaube* requires an assent

because the justification of moral *Glaube* is a product (i.e., construct) of reason as a solution to its own inner problems and contradictions, that is, on the one hand the command of practical reason to promote the highest good and on other, the realization of speculative reason when relying on its own resources that this command is impossible to fulfill because the claims of speculative reason are limited to empirical knowledge of things, i.e., knowledge of appearances.

Parallel to TML, Kant introduces another argument for objective reality of the highest good, the argument that is grounded on human psychology.

1.2 Kant's "Argument for the Highest Good from Human Psychology" (AHP)

Kant's second argument for the highest good, the one he offers in the third *Critique* and which relies on human psychology (AHP) is the following:

> In addition, there is the fact that we feel ourselves forced by the moral law to strive for a universal highest end, but at the same time feel ourselves and all of nature to be incapable of attaining it; there is the fact that it is only insofar as we strive for this that we feel that we can judge ourselves to be in accord with the final end of an intelligent world-cause (if there is one); and there is thus a pure moral ground of practical reason for assuming this cause (since this can be done without contradiction), even if for nothing more than avoiding the danger of seeing that effort as entirely futile in its effects and thereby flagging in it. (KU: 446.28–37)

According to this argument, if we do what is in our power to promote the good but, due to some unpredictable circumstances, are never able to bring about the good, we will begin to believe that right actions and good intentions have no bearing upon moral outcomes. The moral agent will thus regard the moral law as no longer having force in its demands. Hence, unlike the first argument (TML) where denying the possibility of promoting the highest good implied an inner contradiction of reason and subsequently the falsity of the moral law, in this argument (AHP) the moral law is not falsified by this denial and it is in principle taken still as binding. However, with time and continuous experience of hindrances to ends of practical reason the binding force of the moral law will lose its strength.[9] Thus, it is necessary for us to assume God's existence

---

that these representations are true in order to ground hope in moral progress towards the highest good.

9 See Kant's similar points in Rel: 3–5.

and the real possibility of the highest good in order to maintain the proper moral attitude. It is only with respect to its function of *maintaining* (as opposed to grounding) the proper moral attitude that the highest good in this argument relates to the issue of moral motivation.[10]

While on the antirealist reading of the TML argument for the highest good and its corresponding notion of moral *Glaube*, God and the soul were mere representations of speculative reason that were "subjectively necessary" with respect to their pragmatic functions of avoiding reason's inner contradictions, on the AHP argument, Kant appears to be an antirealist because God and the soul are representations of speculative reason that are "subjectively necessary" only relative to a certain human psychological need for maintaining the proper moral disposition.[11]

While TML and AHP arguments for the highest good may support the view that Kant is an antirealist with respect to moral *Glaube*, Kant's notion of practical cognition and his discussion of *Glaube* in the third *Critique* represent a challenge to this view. But before we can discuss the relevance of Kant's notion of practical cognition for a more realist understanding of moral *Glaube* we must first turn our attention to a change in Kant's understanding of moral *Glaube* in the third *Critique* in relation to his early views of moral *Glaube* in the first *Critique*.

---

[10] Because of their respective conclusions Adams (1979) calls the former argument (TML) "theoretical" and the latter (AHP) "practical argument for the highest good." But Adams' choice of title for the former argument, as brought to my attention by Ameriks, is somewhat questionable because in the former argument it is never Kant's intention to give a theoretical proof of God's existence. Kant argues only that it is necessary for us to "assume" (*voraussetzen*) God's existence (KpV: 125.27–28). A detailed discussion of both of Kant's arguments can also be found in Wood (1978, pp. 150 f.) and Wood (1970, pp. 13–17).

[11] This is, for example, Paul Guyer's take on Kant's postulates. He raises the question of why for Kant our rationality does not merely require that the concept of the highest good "be free of contradiction" but rather that it leads to the "postulation of the actual existence" and also further why something that is not possible for us to know theoretically is possible for us to know "from a practical point of view" (Guyer 2000, pp. 335 f.). Guyer contends that the answers to these questions can be found in Kant's moral psychology: "Both the necessity but also the possibility of believing in the actual existence of theoretically indemonstrable conditions for the realization of the ultimate end defined by the moral law lie at the deepest level of the dualistic conception of human nature that underlies Kant's moral psychology: to act effectively to bring it about, we need to believe not just in the possibility of the highest good but in the actuality of its conditions just because we are not purely rational creatures, but creatures with both reason and sensibility who must exploit the natural means afforded by the latter to bring it into conformity with the former" (Guyer 2000, p. 336).

2 Moral *Glaube* in the Third *Critique*

In § 90 and § 91 of the third *Critique*, Kant's discussion of moral *Glaube* changes. It is neither *Glaube* as a justified assumption from the need of practical reason to preserve its unity (TML), nor is it the *Glaube* as a justified assumption from the need of maintaining the existent moral disposition (AHP). In § 90 and § 91, Kant discusses *Glaube* as an assent that takes for its justification the constitution of the object.

In § 90 titled "On the Kind of Affirmation Involved In a Teleological Proof of the Existence of God,"[12] Kant contends that a proof requires that "it does not persuade but rather convinces, or at least acts towards conviction" (KU: 461.17–18). These opening lines of § 90 and Kant's distinction between "persuasion" (*Überredung*) and "conviction" (*Überzeugung*) turn the reader back to his discussion of these terms in the Canon of the first *Critique*. Already in the Canon of the first *Critique*, regarding the question of whether the ground cited by the subject has any reference to the actual constitution of the object, Kant distinguishes between "persuasion" and "conviction." "Persuasion," writes Kant, "is a mere semblance, since the ground of the judgment, which lies solely in the subject, is held to be objective. Hence, such a judgment only has private validity, and this taking something to be true cannot be communicated" (KrV: A821/B848; 532.3–6). Thus, persuasion is an assent to a proposition according to which a subject takes herself to be holding objective grounds for an assent (hence, it is subjectively sufficient) while not even attempting to rationally justify her assent by citing some information about the constitution of the object that should serve as a ground for her assent, or if attempting to rationally justify then her process of justification involves an illegitimate inference.[13] By contrast,

---

[12] The *Cambridge* translation of the third *Critique* puts "moral" instead of "teleological," which gives the wrong impression that the main topic of § 90 is Kant's moral proof of God's existence rather than his criticism of theoretical teleological proofs.

[13] Chignell refers to persuasion as an assent that is "subjectively sufficient and objectively insufficient" (see Chignell 2007, p. 331) but this is how Kant defines *Glaube* and the latter, as will become obvious in what follows, is a type of conviction and not persuasion. Hence, the distinction between persuasion and conviction cannot be captured in terms of objective sufficiency/insufficiency. It is obvious that persuasion is "objectively insufficient" since it is not truth-directed at all. Therefore, the difference between persuasion and conviction is better captured by emphasizing that the former does not even attempt to cite any objective grounds for its assent, or if it does, then it involves some illegitimate inference, and the latter presupposes the process of rational justification and this process is based on legitimate inferences.

"conviction" is an assent for which the judging subject takes herself to be holding objective grounds for her assent while also "hav[ing] reason" (KrV: A820/B848; 532.12–13) for what she holds, i.e., while also engaging in the process of legitimate rational justification, the process of citing some information about the constitution of the object that should serve as a ground for her assent. Unlike 'persuasion,' 'conviction' is inter-subjectively valid and communicable. In the third *Critique*, Kant gives the physico-teleological proof of God's existence as an example of a "pseudo-proof" (*Scheinbeweis*) (KU: 461.23) that belongs to persuasion and not conviction. This is because the physico-teleological proof infers illegitimately from the data and principles that are empirical (i.e., the observations of the purported order in nature according to which everything in nature is good for something) to the properties of the object that lies beyond experience, namely, an intelligent world-cause.

In the Canon, Kant distinguishes three degrees, or "stages" (*Stufen*) (A822/B850; 533.1), of conviction: (1) opinion (*Meinung*), (2) *Glaube*, and (3) knowledge (*Wissen*). Unlike persuasion, all three degrees of conviction presuppose a process of legitimate rational justification based on which proposition "acquires a connection with truth" (KrV: A822/B850; 533.11). "Opinion" is an assent that is "subjectively *as well as* objectively insufficient" (KrV: A822/B850; 533.2). An example of an opinion is the type of assent held by a scientist who considers a hypothesis in order to conduct experiments that would either confirm or deny the truth of a hypothesis.[14] The scientist acknowledges that she lacks objective grounds, evidence, that would confirm the hypothesis. She is also not convinced by false evidence as the ground and, hence, the assent lacks subjective sufficiency as well. But the opinion, i.e., the hypothesis of the scientist, has some connection to truth because it is not an "arbitrary invention" (*willkürliche Erdichtung*) (KrV: A822/B850; 533.12), but rather a carefully chosen hypothesis based on considering some concrete empirical evidence. Knowledge presupposes the highest degree of conviction because it is an assent to a proposition that has both grounds that are objectively and subjectively sufficient. In other words, a subject's assent to a proposition counts as knowledge if the ground she cites for her assent (subjective sufficiency) is the ground sufficient for a proposition to be true (objective sufficiency).[15]

In the Canon of the first *Critique*, *Glaube* is placed between opinion and knowledge with respect to its degree of conviction and, hence, the degree of

---

14 In the third *Critique*, Kant considers the example of a physicist (see KU: 467).
15 See Chignell (2007, pp. 330, 332f.) for a detailed discussion of Kant's notion of opinion and knowledge.

its "connection to truth": "If taking something to be true is only subjectively sufficient and is at the same time held to be objectively insufficient, then it is called believing" (KrV: A822/B850; 533.3–4). *Glaube* is an assent that is possible only within the context of one's "practical relations" (KrV: A823/B851; 533.31), that is, in relation to the ends that one sets for oneself. Those ends can be "arbitrary and contingent" or "absolutely necessary" (KrV: A823/B851; 533.34–35). The practical ends of the former type are those of "skill" and of the latter those of "morality" (KrV: A823/B851; 533.33–34). The types of *Glaube* related to the former ends are "pragmatic" (*pragmatische*) (KrV: A824/B853; 534.26) and "doctrinal" (*doktrinal*) (KrV: A825/B853; 534.35–36) *Glaube* and the type of *Glaube* related to the latter ends is "moral *Glaube*." As an example of "pragmatic *Glaube*" Kant offers a case of a doctor who sets as her end to cure her patient, but does not know the illness the patient suffers from (has no sufficient objective grounds) and makes a diagnosis (subjectively sufficient assent) in order to achieve the end she has set for herself, i.e., the end of curing her patient. Her diagnosis is not a mere hypothesis, an opinion of a scientist, because she must hold her diagnosis as true and not merely entertain a possibility of it being true, in order to proceed with her actions, i.e., prescribe a treatment. In order for her to proceed with her actions her assent requires subjective sufficiency. The end is contingent because it depends on a set of circumstances, a person becoming ill. Just like the antirealist interpretation of TML above, her *Glaube* is holding-to-be-true of a representation in order to direct her will in a certain way, i.e., towards the end she considers desirable to achieve.[16] Kant also refers to "pragmatic *Glaube*" as a "contingent *Glaube*" (KrV: A825/B852; 534.6) and not because of its contingently chosen end, but because someone else, e.g., another doctor, may have or eventually may gain the actual knowledge of the illness the doctor in our example does not have. In contrast to contingent belief of "pragmatic *Glaube*," "doctrinal *Glaube*" is a type of "necessary *Glaube*" (KrV: A825/B852; 534.7) because the person assenting to a proposition could never have knowledge that the proposition is true. One of Kant's examples of "doctrinal *Glaube*" is one's assent to the existence of God from the observation of purposive unity in nature. Given the limitations of our discursive cognitive capacities, no one in principle could ever have knowledge of the truth of the proposition. This is what Kant calls physico-teleological proof of God's existence and he rejects it later in the third *Critique*, as already mentioned above, as a pseudo-proof capable of producing merely persuasions and not convictions. But in the Canon, before the notion of reflective judgment

---

16 See KrV: A824/B853.

was available to him, which prescribes heautonomously the law to itself and not to nature, he ranked the claim that nature is purposive and the claim of God's existence that follow from it among *Glaube*. Thus, although objectively not sufficient, it was considered by Kant subjectively sufficient to make possible the "investigation of nature" (KrV: A826/B854; 535.14) and "the advancement of my actions of reason" (KrV: A827/B855; 536.5–6).[17]

While for Kant the necessity of assent in "pragmatic" and "doctrinal *Glaube*" is of an instrumental sort, that is, necessity relative to the end that must be achieved, the assent of moral *Glaube* is absolutely necessary, "[f]or it is absolutely necessary that something must happen, namely, that I fulfill the moral law in all points. The end here is inescapably fixed, and according to all my insight there is possible only a single condition under which this end is consistent with all ends together and thereby has practical validity, namely, that there be a God and a future world" (KrV: A828/B856; 536.12–18). Thus, the practical end in moral *Glaube*, that is, the fulfillment of the moral ought, is absolutely necessary and is not dependent on empirical circumstances as this is the case in doctrinal and pragmatic *Glaube*. However, this "absolute necessity" of moral *Glaube* does not entail that the degree of "moral certainty" (*moralische Gewißheit*) (KrV: A829/B857; 536.36), or certainty from a "practical point of view" (*in praktischer Absicht*) (KrV: A828/B856; 536.29), is the same as in "logical certainty" (KrV: A829/B857; 536.36) presupposed in knowledge. In the Canon, the kind of certainty that is achieved on "subjective grounds (of moral disposition)" (KrV: A829/B857; 536.37) is lesser in degree in comparison to the certainty of knowledge (*Wissen*) achieved on "objective grounds," that is, grounds based on evidence given either in empirical or pure intuition.

In § 91 of the third *Critique*, *Glaube* is no longer discussed as being clearly subordinated to knowledge and presupposing a lesser *degree* of conviction, i.e., as if it were true to a lesser degree. Rather, Kant focuses on *Glaube* offering a special *kind* of conviction, i.e., "moral conviction" (KU: 463.9). And in § 91, "On the kind of affirmation (*Fürwahrhalten*) produced by means of practical faith," Kant distinguishes three modes of cognition relative to three different kinds of "cognizable things" (*erkennbare Dinge*) (KU: 467.12): 1) matters of opinion, 2) facts (*Tatsachen*), 3) matters of faith (*Glaube*). In the third *Critique*, Kant's discussion of "matters of opinion" does not change much from his discussion of this topic in the Canon. But given that Kant's focus in this paragraph are

---

17 In the third *Critique*, especially in the *First Introduction*, this function is assigned to reflective judgment guided by the logical principle of purposiveness and according to which we represent nature as a system of unified laws and genera into species.

types of cognizable *objects* or *things*, he emphasizes that objects of opinion must be "objects of an at least intrinsically *possible* experiential cognition (objects of the sensible world)" (KU: 467.22; my emphasis). Facts are objects of cognition that presuppose an *actual* intuition for a concept. This intuition can be empirical and then we speak of one's own experience or the experience of others (i.e., testimony). Or this intuition can be pure and either "theoretical," such as the one in geometry, or "practical." By the latter, Kant has in mind his doctrine of the "fact of reason" in the second *Critique*, which was not available to him in the first *Critique*. Finally, "objects that must be conceived [*gedacht werden müssen*] a priori in relation to the use of pure practical reason in accordance with duty (whether as consequences or as grounds) but which are excessive for its theoretical use are mere *matters of faith*" (KU: 469.1–4). The highest good together with the conditions of its possibility (the existence of God and the immortality of the soul) are *objects* of this kind.

Thus, in the third *Critique*, the connection to truth these three types of conviction establish is no longer one of degree but, rather, the following: 1) opinion is a conviction that is possibly true, 2) facts are convictions that are actually true, and 3) moral *Glaube* is a conviction that is true from a "purely practical point of view" (*in reiner praktischer Absicht*) (KU: 463.9). It is clear that in the third *Critique* both our awareness of the moral law (now the Fact of Reason) and moral *Glaube* gain objectivity they did not have earlier in the Canon. This however does not mean that for Kant moral *Glaube* and the Fact of Reason are the same as knowledge (*Wissen*): "All affirmation must ultimately be grounded in fact if it is not to be fully groundless; and the only difference among proofs is thus whether affirmation of the consequence drawn from this fact can be grounded on it as knowledge, for theoretical cognition, or mere faith [*Glaube*], for practical cognition" (KU: 475.9–14). Clearly, knowledge (*Wissen*) is reserved only for theoretical cognition. However, moral *Glaube* and the Fact of Reason are no longer epistemically inferior to knowledge. Instead, they enjoy objectivity that is genuinely cognitive, to wit, objectivity that presupposes a correspondence of a representation with its object. Therefore, Kant grants them a knowledge-like status and the status of a cognition that is not theoretical but "practical."[18]

---

[18] Kant already uses the term "practical cognition" (KrV: Bxxi) and "practical sources of cognition" (*praktische Erkenntnisquelle*) (KrV: Bxxvi, note) in the first *Critique*. However, in the first *Critique* Kant still hesitates to grant theoretical and practical cognition the same epistemic status. We can assume that Kant's view of the relation between *Glaube* and cognition in the Canon is the one that we find described in the *Jäsche Logik* as follows: "Only *I myself* can be certain of the validity and unalterability of my practical belief, and my belief in the truth of a

In order to understand better whether the third *Critique's* emphasis on the "objectivity" of *Glaube* is sufficient to support a realist rather than an antirealist interpretation of moral *Glaube*, we need to look more closely into Kant's use of his notion of "practical cognition."

3 Kant's Notion of Practical Cognition[19]

Kant takes over the concept of practical cognition from Georg Friedrich Meier's *Auszug aus der Vernunftlehre* (1752). For Meier, cognition is practical "insofar as it is conducive to the direction [*Einrichtung*] of our free actions" (Meier 1752, § 30).[20] Meier contrasts a cognition that is practical "insofar as it moves us in a distinct way to do or refrain from doing an action" (Meier 1752, § 216) to both theoretical and speculative cognition. Kant takes over these distinctions in his logic lectures that were delivered based on Meier's *Auszug* Kant used as the textbook.

> When a proposition is a proposition that commands, an *imperativus*, and says that something *ought* to happen, then it is a practical proposition[;] it says which free actions would be good for a certain purpose. [...] All practical propositions, if they are opposed to theoretical ones, are *imperativi*. [...] E.g. in geometry when I say, to measure a straight line take [...], etc. [T]heoretical propositions, on the other hand, do not say how it ought to happen, but rather how the thing is. E.g. A straight line is the shortest path, etc. (WL: 900 f.)[21]

---

proposition or the actuality of a thing is what takes place of a cognition only in relation to me without itself being cognition" (*nur die Stelle eines Erkenntnisses vertritt, ohne selbst eine Erkenntniß zu sein*) (JL: 70). Given that in the Canon the status of an "object" was reserved for a thing given in pure or empirical intuition, the "subjective ground" of *Glaube* was epistemically inferior to the objective ground of knowledge. Although the *Jäsche Logik* is dated to 1800, Kant asked his student Gottlob Benjamin Jäsche to prepare this edition in reference to his notes on George Friedrich Meier's *Auszug aus der Vernunftlehre* that Kant used in his logic lectures from 1765 until the 1790s. Thus, the content of the *Jäsche Logik* reflects Kant's views prior to the publication of his third *Critique*.

19 For a very helpful summary of Kant's notion of practical cognition and Kant's various mentions of it, see Bacin (2016, pp. 560 f.).
20 Citations from Meier's *Auszug* are my own translations.
21 The same distinction can be found in the first *Critique*. There Kant defines theoretical cognition as "that through which I cognize *a priori* (as necessary) that something is" and practical cognition as "that through which it is cognized *a priori* what ought to happen" (KrV: A633/B661).

But practical cognition can be derived from some theoretical cognitions and this requires a further distinction, namely, the one between practical and speculative cognitions:

> For although they do not say what ought to happen, because they are theoretical, practical propositions can nevertheless be derived from them, and they are to this extent opposed to speculative propositions. E.g. That there is God is a theoretical proposition, but it is *practical in potentia*[;] you must just act as if there is a highest legislator for your actions. [...] Speculative propositions are all those from which no rules or *imperativi* for our actions flow[;] in natural theology, propositions are merely speculative. E.g., whether God's omnipresence occupies space or consists merely in an influence on his creatures. (WL: 901.16–28)[22]

Unlike Meier, Kant believed that practical cognition has no place in logic "[f]or nothing belongs to logic except the logical form of all cognition, i.e., the form of thought, without regard to the content" (WL: 903.28–30) and that practical cognition differs from speculative and theoretical with respect to its content. Furthermore, unlike Meier, Kant links practical cognition to morality: "The sole, unconditioned, and final end (ultimate end) to which all practical use of our cognition must finally relate is *morality*, which on this account we may also call the practical *without qualification or the absolutely practical*" (JL: 87.8–11).

Beginning with Kant's second *Critique*, the categorical imperative represents moral cognition in the first sense, i.e., a practical proposition "having to do only with determining grounds of the will [*Bestimmungsgründe des Willens*]" (KpV: 20.2–3). His practical postulates of freedom, God, and soul's immortality represent moral cognition in the second sense, i.e., theoretical propositions that are "grounds for possible imperatives" and are, thus, "practical *in potentia*" (WL: 901). Given the focus of this essay, practical cognition of the latter kind is of concern to us.

In the second *Critique*, Kant claims that the moral law is the "*ratio cognoscendi* of freedom" (KpV: 4, note). In other words, given that the Third Antinomy of the first *Critique* establishes the possibility of our freedom as an uncaused causing, for Kant, our awareness of the categorical imperative is sufficient for us to hold ourselves free, that is, to regard our "real actions" (KU: 468.27) in the world as exhibiting that freedom. Thus, the "[objective] reality" of freedom "can be established through practical laws of pure reason" (KU: 468.24–27). Although, on Kant's view, what is given to us is the moral law and not a direct

---

[22] On the distinction between practical, theoretical, and speculative cognitions see also the Appendix in the *Jäsche Logik* (JL: 86 f.).

insight into our freedom as an uncaused causing (i.e., an insight he reserves for intellectual intuition and not for the human intuition that is sensible and merely receptive), Kant claims that the Idea of freedom is the only Idea of reason whose object is a fact although this fact is neither based in empirical nor pure intuition. But it is based in "intuition" that Kant identifies with "practical data for reason" (KU: 468.14). By "practical data" Kant understands the moral law that serves as an analogue of sensible or pure intuition in theoretical cognition. By referring to it as an "intuition," Kant emphasizes that this law is "given" (KpV: 31.25 – 26) and not derived from some antecedent data of reason.[23] Thus, the content of practical cognition in the second *Critique* is not only limited to imperatives, but also includes the theoretical propositions that are the "grounds for possible imperatives" and are "practical *in potentia*" (WL: 901), namely, our knowledge of freedom. Freedom for Kant is the "*ratio essendi* of the moral law" (KpV: 4, note).

While the practical cognition of freedom is "immediate," tied to our awareness of the moral law, the practical cognition of God and the soul is "mediated," i.e., is of the objects that are "inferred" (KU: 474) from the concept of freedom. This is because the objective reality of the Ideas of God and soul is not an immediate consequence of our awareness of the moral law as binding, but requires a further reflection on our part on the conditions that are required for realizing our moral ends in the world. Furthermore, these are necessary conditions for the realization of our moral ends in nature over which we do not have complete control. The "metaphysical externality"[24] of the objects of the Ideas of God and soul is captured by Kant's stratification of the supersensible into the one that "grounds the object" and the one that grounds the "judging subject" (KU: 340.5). By the latter Kant understands our freedom and he refers to it also as "the supersensible in us" (KU: 341.8). And to this "supersensible within" Kant opposes the former, or the "supersensible without," which grounds the appearances in nature. This is also why the type of connection to truth one can have with the objects of moral *Glaube* is the one of belief and not the one of fact, the type of certainty that is not immediate but inferred.[25] This, however, as

---

[23] See Kain (2010, p. 220) for the claim that Kant's reference to the moral law as "practical data" suggests that the moral law is an analogue of sensible intuition with respect to our knowledge of freedom. This however does not undermine our autonomy by entailing a mere receptiveness of reason. This is because Kant understands our autonomy as "self-legislation" and not as authorship of the moral law. On the latter distinction see Kain (2004, pp. 257 – 290).
[24] See on this issue Ameriks (2008, pp. 180, 182).
[25] Ameriks also emphasizes a "certain non-immediate and risky relation" presupposed by *Glaube* because nature is something external over which we do not have control (see Ameriks 2008, p. 181).

discussed in section 2, does not entail that practical cognition of the objects of *Glaube* is epistemically inferior to the practical cognition that has freedom and the moral law for its objects. Kant's somewhat awkwardly formulated position in the Canon, to wit, his claim that *Glaube* presupposes representations that have objective validity and yet are neither true nor false, but, rather, true to a "certain degree," from a subjective point of view that nevertheless enjoys inter-subjectively validity, is in the third *Critique* replaced by a notion of *Glaube* that presupposes representations that are true, but in an indirect, or "inferred" way. And because the representations of *Glaube* are not "less true" than the matters of fact, regarding the relation *Glaube* establishes to its objects, Kant uses the same term he uses with respect to the relation "matters of fact" establish with their objects, namely, "cognition."

Therefore, theoretical propositions that are the "grounds for possible imperatives" and are, thus, "practical *in potentia*" (WL: 901) and that give objective reality to the Idea of freedom, also serve to give objective reality to the Ideas of God and the soul. Here we should add a qualification. In this context, we should not take "grounds for imperatives" to mean that representations of moral *Glaube*, i.e., holding-to-be-true of the propositions 'God exists' and 'Soul is immortal,' are incentives for moral actions. According to Kant's Critical philosophy, the sole incentive for moral action is the moral law. The Canon of the first *Critique* is here an exception because in the Canon the Idea of the highest good still serves as an "incentive" (*Triebfeder*) (KrV: A813/B841) for acknowledging the moral law as binding for us. Therefore, Kant's claims in the logic lectures that date back to the 1780s may reflect Kant's position in the Canon. However, Kant's claim that practical cognition relative to moral *Glaube* presupposes theoretical propositions that are "practical *in potentia*" could also accommodate Kant's position after the first edition of the *Critique of Pure Reason* insofar as "practical" is here understood in a broader sense, not narrowly as either a condition of a possibility of the categorical imperative (absolute freedom as an uncaused causality) or as an incentive for action (moral motivation). Instead, it is "practical" with respect to "[t]he principle of the self-preservation of reason [*das Princip der Selbsterhaltung der Vernunft*]," which "is the basis of rational *Glaube*, in which assent has the same degree as knowledge, but is of another kind that comes not from the cognition of grounds in the object but rather from the true needs of the subject in respect to theoretical as well as practical applications" (R 2446, AA 16: 371f.).[26] Thus, it is "practical" insofar as it provides us with a coherent image of the relation between our theoretical

---

[26] This *Reflexion* is dated by Adickes approximately 1764–1770.

and practical reason: it provides us with a theoretical representation of the world in which it is possible to make progress in realizing the practical demands of our reason.

And these theoretical propositions, i.e., claims of theoretical reason, extend our cognition beyond the limits of possible experience. With respect to our indirect knowledge of freedom via the moral law, "speculative reason alone provides such a great extension in the field of the supersensible, though only with respect to practical cognition" (KpV: 103.23–24). But also theoretical reason's assent to the existence of the objects of the Ideas of God and soul's immortality, which are necessary for the realization of the highest good demanded by the moral law, "extend a pure cognition *practically*" (KpV: 134.8–9). That is to say that

> theoretical cognition, not indeed of these objects but of reason in general, is extended by this insofar as objects were given to those ideas by the practical postulates, a merely problematic thought having by this means first received objective reality. There was therefore no extension of the cognition of given supersensible objects, but there was nevertheless an extension of theoretical reason and of its cognition with respect to the supersensible in general, inasmuch as theoretical reason was forced to grant that there are such objects, though it cannot determine them more closely and so cannot itself extend this cognition of the objects [...]; for this increment, then, pure theoretical reason, for which all those ideas are transcendent and without objects, has to thank its practical capacity only. (KpV: 135.13–27)

The assent of theoretical reason to the existence of God and soul's immortality does not amount to theoretical cognition "of given supersensible objects" because those objects are not "given" in empirical intuition and, hence, we cannot have theoretical knowledge of them, determine them, or add predicates to them that are not contained in their concept. But the assent to their existence, relative to the demands of practical reason, represents an "increment" of theoretical cognition insofar as theoretical reason is incapable of arriving at those conclusions when relying only on its own resources.

In what follows I proceed to consider whether the fact that Kant grants the representations of *Glaube* the status of genuine objective cognition has any effect on tilting the debate in favor of a realist interpretation of moral *Glaube*.

4 A Case for a Realist Reading of Moral *Glaube*

In light of the preceding discussion, is it fair to confront Kant with the following options? "[E]ither practical cognition by means of the postulates enjoys truth, reference, and correspondence to an object in the same sense as is enjoyed by objectively valid empirical judgments and is aspired to by speculative claims about the supersensible; or it does not, and must instead merit the title of cognition on some other count, pertaining to the rational necessity of the manner in which it facilitates accordance of the will with principles of object-production, i.e., creates possibilities of action" (Gardner 2011, p. 190). In other words, the alternatives presented to Kant are the following: either the objects of *Glaube* are the same kinds of objects as those of theoretical cognition and practical cognition is the same as theoretical cognition, or the content of practical cognition is reduced to the instrumental necessity of a hypothetical imperative, to wit, the necessity of assuming the truth of certain representations in order to direct our will towards the production of the moral good, which is commanded by the moral law. Kant clearly rejects the former by contending that the objects of moral *Glaube* are not given to us in either pure or empirical intuition and are, therefore, not the objects of theoretical knowledge. But does he have to commit himself to the latter alternative? We have seen in section 3 that Kant's notion of practical cognition includes not only imperatives, but also theoretical propositions that are "grounds for imperatives." Furthermore, the "subjective" aspect of moral *Glaube* – i.e., the fact that the free rational assent of moral *Glaube* arises from "the principle of self-preservation of reason" (R 2446, AA 16: 371f.) without which "the moral way of thinking has no way to persevere in its collision with theoretical reason's demand for a proof (of the possibility of the object of morality), but vacillates between practical commands and theoretical doubts" (KU: 472) – is consistent with its absolute necessity. That is to say that in practical cognition associated with moral *Glaube* speculative reason does take the postulates "with full cognitive seriousness" (Gardner 2006, p. 272). Moral *Glaube* is unlike an opinion according to which one entertains a hypothesis with a reservation that it may not at all be true. It is also unlike "pragmatic *Glaube*" according to which one's assent to a representation expresses a hope of its truth relative to some end that must be achieved. It is also unlike "doctrinal *Glaube*" founded on illegitimate inference of a physico-teleologist that leads only to persuasion and never to a genuine conviction. Finally, the view according to which moral *Glaube* is a response to human psychological needs would be inconsistent with its absolute necessity and its status of genuine, knowledge-like, cognition.

But an antirealist can further insist that the absolute necessity of moral *Glaube* could be of an instrumentalist sort if the end to be achieved is not contingent, as in "pragmatic Glaube," but necessary in some existential sense. On this view, the representations of moral *Glaube* are considered as "necessary illusions" that can never have the objectivity required of proper realism. This "absolute" necessity is the one that arises from the "principle of self-preservation of reason." Hence, it is the instrumentality and necessity of the antirealist pragmatic reading of TML discussed in section 1.1 above. The antirealist could argue that considering the representations of *Glaube* as "necessary illusions" can explain why Kant refers to the content of moral *Glaube* as "practical cognition." This is because the object for the representations of *Glaube* is provided by the practical need of reason to preserve its self-coherency.[27] Although Kant emphasizes the subjective aspect of moral *Glaube* insofar as the postulates are not equivalent to moral imperatives, this subjective aspect of *Glaube* does not entail the necessity of a pragmatic sort, to wit, doing what it takes to "keep reason in business." Instead, although postulates themselves are not imperatives they are "related" to the moral law. Hence, necessity must be of the absolute normative sort of "ought" of the moral law that commands that we strive towards the realization of the highest good. In addition, this view ignores the shift in Kant's discussion of moral *Glaube* from the Canon, where, as demonstrated in section 2 above, Kant holds that representations of *Glaube* are true to a "lesser degree" to the third *Critique*, where he considers practical cognition to be at the same level with theoretical knowledge. Illusions could hardly have a knowledge-like quality.

Finally, the alternatives presented above by the antirealist – i.e., either practical cognition is genuinely cognitive and, thus, must be of the objects given in empirical or pure intuition, or it is not and, therefore, it is a form of a "necessary illusion" for the sake of reason's "self-preservation" – presuppose the primacy of theoretical reason according to which theoretical knowledge and, hence, determinative judgment, is the norm for any judgment that should count as genuinely cognitive. Put differently, theoretical reason has primacy "[i]f practical reason may not assume and think as given anything further than what *speculative* reason of itself could offer it from its insight" (KpV:

---

27 Although Gardner never mentions Nietzsche in this context, the antirealist position according to which the objects of *Glaube* are necessary illusions brings to mind Nietzsche's conception of Apolline "visions" in his *Birth of Tragedy* (1872, 1st ed.). Just like on an antirealist reading of Kant's moral *Glaube*, for Nietzsche, Apolline "visions" are necessary illusions. But unlike on an antirealist reading of Kant's moral *Glaube* according to which the necessity of illusion is dictated by the "principle of reason's self-preservation," for Nietzsche, the necessity of Apolline "visions" is dictated by the metaphysical principle of the will that has its own need for self-preservation, namely, keeping itself in existence. Thus, the beauty of Apolline "visions" directs the will towards action by "seducing it," or motivating it, to remain in existence in the face of the Dyonisiac ecstatic revelations of how things really are in themselves.

120.11–13). But Kant contends the opposite. It is the practical reason that has the primacy, which amounts to the following:

> [I]t is clear that, even if from the first perspective its capacity does not extend to establishing certain propositions affirmatively, although they do not contradict it, *as soon as these same propositions belong inseparably to the practical interest* of pure reason it [reason] must accept them-indeed as something offered to it from another source, which has not grown on its own land but yet is sufficiently authenticated – and try to compare and connect them with everything that it has within its power as speculative reason, being mindful, however, that these are not its insights but are yet extensions of its use from another, namely a practical perspective [...]. (KpV: 121.6–15)

The priority of the practical does not entail that practical reason demands 'p' and theoretical reason is only justified claiming 'not p' so that to grant priority to practical reason would require of theoretical reason to contradict itself. Propositions and demands of practical reason, as contended by Kant in the above paragraph, "do not contradict" the claims of theoretical reason. That is to say that, on Kant's transcendental idealism, the claims of the postulates are fully consistent with the claims of science. It is only that the priority of the practical requires an "extension" of the use of theoretical reason to make claims that it is not authorized to make when left to its own resources.

Thus, in light of the above, we can see how by moral *Glaube* Kant can understand claims that are absolutely necessary in a normative and not merely instrumental sense and that are real, genuinely cognitive, and knowledge-like even though they are indirectly "inferred" through rational necessitation from the needs of practical reason. I call this form of realism "rational necessitation realism" (RNR).[28]

The advocates of "rational necessitation realism" (RNR) can find most of the textual support for their interpretation in the second *Critique*. The question remains, what is added, if anything, to the realist interpretation of moral *Glaube* by the third *Critique*? In other words, what does Kant's notion of reflective judgment, which was not available to him in the second *Critique*, add to the realism of moral *Glaube*? It is to this issue that we must turn now.

---

28 This is what I take Ameriks to have in mind when he writes as follows: "Kant can also be read as meaning something fairly realistic and defensible in saying that faith is an attitude which is valid 'only' 'in a practical respect.' [...] On this reading, faith is still understood as a taking to be true of what actually is; it just happens to be a taking that must face the special risks of going beyond whatever is simply within our own mind. This is compatible with its involving various types of rationality and necessity, even if it must go beyond the certainties of determinative judgment" (Ameriks 2008, p. 182).

5 Reflective Judgment and Moral *Glaube*

In the *Critique of the Power of Judgment* there are two types of possible relations that reflective judgment can have to *Glaube:* a) the one of maintaining and b) the one of grounding *Glaube*. Let me address each in turn.

5.1 The Role of Reflective Judgment in Maintaining *Glaube*

The ideal of the highest good – which, according to Kant, belongs to "matters of faith [*Glaubenssachen*]" (KU: 469.4) is *"freely* approved by reason [*von der Vernunft frei gebilligt*]" (KU: 472, note). That is to say that although reason cannot have theoretical certainty about whether conditions for the highest good exist, it can assent to the real possibility of the highest good voluntarily as a result of rational deliberation on the conditions that are necessary for fulfilling the moral law that commends us to strive towards the realization of the highest good.[29] However, it is due to the voluntary character of *Glaube* that Kant claims it "can waver even in the well-disposed" (KpV: 146.11–12). Therefore, given the partially transcendent character of the highest good and given the inconstancy of our *Glaube*, we need some confirmation from experience as a sign that what we take to be possible on moral grounds may in fact be so: "because of the natural need of all human beings to demand for even the highest concepts and grounds of reason something that *the senses can hold on to*, some confirmation from experience or the like [...] some historical ecclesiastical faith or other, usually already at hand, must be used" (Rel: 109.25–31). In this passage Kant has in mind concrete religious practices that, he claims, serve the purpose of maintaining, as opposed to grounding, *Glaube*. But in the third *Critique* the same role is played by the beauty of nature and exceptional works of art, as well as the natural ends and the overall purposiveness of nature as a logical system of laws. Our admiration and our experience of nature's contingent harmony with our cognitive ends, i.e., its amenability to the systematic requirements of our reflective judgment, serve as a sign that nature may also be cooperative with the final ends of our rationality. This further gives us hope

---

29 The voluntary character of *Glaube* is also emphasized by Adams (1979, p. 130). It can also be discerned at KpV: 143 and KpV: 144f. I discuss this issue also in Ostaric (2010, p. 26).

that our justified assumption of an intelligent world-cause and soul's immortality may in fact be true.[30]

However, there is textual evidence in the third *Critique* that suggests the role of reflective judgment in grounding and not only maintaining moral *Glaube*.

5.2 The Role of Reflective Judgment in Grounding *Glaube*

In § 90 of the third *Critique*, Kant's reference to reflective judgment in relation to *Glaube* does not play the role of a sign but rather of a proof, or evidence. The new role Kant assigns to reflective judgment in moral *Glaube* is summarized in the following paragraph:

> A proof, however, that aims at conviction can be in turn of two different kinds, either one that would determine what the object is *in itself* or else one that would determine what it is *for us* (human beings in general) according to the necessary rational principles for our judging (a proof κατ' 'αληθειαν or κατ' 'ανθρωπον, taking the latter word in the broadest sense to stand for human beings in general). In the first case it is grounded on sufficient principle for the determining power of judgment, in the second merely on sufficient principles for the reflecting power of judgment. In the latter case, if it rests on merely theoretical principles, it can never produce conviction; but if it is based on a practical principle of reason [*legt er aber ein praktisches Vernunftprincip zum Grunde*] (which is thus universally and necessarily valid), then it can make a sufficient claim of conviction from a purely practical point of view, i.e., moral conviction. (KU: 462f.)

The proof that would determine the object "in itself" would treat those objects, God and soul, as given in empirical intuition. The proof that determines an object with respect to what the object would be "for us" is based on the reflective power of judgment which reflects on given sensible particulars governed by the principle of purposiveness. By reflective power of judgment that rests on theoretical principles and that cannot produce conviction Kant has in mind physical teleology: "There is a physical teleology which gives our theoretically reflecting power of judgment a sufficient basis for assuming an intelligent world cause" (KU: 447.16–18). And Kant has already noted at the beginning of § 90 that this type of proof can only produce persuasion and not conviction. But if the reflective judgment is based on a "practical principle of reason," then it produces "moral conviction." Put differently, reflective judgment at

---

30 This argument is different from the antirealist "argument from human psychology" (AHP) discussed earlier. The latter relies on human psychology to ground moral *Glaube* and the argument in question relies on human psychology to reinforce the already existent moral *Glaube*.

work in physical teleology reflects on particulars given in nature relative to "the merely subjective ground of human reason" to seek unity in variety, or to "conceive of one principle instead of many as long as it can do so without contradiction" (KU: 461.27–29). This reflection ends in theoretical determination of nature as purposive and the illegitimate inference to the existence of an intelligent world-cause, God, that is the author of this purposiveness. But reflective judgments that are based on practical principles, i.e., judgments of aesthetic, teleological, and logical reflection, do not determine nature theoretically, i.e., they do not make claims that nature 'is purposive' because created by an intelligent world-cause but, rather, compare the representations of particulars given in nature to either our cognitive faculties of understanding and imagination (in aesthetic judgment), or to reason's Idea of nature as a system (in teleological judgments), so that nature in those judgments is represented 'as if created' for our cognitive faculties.

Now, we know that reflective judgment for Kant is not based on any 'practical principle' as he claims in the above-cited passage and we should consider this as a careless formulation on Kant's part. Instead, reflective judgment is based, if aesthetic, on the principle of purposiveness without a purpose; if teleological, on the concept of objective purposiveness of nature, which is the principle of reason for the reflecting power of judgment; and if logical, on reason's logical principle of nature's purposiveness. But the fact that Kant refers in the passage above to the aforementioned principles as 'practical' indicates that for Kant aesthetic, teleological, and logical reflective judgments provide a "proof" for the highest good together with the conditions of its realization (God and the soul) that is "according to a human being" and that, unlike the proof of physical teleology, can produce conviction, namely, a "moral" one. What could Kant possibly mean by this? One way to answer this question is to argue that the justification of assent in moral *Glaube* refers to the object supplied by reflective judgment and not to the object supplied by rational necessitation from the need of practical reason, as in RNR above, or at least not directly. In all three forms of reflective judgments, aesthetic, teleological, and logical reflection on nature as a system of laws, something real is given in the manifold that is excessive for determinative judgment. In the example of aesthetic judgments, there is something contingent with respect to beauty when considered from the perspective of determinative judgment. In other words, we can perfectly imagine the world in accordance with the laws of cause and effect in which there is no beauty. In the example of teleological judgments, an organism is not composed of its organic parts in the way a watch is composed of its wheels and springs because parts of an organism, unlike those of a mechanism, cannot exist independently of the whole to which they belong. Because our understanding must proceed discursively from a universal to a particular by the mediation of concepts, and, hence, explains the whole always in terms of its parts, the regularity exhibited by organisms remains underdetermined and therefore, from the perspective of our discursive understanding, merely contingent. Finally, although the appearances ought to conform to the transcendental laws of the understanding, which are the conditions of the possibility of experience of any object in general, "the specific diversity of empirical laws of nature together with their effects could nevertheless be so great that it would be impossible for our understanding to discover in them an order that we can grasp, to divide its products into genera and species [...] and to make an interconnected experience out of material that is for us so confused (strictly speaking only infinitely manifold and not fitted for our power of comprehension" (KU: 185.26–34).[31] Thus, from the perspective of the transcendental laws of the understanding, the connection of particular empirical laws and concepts into a unified system is contingent.

All three types of reflective judgment take that which in the manifold is excessive for our determinative judgment, and connect it in such a way that the representation of nature that is the outcome of this synthesis is purposive for either our cognitive faculties (aesthetic judgments) or for our cognition (teleological and logical judgments of nature as a system). But in all three examples, reflective judgment heautonomously prescribes a rule to itself, relative to the needs of our limited human understanding, and not to nature. Hence, the outcome of this reflection is the representation of the world *as if* it were purposive for either our cognitive faculties or for our cognition. In the former case, reflective judgment creates an image of the world that is purposive for our cognitive faculties so that upon reflecting on the form of such objects we feel pleasure. In the latter case, our representations of nature as a system and organisms as natural kinds enables us to engage in a scientific exploration of nature. But our reason does not have only the minimal, cognitive ends. It also has the final end, i.e., progress in the realization of the highest good. But the world that we in our reflection on nature represent as purposive for our minimal cognitive ends, we also represent as being purposive for our final ends. Put differently, reflective judgment creates an image of the world that serves as a schema of the Idea of the highest good. That is to say that reflective judgment creates an image of the world that is not only a scene of theoretical exploration but also a scene of action, the image of the world that is amenable to the realization of our moral ends.

---

[31] See EE: 203, 209 for a similar statement.

In this respect, objective reality of the Idea of the highest good is not the same as the one reached by rational necessitation from the need of practical reason (RNR) and we can call it "moral image realism" (MIR).[32] On the surface it may seem contradictory to call "realism" a view according to which the world is an "image." However, the word "image" refers to heautonomy of reflective judgment. Although reflective judgment does not prescribe the rule to nature like the faculty of the understanding, its principle of purposiveness is a transcendental principle and not a hypothetical principle that one can consider optionally relative to some end. The "image" of the world, or the representation of the world created by reflective judgment is condition of the possibility of experience as such and hence has a necessity and objective reality a mere illusion could never have.

6 Concluding Remarks

I have argued in this essay that in spite of some references in Kant's text that may suggest that Kant is an antirealist with respect to the objects of the Ideas of God and immortality, whether of a pragmatic or a psychological sort, a closer look into his notion of practical cognition and the changes in his conception of moral *Glaube* from the Canon of the first *Critique* to the concluding paragraphs of the third *Critique*, suggest the opposite. I have identified two forms of realism that can be ascribed to Kant's moral *Glaube:* "rational necessitation realism" (RNR) and the "moral image realism" (MIR). According to realism of the former kind, the representations of moral *Glaube* are considered necessary in a normative sense and also as having real objects so that moral *Glaube* results in cognition, albeit from a "practical point of view," that is knowledge-like. While the former type of realism relies mostly on the resources of the second *Critique*, the latter type of realism relies on Kant's notion of reflective judgment he develops in the third *Critique*. While on "rational necessitation realism" (RNR) the object of the representations of moral *Glaube* is necessitated by practical reason and its need to represent the world as hospitable to the realization of our moral ends, on "moral image realism" (MIR) the objects of the representations of moral *Glaube* are provided by reflective judgment. Reflective judgment, starting from a concrete given in sensible intuition, creates an image of a world that is not only purposive for our minimal cognitive ends, but also for our final ends, that is, morality. By creating an image of the world

---

32 I borrow the term "moral image" from Henrich (1992).

as a scene of action that is coherent with an image of a world that is suitable for theoretical exploration, reflective judgment grounds *Glaube* on an even stronger realist foundation than the one offered by RNR. While the "primacy of the practical" in RNR emphasizes that the claims of practical reason do not contradict those of the theoretical, MIR emphasizes coherency between the image of the world suitable for action and the image of the world suitable for theoretical exploration, which reaffirms even more strongly that the former cannot be a mere illusion. This is because in reflective judgment the truth of the claims of practical reason must respect the same conditions of objective reality and universality as the claims of theoretical reason, that is, the truth of science. Put differently, the normative principle for both images of the world, the one that is theoretical and the one that is practical, is the same, namely, reflective judgment's principle of purposiveness. Finally, the coherence between two domains is reciprocal, that is, it does not pertain merely to practical reason, but it carries some concrete implications for theoretical reason as well. This is because the representation of the world based on reflective judgment suggests that theoretical exploration of nature cannot proceed without at the same time having reason's practical concern as its own horizon.[33]

Literature

Kant

EE   Erste Einleitung (in die Kritik der Urteilskraft), AA 20
JL   Jäsche Logik, AA 9
KpV Kritik der praktischen Vernunft, AA 5
KrV Kritik der reinen Vernunft, AA 3 (B) und 4 (A)
KU   Kritik der Urteilskraft, AA 5
R   Reflexionen, AA 14–19
Rel Die Religion innerhalb der Grenzen der bloßen Vernunft, AA 6
WL   Wiener Logik, AA 24

---

[33] On this issue see Ostaric (2009). Chignell (2007) brings into question the standard interpretation of the limits of theoretical reason in Kant insofar as it argues for the possibility of "theoretical belief" in Kant and the fact that "Kant is not opposed to rational, speculative, assertoric assents regarding things-in-themselves; he's just claiming that they don't count as knowledge" (Chignell 2007, pp. 349f.). This essay goes beyond Chignell (2007) because on MIR theoretical and moral *Glaube* mutually imply each other and the epistemic status of *Glaube* is knowledge-like when we use the proof "κατ' 'ανθρωπον"(KU: 462 f.), that is, the one based on the principle of the heautonomous reflective judgment.

English translations are taken from the series *The Cambridge Edition of the Works of Immanuel Kant* (1992 ff.). In some cases I have modified the translation. Some citations from Kant's *Nachlass*, those not available in the *The Cambridge Edition*, are translated by me.

All page and line numbers in parentheses refer to the so-called Akademie-Ausgabe (AA), i.e., to *Kant's gesammelte Schriften*, herausgegeben von der *Königlich Preußischen Akademie der Wissenschaften*, Berlin: Walter de Gruyter (1900 ff.).

Secondary Literature

Adams, Robert (1979): "Moral Arguments for Theistic Belief." In: Cornelius Delaney (ed.): *Rationality and Religious Belief*. Notre Dame, IN: University of Notre Dame Press, pp. 116–140.

Ameriks, Karl (2008): "The End of Kant's *Critiques:* Kant's Moral 'Creationism.'" In: Pablo Muchnik (ed.): *Rethinking Kant*. Newcastle: Cambridge Scholars, pp. 165–190.

Bacin, Stefano (2016): "Praktische Erkenntnis." In: Marcus Willaschek et. al. (eds.): *Kant-Lexikon*. Berlin/Boston: Walter de Gruyter, pp. 560 f.

Chignell, Andrew (2007): "Belief in Kant." In: *The Philosophical Review* 116/3, pp. 323–360.

Engstrom, Stephen (2002): "Kant's Distinction Between Theoretical and Practical Knowledge." In: *The Harvard Review of Philosophy* 10, pp. 49–63.

Förster, Eckart (1992): "'Was darf ich hoffen?' – Zum Problem der Vereinbarkeit von theoretischer und praktischer Vernunft bei Immanuel Kant." In: *Zeitschrift für philosophische Forschung* 46/2, pp. 168–185.

Gardner, Sebastian (2006): "The Primacy of Practical Reason." In: Graham Bird (ed.): *A companion to Kant*. Malden, Oxford: Blackwell, pp. 259–274.

Gardner, Sebastian (2011): "Kant's Practical Postulates and the Limits of the Critical System." In: *Bulletin of the Hegel Society of Great Britain* 32, pp. 187–215.

Guyer, Paul (2000): "From a Practical Point of View: Kant's Conception of a Postulate of Pure Practical Reason." In: Paul Guyer: *Kant on Freedom, Law and Happiness*. Cambridge: Cambridge University Press, pp. 333–371.

Henrich, Dieter (1992): *Aesthetic Judgment and the Moral Image of the World: Studies in Kant*. Stanford: Stanford University Press.

Kain, Patrick (2004): "Self-legislation in Kant's Moral Philosophy. " In: *Archiv für Geschichte der Philosophie* 86, pp. 257–306.

Kain, Patrick (2010): "Practical Cognition, Intuition, and the Fact of Reason." In: Benjamin Lipscomb/James Krueger (eds.): *Kant's Moral Metaphysics: God, Freedom, and Immortality*. Berlin/Boston: Walter de Gruyter, pp. 211–230.

Meier, Georg Friedrich (1752): *Auszug aus der Vernunftlehre*. Halle: Gebauer.

Nietzsche, Friedrich (1999): *The Birth of Tragedy and Other Writings*. Edited by Raymond Geuss and Ronald Speirs. Cambridge: Cambridge University Press.

Ostaric, Lara (2009): "Kant's Account of Nature's Systematicity and the Unity of Theoretical and Practical Reason." In: *Inquiry* 52/2, pp.155–178.

Ostaric, Lara (2010): "Works of Genius as Sensible Exhibitions of the Idea of the Highest Good." In: *Kant-Studien* 101/1, pp. 22–39.

Willaschek, Marcus (2010): "The Primacy of Practical Reason and the Idea of a Practical Postulate." In: Andrews Reath/Jens Timmermann (eds.): *Kant's* Critique of Practical Reason. *A Critical Guide*. Cambridge: Cambridge University Press, pp. 168–196.
Wood, Allen W. (1970): *Kant's Moral Religion*. Ithaca: Cornell University Press.
Wood, Allen W. (1978): *Kant's Rational Theology*. Ithaca: Cornell University Press.

Elke Elisabeth Schmidt & Dieter Schönecker
Kant's Moral Realism regarding Dignity and Value. Some Comments on the *Tugendlehre*

Abstract Contrary to recent readings of Kant's theory of value, we argue that dignity and value do play a significant role in Kant's ethics and are in no way dispensable. According to our reading, Kant claims that human beings possess dignity and value as intrinsic, non-natural properties, and that autonomy, i.e., the capacity to give oneself the moral law and obey it, makes the human being an end in itself that has absolute value as an intrinsic metaphysical property. Thus, Kant has to be understood as a moral realist. The focus of this paper is Kant's *Metaphysische Anfangsgründe der Tugendlehre*.

***

> Sie werden bemerkt haben, daß der Begriff von Menschenwürde
> zu den Lieblingsbegriffen des Hrn. Kant gehört.
> You will have noticed that the concept of human dignity
> is one of Mr. Kant's favorite concepts.
> Johann Christoph Schwab,
> *Vergleichung des Kantischen Moralprincips mit dem
> Leibnizisch-Wolffischen*
> Berlin und Stettin, 1800 (p. 79)

Do the concepts of dignity and value play a significant role in Kant's ethics? Or is it rather that for Kant these concepts are dispensable, or at least dispensable when it comes to the foundations of his own ethical thought? In this paper, we shall sketch answers to these questions with regard to Kant's *Metaphysische Anfangsgründe der Tugendlehre*. We will argue that for Kant dignity and value are important, indispensable concepts.[1]

---

[1] We have published our answers to these questions with regard to Kant's *Grundlegung zur Metaphysik der Sitten* in Schmidt/Schönecker (2017).

https://doi.org/10.1515/9783110574517-006

Our analysis was sparked by Oliver Sensen's stimulating and challenging book *Kant on Human Dignity*.[2] Sensen raises a very interesting question: Do humans beings have dignity because or inasmuch as we must respect them, or do they have dignity on the basis of certain metaphysical, intrinsic qualities? His basic answer is this: "It is not because others have a value that we should respect them, but it is because one should respect them that they have an importance and a dignity" (Sensen 2011, p. 2; cf. pp. 28, 32, 174, 176).[3] On Sensen's and other *revisionist* (more or less constructivist or constitutivist) readings, dignity (absolute value) is not a metaphysical or intrinsic quality; to have dignity just means to be elevated, and therefore "'[h]as value' is *merely another way of saying* 'should value'" (Sensen 2011, pp. 30, 32; our emphasis). For those readings, both the concept of absolute value and the concept of dignity are dispensable; these readings also entail that Kant is not a moral realist.

Now, Kant's major writings contain a number of famous passages which, at least at first glance, strongly support the *traditional* reading according to which Kant does claim that human beings possess dignity and value as intrinsic, non-natural properties, and that they should be respected because of this dignity. On this reading, autonomy, i.e., the capacity to give oneself the moral law and to obey it, makes the human being an end in itself that has absolute value as an intrinsic property and that as such grounds the categorical imperative (CI). Indeed we shall presuppose that the *burden of proof* is on those who advocate the revisionist reading. Because of the prima facie evidence that speaks in favor of the traditional reading, it is up to them to show that despite those famous passages we have reason to think that the traditional reading is wrong.

We will begin (1) with a brief look at what we have called elsewhere Kant's *ground-thesis*, i.e., the claim that rational nature exists as an end in itself and is the ground of the CI,[4] followed by a sketch of how to read some of Kant's basic ethical concepts. We shall focus, however, on the *Tugendlehre* in order to show that the traditional reading is adequate and justified (2). The *Tugendlehre* has

---

[2] We are very grateful to Oliver Sensen for very helpful discussions about the topic in general as well about this paper.
[3] Sensen (2011, pp. 153 ff.) quite rightly points out that 'dignity' in Kant's writings has not only a moral meaning. One can have dignity as a king, a teacher, a mathematician, and so on. We do not dispute this, of course. Kant speaks often and in quite different contexts of 'dignity'; we do not mean to say that in all these contexts 'dignity' means the same as 'absolute inner value.' That some x has dignity implies that it is elevated, but different things can be elevated for different reasons. Here, in our context, when we speak of dignity we mean the dignity of a being that it has due to its autonomy.
[4] Cf. Schmidt/Schönecker (2017).

been neglected for a long time (and it still is), but it is Kant's final word on ethics – in the *Tugendlehre* the term "dignity" is used most often (21 times).[5] To conclude, we shall relate the findings of our interpretations to the question of how Kant should be understood in current metaethical terms: Is Kant a moral realist or not? The answer is, we submit, affirmative; Kant is a moral realist, though a moderate one (3).

1 An Outline of Kant's Ethical Foundations

Let us begin with a sketch of how we understand some of Kant's basic ethical claims and concepts. All these concepts are crucial to a proper interpretation of what Kant says about dignity and value. First, we turn to Kant's ground-thesis (1.1), and then to some basic concepts: good will, autonomy, end in itself, rational nature, and dignity (1.2).

1.1 Kant's Ground-Thesis

In *Grundlegung* II, Kant takes a step "into the metaphysics of morals" (GMS: 426.30).[6] His leading question is how "*reason for itself alone* determines conduct" (GMS: 427.15). The context for everything that follows all the way down to the concept of autonomy is Kant's claim that that "which serves the will as the objective ground of its self-determination is the *end*" (GMS: 427.22). Kant distinguishes between "subjective ends" (GMS: 427.28, 428.25) and "objective ends" (GMS: 427.29, 428.27). Objective ends, as opposed to subjective ends, are ends that are "valid for *all* rational beings" (GMS: 427.25, 427.29; our emphasis); after all, it is one of the questions to be answered by this 'metaphysics of morals' whether the moral law is a "necessary law *for all rational beings*" (GMS: 426.22), and Kant's theory of objective ends provides exactly the answer to this question. It is beyond any doubt that Kant *parallels* the "ground of hypothetical imperatives" (GMS: 482.2) with the "the ground of a possible categorical imperative, i.e., of a practical law" (GMS: 428.5). Again, an *end*

---

[5] For reasons of space, we shall not deal with the *Kritik der praktischen Vernunft*. Therein also is a passage that, at first glance, seems to ground a revisionist reading; for a reply, see Kain's paper in this volume.
[6] For the list of abbreviations of Kant's works, see the "Literature" section of this paper.

'serves the will as the objective[7] *ground* of its self-determination.' To say that such ends are 'subjective' is to say that they only have a "relative value" (GMS: 428.20), and this is to say that 'subjective ends' "can provide *no* necessary principles valid universally for *all* rational beings and hence valid for every volition, i.e., practical laws" (GMS: 427.36; our emphasis). And from this Kant concludes: "Hence all these relative ends are only the ground of hypothetical imperatives" (GMS: 428.1). Now look at how Kant continues:

> But suppose there were something *whose existence in itself* had an absolute worth, something that, as *end in itself*, could be a ground of certain laws; then in it and only in it alone would lie the ground of a possible categorical imperative, i.e., of a practical law. [new paragraph][8] Now I say that the human being and in general every rational being *exists* as end in itself, *not merely as means* to the discretionary use of this or that will, but in all its actions, those directed toward itself as well as those directed toward other rational beings, it must always *at the same time* be considered as an *end* [...] The ground of this principle [i.e., the CI] is: *Rational nature exists as end in itself.* (GMS: 428 f.)

Subjective ends, being of value for those who actually set these ends, can only 'ground' hypothetical imperatives. But if there are to be 'necessary principles valid universally for *all* rational beings and hence valid for *every* volition, i.e., practical laws' they must have their 'ground' in *objective* ends; for only these ends, as opposed to 'subjective ends,' have an "absolute value" (GMS: 428.4, 428.30) and therefore '*can* provide' principles valid for *all* rational beings. Only objective ends, i.e., ends in themselves that are of absolute value, can be a 'ground' for the CI. Every rational being exists as an end in itself; hence human beings (as rational beings) exist as ends in themselves. Therefore, human beings as ends in themselves can be a ground for the CI. This is the basic idea. We do not see how this could be reconciled with a revisionist reading.[9]

---

[7] Note that 'subjective ends' are 'objective' in the sense that hypothetical imperatives express an objective relation between ends and means; they are *not* objective ends, however, in the sense that they are ends for all rational beings.

[8] All insertions in square brackets by the authors.

[9] There is one sentence in GMS II that does seem to support the revisionist claim that dignity is not an intrinsic property and rather something that is ascribed to human beings as beings that ought to be respected. This sentence is: "For nothing has a value except that which the law determines for it" (GMS: 436,1); Sensen's interpretation relies strongly on this one sentence. However, Sensen reads this sentence out of context; what Kant says here is that moral *legislation* (and hence autonomy) determines the dignity of the human and of every rational nature (for a detailed anaylsis of that sentence cf. Schmidt/Schönecker 2017).

1.2 Basic Concepts of Kant's Foundations

Before we look into Kant's concept of dignity in the *Tugendlehre*, let us first address some key terms of Kant's ethical theory as he develops them in the *Grundlegung:* 'the good will,' 'autonomy,' 'end in itself,' 'rational nature,' and 'dignity.' They are all interwoven with each other, but let us look at them somewhat independently.

The Good Will

For a reason that will become evident momentarily, we have to differentiate three different aspects, or rather instances, of Kant's concept of a good will: The noumenally-good will, the practically-good will, and the holy will. The *noumenally-good will* – which Kant often identifies with 'pure practical reason' and which he often refers to as the 'homo noumenon,' 'person,' 'personality,' or 'humanity in one's person' – is the will that as such wills the good. Because the noumenally-good will is free, it has a law of its causality (the moral law) and thus always wills the moral good; the noumenally-good will is the autonomous will. As such, it is this moral faculty itself that gives the law (the CI) for imperfect beings and that, by means of moral feelings, is also a motivating force. Every human being has such a will, even if he or she acts morally bad. Thus, even a scoundrel

> transports himself in thoughts into entirely another order of things than that of his desires in the field of sensibility [...] This person, however, he believes himself to be when he transports himself into the standpoint of a member of the world of understanding [...] in which he is conscious of a good will. (GMS: 454 f.)

The importance of this idea of the noumenally-good will can hardly be overestimated, and it is well established in a considerable number of places, for instance:

> [...] this 'ought' is really a volition that would be valid for every rational being, under the condition that reason were practical in him without any hindrances; for beings, such as we are, who are also affected through sensibility, as with incentives of another kind, with whom what reason for itself alone would always do does not always happen, that necessity of action is called only an 'ought,' and the subjective necessity is different from the objective. (GMS: 449.16)

The "moral 'ought' is thus one's own necessary volition as a member of an intelligible world" (GMS: 455.7).[10]

The noumenally-good will is the basis both for the practically-good will and the holy will. The *practically-good will* is the will that human (or all finite, imperfect) beings have when their volition is indeed moral; it is the noumenally-good will considered as a will that manifests itself successfully in a finite being against the influence of inclinations and desires. We shall ignore the difficult question of how deeply rooted in *character* the good will must be understood: Is a good will like a far-reaching embedded disposition which characterizes a person and most of his or her actions such that bad actions are understood as exceptions? Or can a person who, all in all, is a bad person sometimes act morally good, i.e., sometimes act from a good will (from duty)? In any case, for imperfect beings, to act morally (to act with a practically-good will) means to act from duty. The noumenally-good will that is manifest in a person without (active) sensual hindrances is what Kant calls the 'holy will"; it only belongs to God and other holy (perfect) beings. These beings have no inclinations and desires contrary to the good; the "will whose maxims necessarily harmonize with the laws of autonomy is a *holy*, absolutely good will" (GMS: 439.28).[11] The noumenally-good will as such (regardless of its being incorporated in a finite being) cannot be differentiated from the holy will.

Famously, GMS I begins with the claim that there "is nothing it is possible to think of anywhere in the world, or indeed anything at all outside it, that can be held to be good without limitation, excepting only a *good will*" (GMS: 393). Not quite so famously, Kant comes back to this claim towards the end of GMS II:

> Now we can end at the place from which we set out at the beginning, namely with the concept of an unconditionally good will. That *will* is *absolutely good* which cannot be evil, hence whose maxim, if it is made into a universal law, can never conflict with itself. This principle is therefore also its supreme law: 'Act always in accordance with that maxim whose universality as law you can at the same time will'; this is the single condition under which a will can never be in conflict with itself, and such an imperative is categorical. Because the validity of the will as a universal law for possible actions has an analogy with the universal connection of the existence of things in accordance with universal laws, which is what is formal in nature in general, the categorical imperative can also be expressed thus: *Act in accordance with maxims that can at the same time have themselves as universal laws of nature for their object*. This, therefore, is the way the formula of an absolutely good will is constituted. (GMS: 437.5)

---

10 Also cf. GMS: 400.34–37, 412.30–35, 440.7–13.
11 Cf. GMS: 414.1–11.

In order to avoid confusion, one must see that what Kant says in this paragraph is *not* a summary of his analysis of the good will in GMS I; hence, *not* everything Kant says about the good will *here* is already laid out in GMS I. Concluding the 'metaphysics of morals' to which a transition was made in GMS II, Kant claims that it is just the '*concept*' of a good will 'from which we set out at the beginning' that is now recapitulated. In GMS I, Kant had begun with the concept (or rather the term) of a good will as it is already employed in 'common rational moral cognition'; this concept is analyzed and then further elaborated as the concept of duty. What Kant says in GMS II (437), however, contains *more* than GMS I; after all, in GMS II Kant not only presents his theory of action (practical reason, imperatives, and so forth), but also proceeds (in 427) to the 'metaphysics of morals' in the context of which he again offers (as we shall see shortly) a theory of action including the ground-thesis. As a result of all this, and in particular as a result of the 'metaphysics of morals' developed thus far, the concept of a good will is explicated. In GMS I, Kant describes what we call the practically-good will; in that passage of GMS II (437), however, his focus is on the noumenally-good will. Note that Kant in 437 not only speaks of the will that is 'absolutely good' inasmuch as it '*cannot* be evil' and whose maxim as a law 'can *never* be in conflict with itself', but he describes as well this 'absolutely good will' even in a way that this *will itself as such* has '*validity as a universal law* for possible actions,' which is a perfect description of what we call the noumenally-good will. Hence the question is not whether what Kant says in GMS II (437) is compatible with what he says in GMS I, nor is the question whether Kant in GMS I describes the noumenally-good will or the practically-good will. For as explained above, the practically-good will *is* the noumenally-good of a finite being which successfully wills and acts (despite or against the hindrances of sensibility). There is but one concept of the good will both in GMS I and GMS II, but whereas in GMS I the focus is on the practically-good will, in GMS II the focus is on the noumenally-good will.

Autonomy

At first sight, autonomy seems fairly easy to understand: It is "the property of the will through which it is a law to itself" (GMS: 440.16);[12] and the 'law,' of course, is the moral law. However, Kant's distinction between the world of understanding (the intelligible world, the noumenal world, etc.) and the world of

---

12 Cf. GMS: 447.1: "autonomy, i.e., the quality of the will of being a law to itself".

sense, as well as, accordingly, his distinction between a noumenally-good will and a practically-good will, complicate this 'property of the will' considerably.[13] For Kant uses the term 'autonomy' not only for the human being and his or her capacity for a practically-good will, but also for the property of the intelligible will (i.e., the noumenally-good will), simply considered *as* the intelligible will. Recall how Kant understands the will itself as a noumenal causality: "The rational being counts himself as intelligence in the world of understanding, and *merely as an efficient cause belonging to this world* does it call its causality a *will*" (GMS: 453.17; first emphasis ours). Or we may look at this passage: "Our own will, insofar as it would act only under the condition of a possible universal legislation through its maxims, this will possible to us in the idea, is the authentic object of respect" (GMS: 440.7). This will is then identified with the will that is autonomous, i.e., with autonomy *itself:* "if we think of ourselves as *free*, then we *transport ourselves as members into the world of understanding* and cognize the *autonomy* of the will, together with its *consequence*, morality" (GMS: 453.11; our emphasis). Note how Kant continues: "[...] but if we think of ourselves as *obligated* by duty, then we consider ourselves as belonging to the world of sense and yet at the same time to the world of understanding" (GMS: 453.14; our emphasis). Thus the free will is the noumenal will, and autonomy is its property; and in some contexts, this will is *considered* not as the will of a human being that is *also* part of the sensible world, but as a noumenal will only. So, for example, he states that as "a *mere* member of the world of understanding, all my actions would be perfectly in accord with the principle of the *autonomy* of the pure will" (GMS: 453.25; our emphasis), and he also observes, "[...] the idea of freedom makes me into a member of an intelligible world, through which, if I were that *alone*, all my actions *would* always be in accord with the *autonomy* of the will [...]" (GMS: 454.6; emphasis partly ours). It is important to keep in mind that the noumenally-good will *as such* is *not* only a mere capacity to act morally (if 'capacity' implies its not being used or activated); for this will as such wills the good. Nonetheless, it is the noumenally-good will that *enables* the *human* being to act morally; thus, *for the human being* – who is a member both of the noumenal *and* the sensible world – the noumenally-good will is indeed a capacity.

In any event, autonomy cannot be identical with having a practically-good will, although a practically-good will is autonomous. Unless autonomy and

---

[13] We understand the difference between what we call the noumenally-good will and the practically-good will as presumably what Kant in the *Metaphysik der Sitten* (MS: 213f.) explains as the difference between *Wille* and *Willkür*. For this essay, however, this claim of ours is irrelevant.

having a practically-good will are not the same, a scoundrel would not be autonomous – which he actually *is* insofar as even he, to some extent, wants to be morally good, i.e., insofar as he has a *noumenally*-good will. We will return to this again.

End in Itself and Rational Nature

The concept of 'autonomy' is strongly related to the concepts of 'end in itself' and 'rational nature,' and yet it is striking that Kant in GMS II says very little about what exactly an 'end in itself' is and what 'rational nature' means.[14] To be sure, "rational beings [...] are called *persons*, because their nature already marks them out as ends in themselves" (GMS: 428.21). Yet this does not tell us what a 'person' or precisely a 'rational being' is. In the *Religion*, Kant famously distinguishes between animality, humanity, and personality,[15] and it has been a recurring misinterpretation in the literature to ascribe to Kant the position that humanity as the ability to set ends is what deserves respect. But clearly it is not; it is personality, even though Kant, especially in the GMS, often speaks of 'humanity' when he means 'personality,' i.e., freedom as the ability to give the moral law and obey it.[16] At the very beginning of GMS III, Kant declares that freedom is "the key to the definition of the autonomy of the will" (GMS: 446.6). Yet in GMS II he basically speaks of freedom only in passing. He tells us only that the realm of ends is "possible through freedom" (GMS: 434.2; cf. 435.35). But as is commonly known by now, in his so-called lectures *Naturrecht Feyerabend* (1784) it becomes clear that it is freedom of the will which makes human beings ends in themselves: "The freedom of the human being is the condition under which the human being himself can be an end" (NF: 1320). Or again: "I must presuppose the freedom of this being if it is to be an end in its own eyes. Such a being must therefore have freedom of the will" (NF: 1322). It is also quite obvious from this lecture that a being is not an end in itself simply because it is rational and capable of setting ends: "If rational beings alone can be ends in themselves, they cannot be so because they have reason, but because they have freedom. Reason is merely a means. – Through reason the human being could produce in accordance with universal laws of

---

14 For this use of the concept of 'rational being' as identical with the concept of 'end in itself,' cf. GMS: 429.2, 430.6, 430.28, 431.13, 431.27, 433.22, 438.8, 438.16, 439.4. – We are partly drawing here on the commentary by Schönecker/Wood (2015).
15 Cf. Rel: 26 ff.
16 We agree with Sensen on this point; cf. Sensen (2011, pp. 127 ff.).

nature, without freedom, what the animal produces through instinct" (NF: 1321f.). Only if a rational being is free in the positive and emphatic sense that this freedom is "a law for itself" (NF: 1322) is such a being an end in itself. In its capacity as a rational and free being it gives itself moral laws, and only in this regard does it possess value: "The inner worth of the human being rests upon his freedom, upon the fact that he has a will of his own" (NF: 1319). This 'inner worth' is also called here "dignity" (NF: 1319).

Thus, when it comes to be an end in itself, the relevant rationality is *moral* rationality and thus autonomy. These terms, in turn, are related to the term 'dignity.' This is so because rational beings, i.e., autonomous beings, are ends in themselves; and since ends in themselves have dignity, autonomous beings have dignity (more on this later). Yet is it really the noumenal ('autonomous') will that grounds dignity? The following places seem unambiguous: "*Autonomy* is thus the ground of the dignity of the human and of every rational nature" (GMS: 436.6); and "the dignity of humanity consists precisely in this capacity for universal legislation, although with the proviso that it is at the same time itself subject to this legislation" (GMS: 440.10);[17] or yet again, "the will of one rational being must always at the same time be regarded as *legislative*, because otherwise the rational being could not think of the other rational beings as *ends in themselves*" (GMS: 434.23).

Nevertheless it is not so simple, for there are passages and contexts in which Kant seems to say that what is an end in itself is not the human being as an autonomous being (with its *capacity* to give the moral law and obey it) but the human being who has a *practically*-good will – the good person. One relevant passage, of course, is the very first sentence of GMS I on the good will being the *only* thing that is 'good without limitation'; as we have seen, this describes the practically-good will. Another is found in Kant's theory of the realm of ends. To have a practically-good will seems to be a necessary condition in order to be a member in the realm of ends: "Such a realm of ends would actually be brought about through maxims, the rule of which is prescribed by the categorical imperatives of all rational beings, *if they were universally followed*" (GMS: 438.29). Kant also says that it is the "suitableness of its [the rational being's] maxims for the universal legislation [which] designates it as an end in itself" (GMS: 438.11), and that it is the moral "way of thinking" (GMS: 435.25) that deserves "to be recognized as dignity" (ibid.).

---

[17] Cf. Kant's reference to "[...] every other rational being as a universally legislative being (which is why they are also called 'persons')" (GMS: 438.14–16; our emphasis).

We will return to this point later. For now, however, let us briefly argue why it *cannot* be the practically-good will that renders absolute value (being an end in itself), but rather autonomy in a human being as a *capacity* for morality. To begin with, there are not only passages in which Kant seems to say a practically-good will is required for a being to be an end in itself, but also other passages, already quoted (GMS: 436.6, 440,10), in which he says it is just the *capacity*. So let us assume that there is textual evidence for both interpretations. In this case, there are still two systematic reasons that make it highly implausible that Kant would hold that a being with a practically-good will alone is an end in itself. First, Kant says that what is an end in itself is the 'ground' of the CI. If what makes a being an end in itself were it having a practically-good will, then the practically-good will would be the 'ground' of the CI – which makes no sense since to have a practically-good will already *presupposes* being determined by the CI. The latter is the presupposition for the existence of the former; hence the former cannot be the 'ground' of the latter regardless of how we understand 'ground' here (we will return to this shortly). Second, there are many human beings (such as scoundrels) who do not have a practically-good will. Could it really be Kant's position that they are *not* ends in themselves, that they are not persons and hence have no dignity? After all, rational beings are called *persons*, says Kant, "because their *nature* already marks them out as ends in themselves" (GMS: 428.22; our emphasis). But to have a practically-good will is not a matter of 'nature'; it is a matter of acquisition. (And to say that bad persons are no persons seems also strongly at odds with what Kant says about imputability.) Thus, although there is textual evidence for both interpretations, there are two quite convincing arguments suggesting that it is rational, autonomous nature which is an end in itself and thus rational, autonomous nature that has dignity.

On Dignity

Kant uses the term *Würde* (*dignity*) in numerous places in various ways,[18] and we have seen already that it is strongly related to other terms such as 'end in itself,' 'nouemenal will,' 'autonomy,' and so on. Now let us look at dignity more specifically.

To begin with, we suggest (similar to Sensen) that Kant has a *two-level-model* of being an end in itself, which is also to say that Kant has a two-level-model of

---

[18] One of the many merits of Sensen's book is to make this clear.

the concept of dignity (absolute value). According to this model, every human being is an end in itself and has intrinsic value – independently of her moral or immoral maxims – because every human being has a noumenally-good will and therefore the capacity to be moral. And since every human being (even a scoundrel) has this noumenally-good will, every human being is an end in itself and has to be respected. On a second level (in another respect), however, one has to take into consideration whether someone actually intends and acts morally, i.e., whether she also has a *practically*-good will. And if she does, she is an end in itself in an elevated sense and therefore has value in an elevated sense.[19]

How then is this two-level-model related to the concept of dignity? As we have seen already, Kant's theory of a realm of ends seems to leave no other choice than to interpret him as saying that having a practically-good will (being a virtuous person) is not only a sufficient[20] but also a necessary condition for being a member in the realm of ends. It is in this context of the realm of ends – in which all members have a *practically*-good will – that the term 'dignity' appears for the first time (from a systematic point of view, GMS: 434.32). Therefore, and because of the other passages already cited,[21] it seems conceivable at first glance that Kant wants to ascribe dignity only to the second level, i.e., to beings with a *practically*-good will. We have seen, however, that two systematic reasons clearly speak against such an understanding: (i) The practically-good will could not be the 'ground' for the CI because a good will already presupposes the CI; (ii) and beings without a practically-good will are persons and thus have dignity as well. Indeed, Kant makes use of this expression ('dignity') even when he talks about an end in itself in terms of a being which is only *capable* of being moral: "Thus morality and humanity, insofar as it is *capable of morality*, is that alone which has dignity" (GMS: 435); and as already quoted: "the dignity of humanity consists precisely in this *capacity* for universal legislation" (GMS: 440.11; our emphasis). Hence we are justified in holding that

---

[19] There is no direct and clear textual support for this two-level-model. (At least in his major writings, Kant never says something like 'there are two levels of value/dignity/end in itself.') Yet just as Kant, as a matter of fact, distinguishes between an imperfect will and a holy will without introducing a term for this difference or model, we must distinguish between different aspects of value and being an end in itself. There is no single interpretation that has all the textual evidence on its side; all the more reason to conclude, then, that Kant has a model in mind which is in some sense a compromise. In private conversation, Oliver Sensen has emphasized the importance of R 6856; see also Sensen (2011, pp. 168f.). But not only is this merely a *Reflexion* but it also seems to us that it is hardly evident what exactly this *Reflexion* says.

[20] Provided, however, that all rational beings have such a will.

[21] See above p. 128.

Kant has a two-aspect-model of dignity as well. In one respect, "every rational nature" (GMS: 436.7) has dignity, insomuch as rational beings are autonomous (and with regard to human beings it is the "dignity of humanity as rational nature," GMS: 439.4). In another respect, Kant also speaks of the dignity of the "way of thinking" (*Denkungsart*, GMS: 435.25), i.e., of the "morally good disposition or virtue" (GMS: 435.29), or of the "*dignity* in a person who fulfills all his duties" (GMS: 440.1). Thus every rational being in its capacity to give the moral law and to obey it has dignity; and every finite rational being has its own level of dignity, depending on how virtuous it is. In any case, things have no dignity; "rational beings, by contrast, are called *persons*, because their nature already marks them out as ends in themselves" (GMS: 428.21). On the traditional reading, plants and animals have no freedom, i.e., they are not capable of morality; therefore, they are not ends in themselves (and thus have no dignity), and therefore they cannot and must not be the object of respect. There are no duties to them, only duties *with regard to* them (as Kant says in the *Tugendlehre*, § 16).[22]

Here it is very important to see that Kant also speaks quite often of the end in itself having an 'absolute value' or an 'inner value.'[23] This 'absolute' or 'inner value' in turn is identified in both ways with dignity: "[...] inner value, i.e., dignity" (GMS: 435.4), or, the other way round, "[...] dignity, i.e., an unconditioned, incomparable value" (GMS: 436.3). Indeed, in ethical contexts 'dignity' is just a *catchword* for 'absolute inner value.' To say that x has dignity is tantamount to saying that x has absolute inner value. Since an autonomous being as an end in itself has absolute value, and since 'absolute value' is tantamount to 'dignity,' Kant relates an end in itself to (autonomy and) dignity.

2 Dignity in the *Tugendlehre*

Kant's *Tugendlehre* is not simply a *Tugendlehre*; above all, it is a (moral) "doctrine of *ends*" (TL: 381.23). This entire second book of the *Metaphysics of Morals* is based upon the idea that there are objective, intrinsically valuable ends that are at the same time duties or at least lead to duties. It would certainly

---

22 For an analysis of this topic (TL § 16), cf. Schmidt/Schönecker (2016a).
23 Cf. GMS: 428.4, 428.15, 428.30, 435.4, 435.12, 439.16, 439.2, 454.37. See also TL: 435.2, 462.12. – Another important concept Kant uses both in his published writings as well as in the lectures is *Heiligkeit* (holiness). We cannot deal with this here, but it seems very implausible to give a revisionist reading of the person or the moral law as being holy. For some examples of Kant's reference to holiness cf. GMS: 435.27, KpV: 32, 87, 131, TL: 379f., 455.

be worthwhile to explore this basic idea in Kant's late moral philosophy, yet this is not something we could achieve here. We shall therefore focus only on three sections of the *Tugendlehre:* § 11 (part II. 3.1), § 37 (part II. 3.2), and § 38 (part II. 3.3). All three are central to Kant's theory of intrinsic value and dignity, and they strongly support the traditional reading.

2.1 On § 11 of the *Tugendlehre*

§ 11 is one of the most important passages on dignity in the *Tugendlehre*, and in no other section of the *Tugendlehre* does Kant speak so often of "Wert" (*value*, eleven times) as he does in § 11. It is fairly long, and we can only analyze a small passage. Here is our translation of the second paragraph (based on Mary Gregor's):

> [§11.1] Only the human being regarded as a *person*, i.e., as the subject of a morally-practical reason, is exalted above any price; [§11.2a] for as such (*homo noumenon*) he is not to be valued merely as a means to the ends of others, or even to his own ends, but as an end in itself, [§11.2b] i.e., he possesses a *dignity* (an absolute inner value) [§11.2c] by which he exacts *respect* for himself from all other rational worldbeings, [§11.2d] and by which he can measure himself with every other of this kind [§11.2e] and value himself on a footing of equality with them. (TL: 434.32–435.5)

Above we have explicated some key terms in Kant's ethics relevant to his theory of dignity. To begin with, let us recall some additional concepts employed by Kant in this passage, and these will then be developed in due course.

By the concept "person," Kant refers (though not always) to the property of the human being to be a moral subject, i.e., the "subject of the moral lawgiving which proceeds from the concept of freedom and in which he is subject to a law that he gives himself (*homo noumenon*)" (TL: 439.28); this is basically (though not exactly) what we have called the noumenally-good will. Recall that § 11 belongs to the first book of part one of the doctrine of the elements of ethics (*Elementarlehre*), a book that is concerned with perfect duties to oneself. In § 3, one of the introductory sections on the very idea of duties to oneself, Kant introduces this concept of the homo noumenon as a being that is "endowed with inner *freedom* (*homo nouemenon*)" (TL: 418.18) and "capable of obligation" (TL: 418.19; *ein der Verpflichtung fähiges Wesen*), hence with the ability both to oblige and to be obliged.[24] In another passage Kant speaks of the "human

---

24 To be sure, Kant had done so already in RL: 239.

being as a moral being (*homo noumenon*)" (TL: 430.14). Still another *terminus technicus* often used, and used in § 11 as well, is "humanity in his person,"[25] which in turn in § 6 (TL: 423.5) is identified with the term 'homo noumenon' and with the "subject of morality" (TL: 423.1).[26] So at least generally speaking, "person," "personality," "humanity in one's person," "homo nouemenon" all mean (more or less) the same. Henceforth we will simply speak of the *moral subject*; we will also speak of 'dignity,' although Kant speaks twice of "*human dignity*" (*Menschenwürde*, TL: 429.24, 436.29; our emphasis), and we will use 'value' where Kant speaks of *Wert*.

Now let us look at the propositions first; that is, let us for now abstract from the logical structure of the second paragraph of § 11. What Kant says is this:

> [§11.1]* The human being regarded as the subject of a morally-practical reason is exalted above any price.

As for the second proposition, note that there is a difference between the first and the second edition of the *Tugendlehre*: In the first it says "solches" (TL: 434.34), in the second it says "solcher." Following the first edition and ignoring for now the comparison between being a means and being an end, the proposition is this:

> [§11.2a]$_1$ As a subject of a morally-practical reason the human being is to be valued as an end in itself.

If we follow the second edition, our reconstruction yields this:

> [§11.2a]$_2$ As a human being regarded as a person the human being is to be valued as an end in itself.

But since there appears to be no conceptual difference here, we may reconstruct sentence [§11.2a] as follows:

> [§11.2a]* The moral subject is to be valued as an end in itself.

---

25 *Menschheit in seiner Person*: TL: 379.27, 392.3, 418.20, 420.16, 423.5, 429.5, 435.6 (§ 11).
26 Actually, it is not entirely clear whether what we have called the 'noumenally-good will' is identical with the homo noumenon as introduced in § 3; after all, it is the *homo* noumenon which is introduced in § 3, not the *volitio* or *voluntas* noumenon. And the homo noumenon is not only the obligating entity, but also the one that is obligated – although Kant seems to suggest in § 3 that the *homo phaenomenon* is the one who is obligated. For our purposes, we can leave this question open.

We can now also reformulate sentence [§11.1] once more and thus get:

[§11.1]** The moral subject is exalted above any price.

Without further ado and still abstracting from the logical structure, we can extract the following proposition from sentence [§11.2b]:

[§11.2b¹]* The moral subject possesses a dignity.

It is not *prima facie* obvious how we are to understand this proposition in regard to what Kant says in parentheses ('(an absolute inner value)'); that is, it is perhaps not obvious that to have dignity is identical with having an absolute inner value (though we will claim it is). But in any case – because of the grammatical structure and the parentheses – that the moral subject possesses dignity implies that it possesses an absolute inner value:

[§11.2b²]* The moral subject possesses an absolute inner value.

In order to bring more light into this ambiguity and before we continue with extracting the further propositions [§11.2c] and [§11.2d], let us now look at the logical structure. There are three elements to be considered: There is (i) a 'for' (*denn*, TL: 434.33), (ii) an 'i.e.' (*d.i.*, TL: 435.2), and (iii) a 'by which' (*wodurch*, TL: 435.2).

Ad (i) 'for' (denn)

The conjunctive 'for' (*denn*) in [§11.2a] connects sentence [§11.2] with sentence [§11.1]; hence in [§11.2a] the reason is provided *why* it is true that the moral subject 'is exalted above any price.' The claim is this: The moral subject is 'exalted above any price' because the moral subject is to be 'valued as an end in itself.' As Kant had explained in the preceding paragraph (and as it fits the *Grundlegung*), to have a price is to have an "*outer* value of his usefulness" (TL: 434.26). As is then explained in [§11.2a], this is a value a human being has by being 'a means' to her own end or to the ends of others. But if the human being is not a means and still of value, it is an end *in itself*, and this is what we are told in [§11.2a].

To be more precise, however, we are told to *value* (*schätzen*) human beings *as* ends in themselves rather than told that they *are* ends in themselves, and this seems to come in handy for the revisionist reading given that it holds that the relevant value (dignity) is not an intrinsic quality. Here it is important to realize, first, that the German word *schätzen* in [§11.2a] (translated here as 'to value') does *not* mean "to respect." Its general meaning at Kant's time is "to hold" or "to view."[27] Its more narrow sense is to view something with regard to its value, which is why *schätzen* can in some cases be translated as "to value." Though one cannot respect things but only persons, both things and persons can be valued, and the human being too can be valued when it comes to its price; this is why Kant says in the next paragraph of § 11 that the human being "can and ought to value himself by a *low* as well as by a high measure" (TL: 435.8; our emphasis). Second, the proposition that one *should* value human beings as ends in themselves does *not* imply (neither logically nor rhetorically) that they *are not* ends in themselves. Third, note that Kant does not say that we are to *value* the human being *as* 'exalted above any price'; he says the human being '*is* exalted above any price.' But it cannot *be* 'exalted above any price' unless it really *is* an end in itself. Just valuing ourselves as ends in themselves does not make us ends in themselves; we have to *be* them in the first place. Hence we must not overinterpret passages in which Kant says that we must "value" (TL: 435.1) or "use" (TL: 462.23) the human being as an end in itself as if this were to say that having such a value or dignity is *only* something we (ought to) *ascribe* to human beings rather than something that they intrinsically possess.[28] To see that such a reading falls prey to an overinterpretation, read again the passage in the *Grundlegung* discussed above:

> Now I say that the human being and in general every rational being *exists* as end in itself, not merely as means to the discretionary use of this or that will, but in all its actions, those directed toward itself as well as those directed toward other rational beings, it must always at the same time be *considered* as an end. (GMS: 428; our emphasis, Kant's emphasis deleted except for 'exists')

Considering just the latter part of this sentence, one might get the impression that to be an end in itself consists in merely being '*considered*' as such a being in a somehow non-realist (constructivist) way. But quite the opposite is true: All rational beings, says Kant, *exist* as ends in themselves, and *this is why* they also must be 'considered' accordingly; if something is an end in itself, it ought to be considered and respected as an end in itself. By underlining that rational beings exist as ends in themselves and must be considered as ends as

---

27 Cf. Adelung's *Grammatisch-kritisches Wörterbuch der Hochdeutschen Mundart*.
28 Sensen, we believe, has a tendency to do so; cf. Sensen (2011, p. 174) where he refers to those passages in § 11 and § 38.

well, Kant points out that the property of being an end in itself has an effect on how we are to act towards such beings, to wit, as beings that deserve respect.[29] In that passage in § 11 of the *Tugendlehre*, we find the same reason why Kant puts emphasis on the fact that we are to *value* human beings as ends in themselves. The reason is that in the context of § 11 Kant speaks of a specific duty towards beings that *are* ends in themselves: We must avoid servility, which is why "self-esteem [*Hochschätzung*][30] [...] is a duty of man to himself" (TL: 435.21).

Thus we must reconstruct sentence [§11.2a] as follows:

[§11.2a]** The moral subject is an end in itself.

Ad (ii) 'i.e.' (d.i.)

Let us now address the second logical element, the "i.e." at the beginning of [§11.2b]; it poses some severe difficulties. We have used "i.e." for the translation of the German "d.i." rather than "that is to say" (as Gregor does). This is not a minor decision. For the German "d.i." clearly is a translation of the Latin "id est," and this "d.i." can have different functions: It can signal that something which has already been said is *explicated*; for instance, one can say "Peter is a bachelor, i.e., he's an unmarried man." Or it can be used in an *augmentative* manner such that a consequence or implication is expressed; for instance one can say "Paul is a German, i.e., he is a European."

The 'i.e.' relates [§11.2a] ('the human being is an end in itself') to [§11.2b] ('the human being possesses dignity (an absolute inner value)'). Hence to interpret the 'i.e.' presupposes an understanding of the relation between possessing 'dignity' and possessing 'absolute inner value.' Now we have seen already that in the *Grundlegung*, absolute inner value is very clearly identified in *both* ways with dignity: "[...] inner value, i.e., dignity" (GMS: 435.4), and "[...] dignity, i.e., an unconditioned, incomparable value" (GMS: 436.3). It is therefore no surprise that in § 37 of the *Tugendlehre*, Kant uses the 'i.e.' in the

---

[29] Cf. *Mutmaßlicher Anfang der Menschengeschichte* (MAM: 114.20–24): "Und so war der Mensch in eine Gleichheit mit allen vernünftigen Wesen, von welchem Range sie auch sein mögen, getreten [...]: nämlich in Ansehung des Anspruchs selbst Zweck zu sein, von jedem anderen auch als ein solcher geschätzt und von keinem bloß als Mittel zu anderen Zwecken gebraucht zu werden." Note that here, too, Kant says that the human being is an end (in itself) and 'must also be regarded' as such. Once more, that Kant speaks of 'Anspruch' here does not imply that the human is not an end.

[30] Note that Gregor translates *Hochschätzung* with 'self-*esteem*', but *schätzen* with 'to *value*,' so the reader cannot realize that *Hochschätzung* is a variant of *schätzen*.

explicative sense as well to describe the relation between possessing dignity and possessing absolute value; for he speaks of the "recognition of a dignity [...] in other human beings, *i.e.*, of a value" (TL: 462.13; our emphasis). The obvious reason why Kant uses the short term ("dignity") rather than the predicate proper ("absolute inner value") is that he needs a (short) single term in opposition to 'price.'[31] Hence we propose that the formulation in [§11.2b] ('absolute inner value') expresses an *explicative identification* not only in the extensional sense that all beings that possess dignity also possess an absolute inner value, but also such that "dignity" is a catchword (a *terminus technicus*, if you like) for "absolute inner value."

We still have not yet addressed the problem of how to understand the 'i.e.' Unfortunately, it is not even clear where the function of the "i.e." *ends*. Which sentence is it, after all, that is introduced by the 'i.e.'? One might think it is only [§11.2b^1]* (The moral subject possesses a dignity) or [§11.2b^2]* (The moral subject possesses an absolute inner value). But note that the sentence continues with the 'by which' (the third logical element), and on second thought it does not seem implausible at all that what is stated by the 'i.e.'-part is not only that the human being has dignity (and absolute inner value), but all that which is stated in the rest of the sentence beginning with the 'by which.' In other words: The 'i.e.'-sentence does not necessarily end with 'absolute inner value,' but with the *entire* sentence about the human being valuing himself on a footing of equality with all other rational worldbeings. Thus in order to explain the function of the 'i.e.,' we first need to take into account the function of the 'by which.'

Ad (iii) 'by which' (wodurch)

So let us take an even closer look at all this. As a matter of fact, things get even more complicated if we take into account in more detail the 'by which' in [§11.2c]

---

31 Alternatively, to be of absolute inner value could somehow be a consequence of possessing dignity; in this case, the human being has a dignity and, as a consequence, it has absolute inner value. However, it seems unclear what that could mean. As an implication such as in "Paul is a German, i.e., he is a European," it would suggest that there are beings that have an absolute inner value but not dignity, which seems implausible. As an implication such as in "Paul is a musician, i.e., he has a good sense of rythm," this reading would suggest that to have absolute inner value is just an element of having dignity. This seems to make more sense, but then the question is what else is expressed by the term 'dignity.' In any event, the explicative reading is much more plausible.

(*wodurch*). First a note on the proposition itself. In our translation the 'by which' not only refers to [§11.2c] but also to [§11.2d] and [§11.2e]; by comparison, Gregor in her translation begins a new sentence such that the claim that the human being 'can measure himself with every other of this kind and value himself on a footing of equality with them' has no connection with the preceding 'by which.' Given the German original, this is incorrect; in fact we have two or in some sense even three claims here that are all related to the 'by which.' Let us write them down first without the reference to the 'by which':

> [§11.2c] The human being exacts respect from all other rational worldbeings.
> [§11.2d] The human being can measure himself with all other rational worldbeings.
> [§11.2e] The human being can value himself on a footing of equality with all other rational worldbeings.

Obviously, the fact that the human being can 'value himself on a footing of equality with all other rational worldbeings' implies that he can indeed *measure* himself with all those beings; so we can ignore [§11.2d].[32] We may call this 'equality' *moral equality*.[33] That the human being 'exacts respect from all other rational worldbeings' is to say that it is, as Kant lays this out right at the beginning of the next paragraph in § 11, the "object of respect" (TL: 435.6). To make things a bit easier, let us combine all these elements and rephrase the crucial point somewhat; the reconstruction of [§11.2c-e] yields the following:

> [§11.2c-e]* The human being is the object of respect and possesses moral equality.

Since Kant speaks of *messen* and *schätzen* here (to measure, to value) – claiming that all human beings are equal – the question naturally arises: In regard to *what* exactly can the human being 'measure' and 'value' himself and then claim moral 'equality'? As we have already mentioned, in Gregor's translation Kant's answer is unintelligible. To understand his answer one has to take into account the 'by which'; only in regard to something and by strength of something is there commensurability, measurability and eventually moral equality. But what does 'which' in 'by which' refer to? By strength of 'which' is the human being the object of respect and does he possess moral equality?

---

[32] Note that in German *sich messen mit* also means "to compete with someone," or "to be on par with someone," and this fits well with the idea of being on a footing of equality with all other rational worldbeings.

[33] Cf. once more that passage in MAM (114.20 – 24) where Kant speaks of the *Gleichheit mit allen vernünftigen Wesen* when it comes to being an end in itself (see above, note 29).

Again, we are dealing with three key concepts here (end in itself, dignity, and absolute inner value) as well as with two things that are somehow made possible by them: to be an object of respect and moral equality. At first sight, it might seem unclear what element the 'by which' refers back to: Does it refer back mainly to [§11.2a] ('end in itself')? This seems plausible on the assumption that the 'i.e.' is only explicative and not augmentative. Or does it refer back to [§11.2b] (that is, both to 'absolute inner value' and 'dignity' given that, as has already been argued, the very meaning of 'dignity' is 'absolute inner value')? This seems plausible on the assumption that the 'i.e.' is not only explicative but augmentative. Hence we have two plausible readings here:

[§11.2c-e]$_1$* By strength of being an *end in itself*, the human being is the object of respect and possesses moral equality.
[§11.2c-e]$_2$* By strength of possessing *dignity (absolute inner value)*, the human being is the object of respect and possesses moral equality.

By spacing out 'dignity,' Kant himself puts emphasis on the concept of dignity and value rather than on 'end in itself.' This appears to be no incidence, for the claim introduced by the 'by which' (that 'the human being is the object of respect and possesses moral equality') needs the concept of 'dignity' (i.e., the concept of an 'absolute inner value'), not only the concept of an 'end in itself.' Why does Kant introduce 'dignity' and 'absolute inner value' at all? (As a matter of fact, he could simply have written: '…but as an end in itself, …by which he exacts *respect* for himself from all other rational worldbeings…'). First, it is crucial to see that there is no way to understand what 'end in itself' (*Zweck an sich*) as such, as a term means (i.e., regardless of the normative claim that we ought to treat human beings as ends in themselves) unless we understand it as a valuative term. It is quite right that the human being is an end in itself *because* it possesses freedom, i.e., because it is a moral subject; but this alone does not account for the semantic content of the term 'end in itself.' The basic point is this: We easily understand what it means that something is a means to an end, and that something has a value as a means, given that a particular end is an end *for* someone, and is as such of value for her which is why the means is of value for her. But it is only against the background of these conceptual connections that we understand what an end *in itself* is: It is something the value of which is a value neither as a means nor as the value for someone but rather a value independently of these relations; a value in itself (we will return to this point once more shortly).

Second, the 'by which' also makes much more sense from a further philosophical (not only semantic) point of view. In that second paragraph of § 11 (the one we are just discussing), Kant speaks twice of 'valuing' (*schätzen*) and once of 'measuring' (*messen*); in the first two sentences of the next paragraph he again speaks of 'valuing' (TL: 435.9) and even of a 'measure' or 'standard' (*Maßstab*, TL: 435.9). Kant claims that the human being can and must 'value' himself, and that such 'measurement' yields the result that he is 'on a footing of equality' with his fellow men, that there is moral equality. But measurement requires that there is something that *can be* measured, some kind of quality or quantity that *allows* for measurement. The human being is not a means to something else, but an end in itself; this quality Kant calls 'dignity.' But the crucial explication (or, if you prefer, new information) we obtain in sentence [§11.2b] is that to be such an end in itself involves being 'of an absolute inner value' as opposed to the relative outer value of other things that are just means to ends. It is this quality – *possessing an absolute inner value* – that allows for commensurability, measurability, valuing, and eventually for moral equality. Human beings as ends in themselves possess an absolute inner value; as such beings, they are the 'object of respect.' To be more precise: It is the "humanity in the human being's person" (TL: 435.6) that is the 'object of respect.' But this is just to say that it is the moral subject that is the object of respect, i.e., it is the noumenal human being in its ability to oblige and to be obliged – an ability that makes it possess absolute inner value – that is the object of respect. It *is* true, of course, that by strength of being an end in itself, the human being is the object of respect and possesses moral equality, but that is not the point. The point is that there is measure, measurement as well as moral equality, and that this idea can only be brought across by explicating the moral subject in terms of *value* (dignity) rather than in terms of being an end in itself. Hence reading [§11.2c-e]$_2$* is to be (slightly) preferred: By strength of possessing *dignity (absolute inner value)*, the human being is the object of respect and possesses moral equality.

But now we have to recall what Kant lays out in § 3 of the *Introduction* to the first part of the *Tugendlehre* on duties to oneself. His thoughts there provide the basis for everything that follows, and *what* he says is that the human being as a moral subject is the noumenal self, the free subject in its *ability* for morality. This moral subject – i.e., the human being in its ability for morality – is the subject that according to later sections in the *Tugendlehre* possesses dignity, i.e., absolute inner value 'by which' the moral subject is the object of respect and possesses moral equality. This is what Kant says in § 11: The "moral predisposition" (TL: 435.20), our "capacity for internal lawgiving," he says, brings about "the highest self-value, the feeling of his inner value [...], in terms of which he is above any price [...] and possesses an inalienable dignity" (TL: 436). Kant also calls this dignity "*dignitas interna*" (TL: 436.12).³⁴

To sum up, value is by no means a derivative concept for Kant, and therefore the revisionist reading is fallacious; as we have seen, the semantic content of 'end in itself' is strongly related to it. Also, there is no measurement and hence no insight in moral equality unless there is something in regard to which there is equality, and this is the absolute inner value. Finally, there is no 'ground' for morality unless there is 'absolute inner value.' Let us dwell upon this point once more. The term 'inner' in 'absolute inner value' has two aspects: First, the 'inner value' of the human being is the opposite term to the "outer value" (TL: 434.26) of things that only have a price. To be more precise, Kant speaks of the outer value of a human being's "usefulness" (TL: 434.27). The 'outerness' of the value of a thing consists thus in the fact that it is not the value of the thing itself, but of that thing in relation to other things that are someone's ends. As a consequence, its value is dependent on its 'usefulness'; if its usefulness is diminished, so is its value. Its value might even be totally lost. Furthermore, for a human being whose value is dependent on his or her usefulness there can always be a replacement, someone else who can be just as useful to realize the end. Finally, if there were only outer value, then (at least as a matter of brute fact) there would be no equality among human beings; there would only be different degrees of usefulness, different values, and hence different prices.

As opposed to this, the innerness of a value consists in its being of value regardless of its usefulness and due only to what it simply is, an end in itself. This value is an intrinsic property of human beings, something that they have as human beings in their ability for morality. Consequently, its value is not relational, not dependent. As a human being, a human being's value cannot be diminished and it cannot be lost; this is why Kant says that moral dignity is an "inalienable dignity (*dignitas interna*)" (TL: 436). Furthermore, the moral value of a human being has "no equivalent for which the object evaluated [...] could be exchanged" (TL: 462.14). Finally, the absoluteness of the moral value of dignity warrants moral equality. For if everybody has an absolute (unlimited) value, one person's value cannot be greater or smaller than another person's

---

34 It is striking that in § 4, where Kant still reflects in a general manner on duties to oneself, it is said that man's duty to himself as a moral being "consists in what is *formal* in the consistency of the maxims of his will with the *dignity* of humanity of his person" (TL: 420.14). Hence it is impossible that dignity is just the quality of a person inasmuch as it ought to be respected; rather, the very law that obligates us to respect human beings even in its 'formal' aspect already presupposes dignity.

value; everyone who possesses it has it in a way that no other person that has it can possess more or less of it. (To be sure, of course, there are differences or degrees of value among human beings when it comes to their moral value as it exists *not* in the value of their 'moral predisposition,' but rather in the goodness of their practically-good will or their virtue; we have discussed this above.)

2.2 On § 37 of the *Tugendlehre*

§ 37 is a very strong confirmation of what we have found in § 11. Once more, there is textual evidence that strongly supports the traditional reading, and the burden of proof is on the revisionists to show that these passages must be read in a different way. Here is the central passage:

> The respect that I have for others or that another can require from me (*observantia aliis praestanda*) is thus the recognition of a dignity (*dignitas*) in other human beings, i.e., of a value, that has no price, no equivalent for which the object of estimation (*aestimii*) could be exchanged. (TL: 462)

Respect, says Kant, '*is* the recognition of a dignity.' To respect someone is to recognize her dignity. Her dignity is already there; it is a quality to be respected, not something that is somehow brought about *by* respecting her. And once more, Kant explicates the term 'dignity' by the term 'value'; to possess dignity is to possess (absolute) value. We do not see how these claims can be read in a revisionist way.

There is, however, one complication here: The Latin equivalent for *Achtung* in this passage (§ 37) seems to be 'observantia.' This is respect that is 'aliis praestanda,' i.e., respect that we *owe* to others (that we must 'grant'). In § 25, Kant has introduced this kind of respect as "respect in the practical sense" (TL: 449), using in parentheses the same Latin formula 'observantia aliis praestanda,' and he explicitly says that this kind of respect is *not* a feeling (just as love is not a feeling in the context of duties of love and respect to others), but rather a maxim or an attitude. However, in the *Introduction* of the *Tugendlehre* (section XII), Kant speaks of respect as a feeling[35] which is not a duty to have. This respect is specified in Latin as "*reverentia*" (TL: 402).[36] Kant

---

[35] To be more precise: 'respect' is one of the moral predispositions that brings about a feeling with that very name.
[36] Yet Kant also speaks of "*reverentia adversus hominem*" (TL: 468).

identifies this respect as respect for oneself, as "self-respect" (TL: 399). Given that Kant both in the *Grundlegung* and in the *Kritik der praktischen Vernunft* speaks of respect as a feeling, and taking into account that in § 23 of the *Tugendlehre* Kant speaks of love and respect not only as duties but as "feelings that accompany" (TL: 448) the duties of love and respect, we thus have *four* meanings of the term "respect" in the *Tugendlehre* inasmuch as respect is related to persons: respect as self-respect (as a feeling), respect for others as a feeling, and respect for others as well as respect for oneself as a maxime.[37] Once we recognize this, it is not entirely clear whether 'respect' in that passage quoted above is simply respect in the practical sense. After all, Kant speaks of the 'respect that I have for others *or* that another can require from me.' Since he speaks before and after the 'or' of '*others*' to which the respect is related, respect as *reverentia* cannot be meant, for *reverentia* is self-respect. But is 'observantia aliis praestanda' the Latin term for respect such that (i) respect 'that I have for others' is identical with (ii) the respect 'that another can require from me' (§ 37) and thus simply another way of putting it? Or does 'observantia aliis praestanda' only refer to the latter, such that we must read: The respect that I have for others (*respect as a feeling*) *or* that another can require from me (*observantia aliis praestanda*). In *any* case, i.e., on any reading, there is no evidence here that speaks in favor of the revisionist interpretation. For it is not Kant's claim that dignity is nothing but being the object of obligatory respect, but that the respect that is obligatory is the '*recognition* of a dignity.' Even respect as an obligatory maxim that we must have (practical respect) presupposes dignity in that it is dignity that must be practically recognized: Respect, says Kant, is to be "understood as the maxim of *limiting our self-esteem by the dignity of humanity* in another person" (TL: 449; our emphasis, Kant's emphasis deleted).

2.3 On § 38 of the *Tugendlehre*

§ 38 begins with an argument that we reconstruct here without commenting on it: All human beings have a right to be respected by all human beings, and to this right corresponds a duty of all human beings to recognize this right.

---

[37] The concept of respect becomes even more complicated if we take into account that there are numerous different objects of respect: In the *Tugendlehre*, Kant mentions respect for the right (TL: 390), for the moral law (TL: 394, 408, 410, 464), for oneself (TL: 399, 402, 425, 437, 449), for the law in oneself (TL: 403), for the predisposition to the good (TL: 441), for humanity (TL: 425, 435), for every human being (TL: 448f.).

Therefore, all human beings are obliged to respect all human beings. Kant then continues:

> **[§38.1]** Humanity itself is a dignity; **[§38.2a]** for the human being cannot be used merely as a means by any human being (either by others or even by himself) but must always be used at the same time as an end, **[§38.2b]** and it is just in this that his dignity (personality) consists, **[§38.2c]** by which he raises himself above all other worldbeings that are not human beings and yet can be used, and thus over all things. **[§38.3a]** But just as he cannot give himself away for any price (this would conflict with his duty of self-value), **[§38.3b]** so neither can he act contrary to the equally necessary self-value of others, as human beings, that is, **[§38.3c]** he is under the obligation to acknowledge, in a practical way, the dignity of humanity in every other human being. (TL: 462)

We cannot discuss this passage in as detailed a manner as above. Nonetheless, let us make some observations. First, note the remarkable formulation in [§38.1] that 'humanity itself *is* a dignity.' Since by 'humanity' Kant means the moral subject (the rational being with a noumenally-good will), Kant puts emphasis both on the fact that the moral subject *itself* is a dignity, and that the moral subject itself *is* a dignity. To say that it 'itself' is a dignity is to say that the moral subject is so regardless of its relations to others, in particular regardless of its usefulness; and to say that the moral subject 'is' a dignity shall also express that this is an objective, intrinsic property of the moral subject. This formulation ('*is* a dignity') sounds perhaps less peculiar once we replace 'dignity' by 'value.' We have already seen that indeed both in the *Grundlegung* and in the preceding section (§ 37) Kant identifies 'dignity' with 'absolute value' (in both ways), and to say that something '*is* a value' at least sounds less peculiar in German. Thus we may reformulate:

> [§38.1]* The moral subject is an absolute value.

The well-known reason Kant provides for this claim ('for,' *denn*), it seems, is basically this:

> [§38.2a]* The human being is an end in itself.

Since in [§38.2b] Kant relates this back to the concept of dignity ('it is just in this that his dignity consists'), everything we have learned from § 11 appears to be corroborated:

> [§38.2b]* The dignity of the human being is grounded in it being an end in itself.

But not so fast; it is not that easy. Kant does not simply say in [§38.2a] that the human being *is* an end in itself; rather, what he says is this:

> [§38.2a]** The human being must be used (*gebraucht*) as an end in itself.

And since Kant then relates this to the concept of dignity ('it is just in this that his dignity consists'), he really seems to say this:

> [§38.2b]** The dignity of the human being is grounded in that he must be used as an end in itself.

Well, this is not significant, one might think. But recall the basic line of the revisionist reading. Sensen, one of its advocates, quotes our current passage (§ 38) as evidence for his basic claim: "It is not that someone should be respected because he has dignity, but he has dignity because he should be respected" (Sensen 2011, p. 174). And sentence [§38.2b] understood in terms of [§38.2b]** indeed seems to be evidence for this claim of Sensen's: The dignity of the human being is not an intrinsic metaphysical property but consists merely in that the human being must be 'considered,' 'valued,' or, for that matter, be 'used' as an end in itself. But is [§38.2b] really evidence for this revisionist reading?

First of all, we have already seen that Kant also says elsewhere (in the *Grundlegung*, in the *Tugendlehre*)[38] that the human being must be 'considered' as an end in itself, but that this does not imply at all that she *is* not an end in itself; she *is*, and this is precisely *why* she also must be *considered* as such an end. A similar point can be made with regard to Kant's recurrent claim that the human being is 'elevated.'[39] Let us look at [§38.2c]; the statement is quite clear:

> [§38.2c] By his dignity the human being raises himself above all other things.[40]

It is true, of course, that one aspect of possessing dignity (morally understood) is that whoever does possess dignity is *elevated*; thus, Kant speaks of the "sublimity of his moral predisposition" (TL: 435.20) as well as of the "sublimity of his vocation" (TL: 437.4). But this does not at all imply that "'dignity' *means* nothing but 'raised above'" (Sensen 2011, p. 176; our emphasis). A person who

---

[38] See above, p. 135.
[39] Cf., for instance, GMS: 434.33 or TL: 435.20.
[40] To say that the human being 'raises himself' above is tantamount to saying that it is raised above (this is true both on the standard and the revisionist reading).

is taller than another person certainly is taller *in relation* to that other person. Unless there is another person, and a person that is smaller than him, he is not taller; still he would not be taller in relation to that other person if he had not a certain height *as such* in the first place. By the same token, a human being is raised above (say) animals by his dignity, but his dignity does not only *consist* in being raised above animals. Furthermore, that *which* raises human beings above animals is *not* simply the *descriptive* fact that they possess freedom as a moral capacity. If this were all, then all we could say would be that human beings possess freedom and animals do not. But to say that human beings are 'above' animals only makes sense if there is a standard, i.e., a *value*, in regard to which we can say that something has a higher value, that is, is raised above someone else. It is the term 'value' by which we can state that to be a moral subject is a "*prerogative*" (TL: 420.17).[41]

In [§38.3c] Kant says that the human being 'is under the obligation to acknowledge, in a practical way, the dignity of humanity in every other human being,' or in short:

[§38.3c]* It is a duty to acknowledge the dignity of the moral subject.

---

[41] Cf. again MAM where Kant says that the human being "vermöge seiner *Natur*" (MAM: 114; our emphasis) is raised above animals. – Of course, Schönecker (2015) has not, as Sensen claims (2015, p. 125), argued that every predication of the kind 'is raised above' is as such a *moral* value judgment; an excellent professor of mathematics is typically raised above his students with regards to his ability to do mathematics, but this, of course, is not a moral quality. Rather, Schönecker's point (and now our point) is twofold: First, if A is raised above B in regard to a certain quality, A must have this quality, *regardless* of A's relation to B; A must have that quality that allows for the comparison such that it is possible to say that A *is* raised above B. Second, freedom cannot *just* be a descriptive concept, not even only in the "first instance" (Sensen 2011, p. 103). Kant often says that human beings are elevated above animals. This cannot *simply* mean that animals do not possess a certain quality (freedom) which human beings do possess. Probably all animals possess qualities that human beings do not possess; many animals run much faster than we do, but that does not imply that they are raised above human beings, because the ability to run fast is irrelevant to the question of what species is superior. As living beings we are elevated *in toto* above animals, and this requires that we have a quality with a certain absolute value. In §1 of the *Anthropologie*, Kant writes: "The fact that the human being can have the 'I' in his representations *raises him infinitely above* all other living beings on earth" (Anthro: 127); again, the point is not that the human being is elevated above animals because it has just some non-normative quality.

It would be very strange, however, if there were first a duty to respect human beings by which dignity is conferred to them, and then to claim that there is another duty that we have to respect this dignity.[42]

3 Dignity, Value, and Moral Realism

Is Kant a moral realist? More precisely: Is Kant a moral realist regarding dignity and value? The answer to this question obviously depends on what moral realism is.[43] It is undisputed that there is more to moral realism than cognitivism; but what is it? We submit there are three elements: First, moral properties are *genuine* properties, i.e., they cannot be reduced to other properties; presupposing a strict distinction between natural and non-natural properties, moral realism holds that moral properties are not identical with and (or) cannot be reduced to natural properties. Second, moral properties are *non-contingent*. According to realism, there is something like a moral nature of things; they are as they are, independent of what human beings as individuals or groups actually (at a given time) strive for, feel, or think. However, non-contingency can be understood in two ways: Either as absolute non-contingency such that those things that have non-contingent moral properties cannot not have them (we call this *strict* realism); this would be true for God as the morally perfect being as well as for the Platonic Idea of the Good. Or things could also have non-contingent moral properties, and yet these would not be absolute: The existence of moral properties depends on the very fact that things exist; for instance, if some human actions are prohibited, then the fact that there are

---

42 To the present day, there has been considerably less literature on Kant's *Tugendlehre* than on the GMS or the KpV. Hence it is no surprise that there is little to find on the interpretation of §§ 11, 37 or 38, or, in any case, little that is specific. Wood (2002, p. 12f.) is eager to point out the primacy of the moral principle based upon on dignity; Kain (2010, p. 212f.) presents a brief standard reading; also cf. Höffe (2010, p. 87). Both Forkl (2001, pp. 168, 227f.) and Malibabo (2000, pp. 204–206, 214–216) in their commentaries more or less cite or paraphrase the relevant paragraphs and provide a standard realist reading. Porcheddu (2016) deals almost only with the *Grundlegung*. For a rather constructivist (antimetaphysical) interpretation of Kant's ethics in general and the *Tugendlehre* in particular, see for instance Esser (2004).
43 There is, of course, considerable literature on what moral (anti-)realism is, which we cannot discuss here, but it is at least worth mentioning; thus, cf. Hare (2001, pp. 1–48), Korsgaard (1996, pp. 28–48), Kutschera (²1999, pp. 213–245), Schaber (1997), and Shafer-Landau (2003, pp. 13–22). There is also some literature on how to read Kant in this respect; cf. Bojanowski (2012, pp. 1–22), Kain (2006, pp. 449–465), Rauscher (2002, pp. 477–499), Rawls (2000, pp. 235–252), and Sensen (2014, pp. 63–81).

prohibited actions depends on the existence of human beings and their actions, and this existence is not necessary. However, this does not make these properties 'unreal,' or not 'out in the world' or so. Granted that this existence requirement is fulfilled, the existence of moral properties could stem from the nature of human beings as such (for instance as beings that strive for happiness) or from something else of a more general nature, such as reason; this we call *moderate* realism. Third, moral facts either are *absolute* (categorical, non-hypothetical) *commands* or imply such commands (although their absoluteness can be relative to a given situation).

Given this definition, it is almost undeniable that Kant is at least a moderate moral realist,[44] since to him moral properties are indeed (i) genuine, (ii) non-contingent, and (iii) categorically commanding. To begin with (i), recall that Kant himself draws a very sharp distinction between *nature* (and its realm and laws) and moral *freedom* (and its realm and laws). As we have seen, dignity (absolute value) at the first level is a property of beings that are autonomous; in Kant's *own* terminology, this is a non-natural quality, and in this sense a genuine property. But Kant must also be regarded as a non-naturalist in the contemporary usage of 'natural' vs. 'non-natural.' As many discussions over the last decades have shown, there is no non-begging or non-trivial way to define 'natural' (as opposed to non-natural) unless one defines it on the basis of methodology: Whatever is 'natural' (things, substances, events, properties) is so because it is an object of physics, chemistry, biology and other sciences; and with this Kant would agree: freedom is not such an object. As for non-contingency (ii) and categorical commands (iii), there is no doubt that there are, for Kant, entities with a non-natural, non-contingent (though not absolute) nature that involves moral laws: There are rational, autonomous beings with a noumenally-good will (pure practical reason) that commands the CI.

Hence Kant is at least a moderate moral realist.[45] Moderate constructivists (revisionists, such as Sensen) argue that according to Kant value (dignity) is *not* a "distinct metaphysical property" (Sensen 2011, p. 32; cf. pp. 35, 134, 189f.) that exists "'out there'" (Sensen 2011, e.g. pp. 32, 134). Not only does this contradict Kant's basic claims about dignity (including, of course, the

---

[44] It is not as obvious as one might think that Kant is not a strict moral realist; cf. Schmidt/Schönecker (2016b). But we can leave this undecided here.

[45] And if (and only if) Kant is a moderate (ontological) moral realist, is he also a moral realist from an epistemological point of view. Here we cannot get into this, but we would submit that the key term here is respect and other moral feelings such as conscience. We know that there is moral validity and value by our ability to have moral feelings. See Schönecker (2013), Schmidt/Schönecker (2014a), and Schmidt/Schönecker (2014b).

ground-thesis), but there is also more to criticize about the revisionist reading in the context of metaethical considerations:

First, if 'metaphysical' just means 'non-natural,' then of course moral properties *are* metaphysical, and they are certainly so for Kant. If 'metaphysical' just means 'real' or 'intrinsic' in terms of ontological mind-independence the way we speak of, say, the extension of bodies as real properties, then of course moral properties are real (for Kant). So what else could 'metaphysical' mean? It seems to be little more than a red herring (similar to Mackie's question-begging 'queerness'-argument).

Second, note that even if it is true that human beings have dignity because we have to respect them (and not the other way round), Kant still would be a moral realist. He would not be a realist about value, but about the non-natural and non-contingent moral property *being an object of moral respect*; and as a matter of fact, Sensen does not deny this.

Third, according to Sensen, both freedom and being an end in itself are *not normative properties*; rather, they are *descriptive*.[46] Now Sensen does very little to explain what exactly it means for a term to be 'normative' rather than 'descriptive.' Since he at times explains 'normative' with recourse to 'valuative,' we are not supposed to understand him as saying that 'normative' terms are only duty-terms (such as 'ought to,' 'command,' etc.). Thus, it seems that to Sensen a term is 'normative' if it is either a duty-term or a valuative term. But then we have two good reasons to believe that Sensen's claims about freedom and being an end in itself as merely 'descriptive' are wrong. For how should positive freedom, since it is a special kind of causality – namely the *moral* causality –, *not* be understood as normative? Also, freedom is what makes rational beings ends in themselves, i.e., beings with absolute value. This, of course, is a normative (valuative) fact; therefore, freedom too has to be 'normative.' We can also see here that Sensen goes astray in claiming that defenders of the traditional reading need to find passages "in which Kant does not merely use phrases like 'has absolute inner value,' but in which he also specifies it as something prior to and independent of the moral law" (Sensen 2011, p. 39; cf. pp. 50 and 85). But why so? The absolute inner value (i.e., dignity) of human beings stems from their autonomy, and autonomy is certainly not 'prior to and independent of the moral law.'

Tougher constructivists (such as Rawls, Korsgaard, or Rauscher) deny that Kant is a moral realist of any kind. To say that Kant never *claims to be* a moral realist is not a good argument, of course, since 'moral realism' is a

---

46 Cf. Sensen (2011, pp. 98, 103 f., 107, 114, 133) and Sensen (2015, p. 119).

contemporary term. It also makes little sense to find fault with the fact that Kant has no theory of what, ontologically speaking, 'moral facts' or 'moral properties' are; Kant certainly has no theory of, say, supervenience in contemporary terms. But so what? He has some things to say about moral facts and properties (for instance, that they belong to the world of understanding), and even if Kant has no theory of what exactly a 'property' is, this should not be censured. To the present day, we all speak of 'moral facts' and 'moral properties' in metaethical discourse and most of the time in a way that does not presuppose a worked out theory of 'properties.'

In any case, the debate which is now received as a debate between moral realism and moral antirealism has always been present in philosophy, and certainly so in Kant's times. Kant is very strict about the reality of freedom and morality. It is true, of course, that there is no *theoretical* knowledge of freedom (hence of morality), because in Kant's epistemology, theoretical knowledge is partly based on perception, and there is no perception of freedom (at least not in the sense that Kant speaks of 'intuition' and 'perception'); in this, and only in this sense, freedom is an 'idea.' But this does not by any means imply that freedom is not real and that we could not know of it, for there is *praktische Erkenntnis* (practical cognition). Practical cognition delivers knowledge of objects that are theoretically unknowable; moral laws and our knowledge of them are the "*ratio cognoscendi*" (KpV: 4) of freedom as a supersensible object. We practically know that the CI is valid for us, but then we also practically know that we are free, that our souls are immortal, and that God exists. In the programmatic *Preface* to the second edition of the *Kritik der reinen Vernunft*, Kant writes:

> Now after speculative reason has been denied all advance in this field of supersensible, what still remains for us is to try whether there are not data in reason's practical cognition for determining that transcendental rational concept of the unconditioned, in such a way as to reach beyond the boundaries of all possible experience, in accordance with the wishes of metaphysics, cognitions *a priori* that are possible, but only from a practical standpoint. (KrV: Bxxi)

Kant speaks repeatedly of the *reality* of freedom and morality.[47] The fear of substantial metaphysics is great in contemporary philosophy. But to do away

---

47 To take just one example of many, look at the opening paragraphs of the *Preface* of the *Kritik der praktischen Vernunft* where Kant says that "transcendental freedom is also established" (KpV: 3), that its "objective reality" (ibid.) is "proved by an apodictic law of practical reason" (ibid.).

with Kant's metaphysics of freedom and morality is to do away with the very 'ground' of his entire ethical thought.

Literature

Kant

Anthro Anthropologie in pragmatischer Hinsicht, AA 7
GMS   Grundlegung zur Metaphysik der Sitten, AA 4
KpV   Kritik der praktischen Vernunft, AA 5
KrV   Kritik der reinen Vernunft, AA 3 (B) und 4 (A)
MAM   Mutmaßlicher Anfang der Menschengeschichte, AA 8
MS   Die Metaphysik der Sitten, AA 6 (*Vorrede* und *Einleitung in die Metaphysik der Sitten*, 205–228)
MSV   Metaphysik der Sitten Vigilantius, AA 27
NF   Naturrecht Feyerabend, AA 27
RL   Metaphysische Anfangsgründe der Rechtslehre, AA 6
TL   Metaphysische Anfangsgründe der Tugendlehre, AA 6

English translations (though with modifications) are taken from the series *The Cambridge Edition of the Works of Immanuel Kant*, Cambridge University Press (1992 ff.), except for the *GMS*, where we use Allen Wood's translation, Yale University Press (2002).
All page and line numbers in parentheses refer to the so-called Akademie-Ausgabe (AA), i.e., to *Kant's gesammelte Schriften*, herausgegeben von der *Königlich Preußischen Akademie der Wissenschaften*, Berlin: Walter de Gruyter (1900 ff.).

Secondary Literature

Bojanowski, Jochen (2012): "Is Kant a Moral Realist?" In: *Kant Yearbook* 4/1, pp. 1–22.
Esser, Andrea Marlen (2004): *Eine Ethik für Endliche. Kants Tugendlehre in der Gegenwart*. Stuttgart/Bad Cannstatt: Frommann-Holzboog.
Forkl, Markus (2001): *Kants Sytsem der Tugendpflichten. Eine Begleitschrift zu den 'Metaphysischen Anfangsgründen der Tugendlehre'*. Frankfurt/Main: Peter Lang.
Hare, John (2001): *God's Call. Moral Realism, God's Commands, and Human Autonomy*. Grand Rapids: William B. Eerdmans Publishing Company.
Höffe, Otfried (2010): "Kant's innate right as a rational criterion for human rights." In: Lara Denis (ed.): *Kant's Metaphysics of Morals. A Critical Guide*. Cambridge: Cambridge University Press, pp. 71–92.
Kain, Patrick (2006): "Realism and Anti-realism in Kant's Second *Critique*." In: *Philosophy Compass* 1, pp. 449–465.
Kain, Patrick (2010): "Duties regarding animals." In: Lara Denis (ed.): *Kant's Metaphysics of Morals. A Critical Guide*. Cambridge: Cambridge University Press, pp. 210–233.

Korsgaard, Christine (1996): *The Sources of Normativity.* Cambridge: Cambridge University Press.
Kutschera, Franz von (²1999): *Grundlagen der Ethik.* Berlin/Boston: Walter de Gruyter.
Malibabo, Balimbanga (2000): *Kants Konzept einer kritischen Metaphysik der Sitten.* Würzburg: Königshausen & Neumann.
Porcheddu, Rocco (2016): *Der Zweck an sich selbst. Eine Untersuchung zu Kants 'Grundlegung zur Metaphysik der Sitten'.* Berlin/Boston: Walter de Gruyter.
Rauscher, Frederick (2002): "Kant's Moral Anti-Realism." In: *Journal of the History of Philosophy* 40, pp. 477–499.
Rawls, John (2000): *Lectures on the History of Moral Philosophy.* Edited by Barbara Herman. Cambridge: Harvard University Press.
Schaber, Peter (1997): *Moralischer Realismus.* Freiburg: Karl Alber.
Schmidt, Elke Elisabeth/Schönecker, Dieter (2014a): "Vernunft, Herz und Gewissen. Kants Theorie der Urteilskraft zweiter Stufe als Modell für die Medizinische Ethik". In: Franz-Josef Bormann/Verena Wetzstein (eds.): *Gewissen. Dimensionen eines Grundbegriffs medizinischer Ethik.* Berlin/Boston: Walter de Gruyter, pp. 229–250.
Schmidt, Elke Elisabeth/Schönecker, Dieter (2014b): "Kants Philosophie des Gewissens. Skizze für eine kommentarische Interpretation". In: Mario Egger (ed.): *Philosophie nach Kant. Neue Wege zum Verständnis von Kants Transzendental- und Moralphilosophie.* Berlin/Boston: Walter de Gruyter, pp. 279–312.
Schmidt, Elke Elisabeth/Schönecker, Dieter (2016a): "Kant on Moral Necessitation by Another Subject's Will (*Tugendlehre*, § 16)." In: *Studi Kantiani* XXIX, pp. 91–108.
Schmidt, Elke Elisabeth/Schönecker, Dieter (2016b): "Über einen (unentdeckten) Gottesbeweis in Kants Philosophie des Gewissens". In: Saša Josifović/Arthur Kok (eds.): *Der 'innere Gerichtshof' der Vernunft: Normativität, Rationalität und Gewissen in der Philosophie Immanuel Kants und im Deutschen Idealismus.* Leiden/Boston: Brill, pp. 115–153.
Schmidt, Elke E./Schönecker, Dieter (2017): "Kant's Ground-Thesis. On Dignity and Value in the 'Groundwork.'" In: *Journal of Value Inquiry,* online August 2017.
Schönecker, Dieter (2013): "Kant's Moral Intuitionism. The Fact of Reason and Moral Predispositions." In: *Kant Studies Online* Feb. 2013, pp. 1–38.
Schönecker, Dieter (2015): "Bemerkungen zu Oliver Sensen, *Kant on Human Dignity,* Chapter 1." In: *Kant-Studien* 106/1, pp. 68–77.
Schönecker, Dieter/Wood, Allen W. (2015): *Kant's Groundwork for the Metaphysics of Morals. A Commentary.* Cambridge: Harvard University Press.
Sensen, Oliver (2011): *Kant on Human Dignity.* Berlin/Boston: Walter de Gruyter.
Sensen, Oliver (2014): "Kant's Constructivism." In: Carla Bagnoli (ed.): *Moral Constructivism: For and Against.* Cambridge: Cambridge University Press, pp. 63–81.
Sensen, Oliver (2015): "Kant on Human Dignity reconsidered. A Reply to my critics." In: *Kant-Studien* 106/1, pp. 107–129.
Shafer-Landau, Russ (2003): *Moral Realism. A Defense.* Oxford: Oxford University Press.
Wood, Allen (2002): "The Final Form of Kant's Practical Philosophy." In: Mark Timmons (ed.): *Kant's Metaphysics of Morals. Interpretative Essays.* Oxford: Oxford University Press, pp. 1–21.

Something in Between

Stefano Bacin
Moral Realism by Other Means: The Hybrid Nature of Kant's Practical Rationalism

Abstract After qualifying in which sense 'realism' can be applied to eighteenth-century views about morality, I argue that while Kant shares with traditional moral realists several fundamental claims about morality, he holds that those claims must be argued for in a radically different way. Drawing on his diagnosis of the serious weaknesses of traditional moral realism, Kant proposes a novel approach that revolves around a hybrid view about moral obligation. Since his solution to that central issue combines elements of realism with elements of voluntarist assent, Kant's position can be characterized as an idealist version of moral realism or, more specifically, as the combination of a strong realism about the moral law with an idealist account of moral obligation.

* * *

1 Moral Realism in Eighteenth-Century Moral Philosophy

"A philosopher who asserts that she is a realist about theoretical science, for example, or ethics, has probably, for most philosophical audiences, accomplished little more than to clear her throat," as Crispin Wright once observed (Wright 1992, p. 1). Such an observation effectively conveys the familiar uneasiness with these terms of art, along with a kind of prejudice against views apt to be considered as realist. In a similar vein, Korsgaard writes that "[t]here is a trivial sense in which everyone who thinks that ethics isn't hopeless is a realist" (Korsgaard 1996, p. 35). In this perspective, examining a philosophical view with regard to these terms risks being not very productive. 'Realism' and 'antirealism' are maybe even more ambiguous than similar terms of art, to the extent that merely declaring a view realist or not-realist does not amount to a helpful statement. Things may become especially problematic when such labels are applied to philosophical views of the past, as in discussing Hume's or Kant's own thought, since they did not employ these terms to characterize their perspectives. Here the risk of anachronism seems difficult to avoid. As John Skorupski has remarked, the very attribution of the label 'moral realism' (or 'moral realist') to views which do not share specific philosophical assumptions with the current debates, for instance regarding the semantics of moral words or the truth-value of judgments, is hardly appropriate, since it connects or even equates views that are in fact heterogeneous in important respects.[1]

In light of these difficulties, a helpful way to gain a clearer understanding of the questions at issue with regard to Kant is, I believe, to briefly consider what moral realism could be taken to mean in eighteenth-century discussions and whether such terms are applicable to them at all. The risk of anachronism, in this case, is mitigated by the historical emergence of the use of the term 'realism' with regard to the foundations of morals. The first philosopher who characterized a position as realism regarding morals, and explicitly endorsed it, was probably Shaftesbury. In *The Moralists*, he distinguishes philosophers who "hold zealously for Virtue, and are Realists in the Point" from those who "are only nominal Moralists by making Virtue nothing in it-self, a Creature of Will only, or a mere Name of Fashion" (Shaftesbury 1711, II, p. 145). The explicit history of the concept of moral realism begins here. Notably, when the label 'realism' was used again about a century and a half later to characterize a specific view in moral philosophy, it happened exactly with reference to this passage.[2] According to Shaftesbury, the realist about virtue "endeavours to shew, 'That it is really something in it-self, and in the nature of Things: not arbitrary or factitious, (if I may so speak) not constituted from without, or dependent on Custom, Fancy, or Will; not even on the Supreme Will it-self, which can no-way govern it: but being necessarily good, is govern'd by it, and ever uniform with it'" (Shaftesbury 1711, II, p. 151). The opposition between moral realism and moral antirealism is thereby construed in a fairly straightforward way as simply concerning the fundamental contrast between views holding that moral properties (virtue, merit, goodness) are entirely independent from the activity of any mind and views holding, on the contrary, that they are dependent on the activity of minds. According to this understanding of the terms, the two conceptions are mutually exclusive.

Now, it might still appear unwarranted to directly apply this understanding of the terms at issue to Kant, if only because no analogous definitions of 'moral realism' are to be found in eighteenth-century German moral philosophy. Indeed, that those labels carried the risk of some misunderstanding even then

---

[1] Cf. Skorupski (2012, pp. 18 ff.).
[2] Cf. Whewell (1852, p. 91); cf. Irwin (2015).

becomes clear when one considers the German translation of Shaftesbury's remarks. If Johann Joachim Spalding's translation has 'Realisten' for 'realists,' it renders 'nominal Moralists' with 'Titularsittenlehrer,' that is, 'moralists only by name.' Thereby Spalding alters the opposition, which, put in those terms, does not contrast moral realists with antirealists, but genuine moral philosophers with merely pretending ones.[3] Spalding's mistake indicates a difference between German and British terminology in this respect. Unlike Shaftesbury, German eighteenth-century philosophers mostly employed 'realism' and its antonym 'idealism' as metaphysical terms, not extending their use to the discussions on the foundations of morals. Nevertheless, we can safely discuss moral realism and antirealism also with regard to Kant and other eighteenth-century German writers, since we thereby understand the fundamental issue concerning the independence of moral criteria and principles from the activity of any mind.[4]

Approaching Kant's view from this angle is helpful not only to avoid anachronisms and conceptual confusion, but also to highlight how his view relates to the alternatives that characterize the previous discussion. First of all, we should recognize that Kant shares with earlier moral realists some of their core theses. Against voluntarist accounts of morality, pre-Kantian moral realists argued that understanding morality as dependent on commands issued by an authority makes them arbitrary and contingent.[5] Moral realism developed out of the aim of defending the objective and necessary status of moral truths, which are regarded as firm and 'eternal' as mathematical truths, and like these are equally shared by finite rational beings and God. In Leibniz' formulation, for instance, the "formal reason" that "should teach us what justice is [...] must be common to God and to man," the difference between them being "only one of degree" (Leibniz 1703, p. 49). Finally and most importantly, moral requirements are fully cognizable by human reason, either because they are evident to the mind or because they can be known as grounded in the nature of things. In the most optimistic version of this thought, there are no genuine epistemic hindrances to moral cognition, but only "corruption of Manners, or perverseness of Spirit" (Clarke 1738, II, p. 609) can interfere with it. This kind of moral realism, therefore, does not merely consist in affirming the reality of moral distinctions,

---

3 Cf. Shaftesbury (1745, pp. 98 f.).
4 Moral realism is characterized in the same terms, as mind-independence of morality, also by Rauscher (2015, pp. 17 f.), with regard to the current state of the art. See Rauscher (2015, pp. 11 ff.), for a careful discussion of the issue.
5 Cf. e.g. Leibniz (1703, pp. 45 f.).

but in maintaining that they are expressions of a mind-independent order.⁶ The underlying assumption is that only such an order, since it is not contingent, can provide the proper basis for accounting for three fundamental ideas: morality is objective, necessary, and cognizable by every rational being.⁷

Kant shares all of these three main points, which he seems to take as included in the common understanding of morals. Against voluntarist accounts, Kant employs much the same arguments as Cudworth and Leibniz, arguing that also divine-commands conceptions of morality are unable to vindicate its absolute necessity and make of the moral laws merely positive laws.⁸ Much like previous realists, Kant maintains a rationalist view on the Euthyphro question, holding that "suicide is not abominable because God has forbidden it, but because it is abominable He has forbidden it" (NK: 174, cf. 38f. and MC: 262). He even deploys the traditional analogy between morality and mathematics to stress that moral laws are "immutable," so that not even God can change their content.⁹ In the later essay *The End of All Things*, Kant even observes that the moral law "as an unchanging order lying in the nature of things, is not to be left up to even the creator's arbitrary will to decide its consequences thus or otherwise" (ED: 339). When he remarks that both God and finite rational beings are subject to the same moral law, even if in modally different terms,¹⁰ he elaborates the same thesis. Furthermore, as with earlier realists, Kant holds that the common human reason as such can easily cognize moral principles.¹¹

A possible objection to this way of framing the matter at issue is that Kant's main aim regarding the foundations of practical philosophy is shared not only by previous moral realists, but by previous antirealists as well, as long as they are not willing to give up the idea that moral judgments and their criteria have to be regarded as objective and universally valid. In other words, according

---

6 Gill (2006, p. 296) suggests a corresponding distinction between a "Copernican or anti-egoist realist" and a "Ptolemaic or mind-independent realist." The former "holds that there is a difference between the motives of those people we judge to be virtuous and the motives of those people we judge to be vicious," while the latter "holds that moral properties exist independently of the human mind and that our moral judgments represent those properties accurately."
7 Here I cannot discuss the assumption. For a critical examination see Gill (1998).
8 Cf. e.g. MM II: 627. On Kant's criticisms of moral voluntarism, see Bacin (2018, § 3). – For the list of abbreviations of Kant's works, see the "Literature" section of this paper.
9 Cf. NK: 79 = MC: 283; MSV: 547; PPP: 137; MM II: 634. On the analogy and its pre-Kantian usage, see Gill (2007).
10 Cf. GMS: 414; KpV: 32.
11 Cf. KpV: 152ff.; G: 255f.

to the objection, the only aim would be to guarantee the objectivity of morals, and that would not be enough to commit to moral realism in any specific sense. However, Kant's aim is not simply to account for the pretensions of realism, as this task is understood in current debates,[12] but more specifically to argue for strong realist theses and their implications, only on different grounds and through a different strategy than earlier moral realists.

However, while Kant shares with traditional moral realists several fundamental claims about morality, he believes that those claims must be argued for in a radically different way than it had been before. A crucial part of Kant's main aim in practical philosophy is to defend the distinctive contentions of moral realism – i.e., that moral criteria are objective, necessary, and epistemologically accessible – through a novel philosophical strategy, quite different from the strategies deployed by previous moral realists.

2 The Weaknesses of Pre-Kantian Moral Realism

Other means are needed when a certain way of managing things proves insufficient or is inadequate with regard to the intended goal. On the reading I suggest, this also holds with respect to Kant's practical philosophy, which can be interpreted as arising out of dissatisfaction with the previous versions of moral realism. The standard variants of moral realism can be regarded as unable to defend its basic tenets, which thus require following a different path. The reasons why Kant deemed it necessary to reject the traditional realist approach can be summarized in three main points.

First, in Kant's view, moral realism faces significant difficulties in moral epistemology. On the traditional approach, status and possibility of moral cognition often remain unclear, or exceedingly demanding.[13] If the cognition of moral principles requires an insight into the fabric of reality, it seems that it must be as demanding as metaphysical knowledge. In spite of the insistence on the evidence of moral principles, traditional moral realism faces serious issues in explaining this evidence. Especially from the standpoint of Kant's critical philosophy, an insight into the nature of things is not possible beyond the limits of experience. Furthermore, since in traditional realist accounts moral obligation is intrinsically linked with the awareness of the natural law,

---

12 Cf. e.g. Star (2013, p. 820).
13 I will not go into the details of the differences among the various instances of traditional rationalist moral realism. Here it suffices to my purpose to provide a brief sketch of their characteristic features, in order to assess Kant's attitude towards their basic project.

the difficulty in clarifying the possibility of an adequate cognition of the nature of things also affects any attempt to vindicate moral obligation.

Second, the tendency of traditional moral realism to conflate theoretical and moral knowledge has another important implication that must be regarded as a fatal flaw from Kant's standpoint. On the traditional realist view, the difference between theoretical cognition and practical cognition gets lost because both are merely representational, since they provide the mind with the representation of some aspect of the reality of things. On the contrary, Kant holds that moral cognition is to be understood as essentially practical and that, therefore, it must be construed in non-descriptivist terms as being not about states of affairs, but about grounds for actions.[14] Traditional moral realism appears unable to explain how the cognition of features of reality immediately provides grounds for action, if not by assuming a prior desire for the object regarded as good. Therefore traditional moral realism falls under the general principle of the heteronomy of the will.

Third, the limits of that conception of moral knowledge lead to an additional reason for dissatisfaction with traditional realism. Since practical cognition is not about states of affairs, but about grounds of action, Kant has to also reject the thought that moral qualities are to be understood as properties of actions, which is characteristically maintained by traditional moral realists in opposition to the sentimentalist thesis that goodness and rightness of actions are nothing but "perceptions in the mind" (Hume 1739–1740, III.I.i). In Kant's view, this conception does not reflect ordinary moral thinking and misses again the essentially practical character of moral concepts and judgments, which do not describe anything but rather express requirements. The concepts of good and bad that we apply to actions do not refer to objects and their qualities but follow from a "determination of the will a priori" (KpV: 65) that requires actions. Again, traditional moral realism can ground requirements only by referring back to some prior desire for an object with specific features. Accordingly, a view capable of accounting only for a heteronomous determination of the will ends up regarding some features of objects as good-making properties.

Finally, all of Kant's reasons for dissatisfaction with traditional moral realism ultimately lead to highlighting what must be, in Kant's eyes, its crucial limit, namely the inability to adequately account for moral obligation. Traditional moral realists characteristically hold that the natural law immediately entails moral obligation, which is understood as part of the reality of things as much as the law itself. Intrinsically normative facts immediately impose an

---

[14] Cf. JL: 86; KpV: 20.

obligation, without an obligating subject. Thus, for instance, Clarke declares that the "eternal and necessary differences of things make it fit and reasonable for Creatures so to act; they cause it to be their Duty, or lay an Obligation upon them, so to do; even separate from the consideration of these Rules being the positive Will or Command of God" (Clarke 1738, II, p. 608). Similarly, Wolff maintains that the natural law is binding by a "natural obligation" independent of any act of imposition, because "nature has connected motives with men's inherently good and bad actions" (Wolff 1733, § 9). In Kant's view, however, features of reality cannot give rise to obligations that satisfy the requirements of universality and necessity. The immediate transition from a fundamental law to a genuine moral obligation, in his eyes, is unwarranted, at least in the relevant case of finite rational subjects. Kant's remark that the concept of obligation had not been made clear yet and that the central issue of practical philosophy remains unsolved[15] certainly holds with regard to traditional moral realism and its difficulties in accounting for the binding character of moral requirements.

For these reasons, I suggest that in Kant's view the traditional versions of moral realism are not able to meet the demands that motivated them in the first place. Since those philosophical and practical demands still hold for him, it is necessary, from his standpoint, to develop different means to meet them in order to build a satisfying conception.

3 Kant's Non-Realist Strategy: The Outline

Instead of the immediate connection of natural law and obligation, which is characteristic of earlier moral realism, Kant's conception revolves around a two-level model, centered on the distinction between law and obligation, that is, between the principle of moral normativity and the binding validity of moral demands. His development of that model makes of his novel defense of the tenets of moral realism a hybrid view on the foundations of morals.

On the one hand, much like earlier realists, Kant still maintains that the moral law must be understood as non-positive and "practically necessary" (cf. e.g. MC: 283), that is, fully independent, both as to its existence and its content, of the action of any mind, even of God's, as I mentioned before. On the other hand, Kant combines this feature of the traditional realist view with a non-realist conception that makes moral obligation dependent on the action of the finite

---

[15] Cf. UDG: 298 and GMS: 450.

rational will. Departing from previous moral realists, Kant argues that the moral law does not carry an obligation in itself, since the obligation generates only through the practically necessary consent of the finite rational beings subject to the moral law. The genuine source of moral obligation is, in this view, the autonomy of pure practical reason.[16]

The combination of realist and non-realist elements in Kant's view is reflected in his use of the distinction between the role of author of the law and the role of author of the obligation. The distinction was already present in previous writers like Baumgarten and Meier,[17] but Kant deploys it to put forward a different view than theirs. According to Kant, the author of the law and the author of the obligation correspond in the case of positive laws, generated through a contingent imposition of the will, which determines both their normative content and the corresponding obligation. In the case of non-positive (i.e., "natural") laws, as is the moral law, the two roles are to be kept distinct, since the content of the law is not dependent on any imposition, whereas the corresponding obligation is.[18] For Kant "moral laws have no author" (PPP: 145), if they are to be understood as necessary and unconditionally valid. The only authorship that can be claimed for such non-positive laws is the authorship of obligation. Now, to be author of the obligation is precisely the function of a legislator, who makes the law binding through the consent of his or her will (cf. e.g. MSV: 544 and 583, also R 6187, AA 18: 483).

Kant's solution to the problem of defending moral realism revolves around a very close connection between cognition of the moral law and legislation, that is, on the thought that moral subjects can have access to the law only through the practically necessary recognition of grounds for acting. Generally, most earlier moral realists were rationalists because, some minor differences notwithstanding, they regarded reason as the faculty of the mind, i.e., "the capacity to have insight into the interconnection of truths" (Wolff 1751, § 368). Such a view is for Kant not a viable option. First, his transcendental idealism argues against the possibility of adequate knowledge of the features of reality beyond the boundaries of possible experience.[19] Second, Kant also has a specifically moral objection to such views, which construe moral cognition as knowledge

---

[16] Cf. GMS: 439 f.; KpV: 33.
[17] Cf. Baumgarten (1760, §§ 71, 100), and Meier (1764, § 140).
[18] Cf. MS: 227 and R: 131, 156, 247; MC: 283; MM: 1433; MSV: 544 f.; NK: 79; and also Päd: 494.26–33. For a detailed analysis of this distinction, see first and foremost Kain (2004, pp. 282 ff.). On the same point, considered from different perspectives, see also Reath (2006, pp. 145 f.), Irwin (2004, pp. 151 ff.), Irwin (2009, pp. 156 f.), Reath (2012, pp. 37–40).
[19] See also Rauscher (2015).

of some feature of reality. As long as they make the cognition of moral demands dependent on facts and features of the world, they make moral demands heteronomous. In contrast with such views, Kant's novel moral rationalism is centered on the idea that access to the moral law can be only provided by the same faculty to which moral demands are addressed.

Traditional realist positions were essentially descriptivist, as they tracked the source of both moral normativity and obligation back to some metaphysical feature of reality, conflating the fundamental principles of morality with their obligation. In contrast to such positions, Kant's account can accommodate both descriptive and non-descriptive aspects in morality, making sense of its action-guiding nature. As practical cognition, moral cognition does not represent features of things, but is about prescriptive grounds for acting. These grounds are essentially prescriptive only as a consequence of "the subjective constitution [*Beschaffenheit*] of our practical faculty" (KU: 403, cf. GMS: 414) of finite rational beings. At the same time, the fundamental law on which prescriptive moral demands are based is not prescriptive per se, as it describes a perfectly rational will, to which as such no obligation applies.[20] Obligation is the mode of morality only for beings whose maxims are not eo ipso universally valid like laws. The conceptual distinction between the moral law (*moralisches Gesetz*) as the fundamental law of pure practical reason and the prescriptive principle of morality "that we call *Sittengesetz*" (KpV: 31), i.e., the categorical imperative, is a crucial clue for the proper understanding of Kant's view.[21] The former is the principle of practical rationality as such and does not contain any prescription, since it expresses the constitution of the perfect rational will. The latter is the principle legislated through the autonomy of pure practical reason in finite beings, upon which it imposes an obligation. Prescriptions and imperatives can only enter the stage once the moral law is recognized by finite rational agents as binding.

On the reading I am proposing, Kant elaborates a hybrid view of moral obligation structurally similar to the one put forward by some previous writers, such as Suárez and Barbeyrac. Suárez distinguishes between the natural law as belonging to the nature of things and full-fledged, binding moral demands. The latter do not directly derive from the natural law, but require God's command, in order to become laws proper through an imposition. The natural law as such is

---

[20] Cf. e.g. KpV: 32: "In the supremely self-sufficient intelligence, choice is rightly represented as incapable of any maxim that could not at the same time be objectively a law, and the concept of holiness, which on that account belongs to it, puts it, not above all practical laws, but indeed above practically restrictive laws and so above obligation and duty." (I have corrected the translation, which misses a few words in the last sentence.)

[21] See e.g. Wolff (2009, pp. 524 f.).

merely a lex indicans, which presents normative contents, but is not binding yet until the authoritative imposition of the divine will generates genuine prescriptions drawing on the perfectly rational content of the natural law.[22] Closer to Kant's time, Barbeyrac had made some points that suggested a similar conception. Moving, as it were, in the opposite direction than Suárez, Barbeyrac tried to defend Pufendorf's position from Leibniz' criticisms by incorporating naturalist elements into a voluntarist account.[23] Barbeyrac argued that, if "one grounds the obligation (properly so-called) to practice the rules of justice in the will of God," "this supreme being's right of command is founded in reasons whose justice is immanent." In fact, for Barbeyrac, God "wants us to conform our external and internal acts" to the "relations of propriety, order, beauty, honesty, [...] to which justice reduces," that reason reveals to us (Barbeyrac 1735, pp. 296, 302).

In a similar way to Suárez and Barbeyrac, Kant distinguishes between a fundamental principle of rationality and the principle of moral obligation imposed by an authoritative will, thereby combining insights of the traditional realist views with a voluntarist take on obligation. Now, I do not contend that either Suárez or Barbeyrac should be regarded as direct sources of Kant's view. In fact, the basic distinctions on which Kant draws in developing his account of the foundations of morals (i.e., law vs. obligation, author of the law vs. author of the obligation) were available in the conceptual vocabulary of pre-Kantian discussions on natural law, so that it was not necessary to refer to Suárez or to Barbeyrac as such to be aware of the possibility of distinguishing the two levels of the normative principle and its obligation. After Suárez, other writers deemed it necessary to combine rationalist and voluntarist approaches in explaining moral obligation. However, taking into consideration the paradigm exemplified in those earlier hybrid views helps us see a similar pattern in Kant, which makes the complexity of his novel conception apparent. At the same time, the contrast with the pre-Kantian examples of the hybrid paradigm is helpful to highlight three features distinctive of Kant's own new view, which regard the meaning of the concept of law, the role of the legislator, and the character of moral cognition.

(1) In contrast to the Suárezian hybrid view, in Kant's view the concept of law is basically a metaphysical notion. Following a tradition culminating in Aquinas, Suárez still understood laws in general in a primarily political sense and holds

---

[22] A related analogy between Kant's and Suárez's views regarding the relation between reason and will has been suggested by Ludwig (1997). Here I cannot directly address the question.
[23] See Stern (2012, pp. 71 ff.).

that in the proper meaning of the word laws are addressed to rational beings and are intended to govern their behavior. For Suárez, if we speak of a law of nature, it is only by analogy in a derivative, metaphorical sense.²⁴ In contrast to this conception, Kant understands the concept of law in primarily descriptive terms, that is, as a rule expressing a non-contingent regularity (or normativity) in a given domain. While the commentators have often interpreted Kant's talk of moral laws stressing the analogy to political laws, he in fact always parallels moral laws with laws of nature.²⁵ For him, the concept of law belongs to metaphysics as well as to practical philosophy, so that the distinction between laws of nature and moral laws, or laws of freedom (cf. e.g. GMS: 387) differentiates between two species of the same kind, thereby highlighting that both are "principles of the necessity of that which belongs to the existence of a thing" (GMS: 469, cf. KrV: A113).²⁶ It is in virtue of the fundamental univocal meaning of the concept of law that Kant can regard as entirely appropriate introducing the form of a law of nature as a schema or a 'type' of the moral law in the application to particular cases.²⁷ Kant's understanding of natural laws in general develops further a conception present in earlier German rationalists, who defined as law any rule that states a determination, in contrast with the voluntarist understanding of laws as commands.²⁸ By elaborating such an anti-voluntarist concept of natural law, Kant accentuates the fundamental realist assumption that moral laws do not originate from any act of imposition by a subject, but express non-contingent normative features of reality. Moral laws must therefore be regarded as independent of any will, as to their authority and content.

(2) The most apparent difference from the earlier hybrid paradigm, however, is that, in Kant's conception, the role of legislator is not (only) played by God,

---

24 Cf. Suárez (1612, I.i, p. 2): "This third acceptation of law is […] metaphorical, since things which lack reason are not, strictly speaking, susceptible to law, just as they are not capable of obedience" (*Haec tertia acceptio [scil. lex ordinis seu propensionis naturae] metaphorica est: nam res carentes ratione non sunt proprie capaces legis, sicut nec obedientiae*); I.i, p. 5: "The name 'law' is properly applied, in an absolute sense, to that which pertains to moral conduct" (*Propria et absoluta appellatio legis est, quae ad mores pertinet*).
25 The analogy with political laws has led some interpreters to (mistakenly, in my view) characterize Kantian moral laws as positive laws: cf. e.g. Korsgaard (1996, p. 66), Rauscher (2002), Krasnoff (2012, pp. 64f.).
26 For an analysis of Kant's concept of law that stresses its univocality across theoretical and practical contexts, see Watkins (2014).
27 Cf. KpV: 69. See also Klotz (2001).
28 Cf. Wolff (1733, § 16), Wolff (1736, § 475), Baumgarten (1757, §§ 83–84). For an explicit contrast with Crusius, see Meier (1764, § 111).

but also by reason in finite subjects. The categorical imperative qua imperative is a "command (of reason)" (GMS: 414), and is in fact the only genuine command that reason issues, as it is unconditional and necessary. It is not an external legislator, but pure reason that "gives (to the human being)," as well as "all finite beings that have reason and will," the moral law (the *Sittengesetz*) (KpV: 31f.). Unlike earlier rationalists, Kant stresses that the character of command belongs to moral demands not simply subsidiarily, but essentially. The crucial legislative role of reason lies in determining the moral demands as commands. Thereby Kant holds that finite reason is not merely able to grasp the contents of the moral law, as previous realists had already maintained, but that that ability is sufficient to determine the obligatory character of moral demands. The inherent normativity of the moral law as internal law of practical rationality suffices to establish imperatives without needing the authority of a "third being" to impose the law, to borrow the formulation Kant sometimes deploys in his lectures (cf. e.g. MC: 277; NK: 61).

However, regarding not the divine will, but pure reason in finite subjects as the legislator of the moral law does not merely amount to an internalization of moral lawgiving. In fact, here lies Kant's most significant departure from traditional moral realism. The role of the legislator does not consist in the mere transmission of the normative content of the law, as if his function were only about applying it to a particular domain.[29] Lawgiving entails the recognition and the confirmation of the law through the will of the legislator.[30] This is precisely what pure reason does in Kant's view: It recognizes the moral law as its own fundamental law, which inescapably demands consent. Through the necessary consent to the fundamental law, reason recognizes its validity, if only in prescriptive terms, because of the limits of finite beings. For Kant, moral obligation is not a given, but only arises through this lawgiving activity. Since he understands obligation as "necessitation of a rational being by the mere cognition of the law," the moral law can bind a rational being only insofar as the subject "cognizes its universal validity for every will, hence also the necessary consent [*die nothwendige Einstimmung*] of his will" (R 6187, AA 18: 483).

In contrast to traditional realist views, therefore, moral obligation is not detected and then applied to specific moral requirements, but is established through an imposition of the rational will, rather along the lines of voluntarist

---

[29] Here I refer to Baxley (2012, pp. 571ff.), who has aptly remarked, against Stern (2012), that the question concerning the authority of morality and the question concerning the experience of morality in prescriptive terms must be kept separated.
[30] Cf. e.g. MC: 283, NK: 79.

conceptions. Only an authoritative will can institute a valid obligation, and the rational will is authoritative because of the moral law. Kant does not explain moral obligation through the limits of finite rational beings, but through their being rational, which warrants them an access to the fundamental moral law. They can thus institute moral obligation according to the constitution of their own practical faculty. Therefore, the transition from a conception where the divine will legislates the moral law to a conception where pure reason plays that role allows Kant to account not simply for the phenomenological fact that moral demands have prescriptive character, but also for their binding authority as grounded in the fundamental law of practical reason.[31]

(3) In Kant's view, furthermore, the lawgiving of the moral law also plays a crucial epistemological role, which marks a significant difference from earlier conceptions. Unlike traditional moral realists, Kant does not maintain that moral cognition can be explained as a sort of knowledge of facts or features of the world. In fact, he develops the voluntarist idea that the promulgation of the law belongs to lawgiving and is an essential part of establishing it as binding. For instance, Suárez had remarked that "the lawmaker should manifest, indicate or intimate this decree and judgment of his, to the subjects to whom the law itself relates." If he does not do so, his will "could not be binding" (Suárez 1612, I.iv., pp. 12, 57; cf. I.xi). It is necessary to the bindingness of the law that the subject have access to it, and the lawgiving act, establishing obligation, satisfies also this essential condition. Kant's view follows this voluntarist conception of moral lawgiving in order to make full sense of moral obligation and to account for the simplicity of moral cognition, overcoming the limits of traditional moral realism. Although, for Kant, no valid factual cognition is warranted beyond the domain of possible experience, moral subjects can gain a proper access to moral demands in virtue of their partaking in the moral lawgiving. "We can become aware of pure practical laws [...] by attending to the necessity with which reason prescribes them to us and to the setting aside of all empirical conditions to which reason directs us" (KpV: 30). Kant's solution to the epistemological problem affecting traditional moral realism revolves around the idea that moral cognition is to be achieved only through autonomy and the resulting obligation. The difficulty of accounting for the possibility of a fully adequate cognition of moral requirements is overcome by abandoning the basic descriptivist assumption of traditional moral realism. For Kant, moral cognition is neither to be understood as knowledge of facts, nor as knowledge of properties

---

[31] I have presented in greater detail a reading of Kant's conception of the self-legislation of the moral law in Bacin (2013a).

of its objects, but rather as the cognition of principles providing inescapable normative grounds for actions, which are specifications of the categorical imperative legislated by pure reason as a general principle of moral obligation. Moral cognition is thereby vindicated not as the cognition of something real, but as the cognition of something constructed by the activity of reason, supported by its fundamental constitutive principle. Moral cognition is not about external reality, but is in fact centered on "the self-consciousness of a pure practical reason" (KpV: 29). Autonomy as self-legislation of a fundamental law of rationality is what explains that "what is to be done [...] is seen quite easily and without hesitation by the most common understanding" (KpV: 36).

The comparison with the previous hybrid paradigm first introduced by Suárez's view thus underscores three crucial innovative features that give to Kant's new hybrid view a different character, determining the peculiar nature of his defense of moral realism through a radical transformation of the philosophical strategy. I shall highlight the main features of the resulting position in the final section.

4 Kant's Idealist Transformation of Moral Realism

On the interpretation I am suggesting, Kant's view on morality should be seen as marking a turning point in the history of moral realism and its confrontation with different variants of antirealism, since he undertakes a transformation of moral realism into a more complex hybrid view. After such elaboration, in Kant's view moral realism can no longer be merely defined as the thesis of the mind-independent nature of morality in general. More precisely, after Kant moral realism as the thesis of the mind-independence of moral criteria, and moral antirealism as the thesis of their mind-dependence can no longer be regarded as mutually exclusive. In fact, the combination of both is distinctive of Kant's new conception.

A characterization of Kant's position that only focuses on its distance from traditional moral realism would offer only a partial explanation. For instance, because Kant's view cannot be reduced either to realism or to voluntarism, some commentators have suggested that Kant should be understood as maintaining a form of cognitive irrealism. However, although this reading rightly highlights the novelty of Kant's approach with regard to simpler options, it obscures that Kant's rejection of factualism, that is, of the thesis that (moral) propositions are made true by corresponding facts that obtain, does not amount to a full rejection of realism.³² Even if for Kant moral principles are not propositions whose truth conditions are provided by their correspondence with facts, this does not entail that his position is ipso facto irrealist, but only that his conception of practical cognition is non-descriptivist. In fact, if realism consists in affirming the mind-independent status of some fact or principle, as I have proposed at the outset, this leaves open the possibility of acknowledging in Kant's view a significant element of moral realism in that every practically necessary principle enjoys mind-independent authority, although he holds to non-descriptivism. According to the interpretation of Kant as a cognitive irrealist, he cannot hold a realist view because "we can only know the noumena as they appear to us, and that they appear to us only through receptivity" (Skorupski 2010, p. 487, note 15). Also, this remark neglects the relevant differences between theoretical and practical cognition. Not only does Kant maintain that practical cognition is not about what appears and in fact is possible in virtue of the activity of reason, but he also states that our cognition of the moral law presents exactly a crucial instance of something that can be acknowledged as real without being empirically known.

A further significant level of Kant's moral realism lies in the fact that he strongly holds that the cognition of the moral law opens up the possibility to refer (albeit in non-theoretical terms) to an order of reality that he clearly does not understand as mind-dependent. On some occasions, Kant even refers to an "order of things," deploying an almost Malebranchian formulation (cf. e.g. KpV: 42, 49). It is understandable that later attempts at elaborating Kant's views have downplayed, if not utterly dismissed, this aspect, which is, within Kant's philosophical outlook, intrinsically connected with demanding metaphysical and epistemological theses and with a robust conception of reason.³³ Nevertheless, Kant's view in its complexity would lack an essential component if that connection were severed.³⁴

While a substantial part of Kant's aim is to defend the contents of common moral thinking against inadequate philosophical accounts, the elements of realism in his view are not confined to the realm of experience. He develops a new view without abandoning a realist conception of the fundamental moral law.³⁵ In this respect, Kant does hold to a strong realist view. If robust realism is the thesis that "there are objective irreducibly normative truths" (Enoch 2011, p. 4), Kant holds a robustly realist position about the moral law. This is

---

32 Cf. Skorupski (2010, pp. 11ff.).
33 On the latter, see e.g. Watkins (2010).
34 See Ameriks (2003, p. 269).
35 Sensen (2013) has also pointed out a realism of the moral law in Kant's position.

not the whole story, of course, as he holds at the same time that the mere existence of normative data (or facts) is neither sufficient to provide the specific kind of normativity that we call moral obligation nor sufficient to make the cognition of moral obligation possible. However, if we define our understanding of moral realism by referring to a distinction between procedural realism and substantial realism,[36] we should argue that Kant does not merely hold a procedural realism but a substantial realism about the moral law as well. That is, Kant does not merely argue that "there are answers to moral questions; that is, that there are right and wrong ways to answer them," as procedural realists are supposed to, according to Korsgaard's definition, but in fact also believes, like the substantial realist, that "there are answers to moral questions because there are moral facts or truths, which those questions ask about."[37] This holds for him only with important qualifications, though. The basic normative truth consists in the fundamental law of practical reason, which cannot be directly grasped. The answers to moral questions refer to that basic normative truth, but cannot be simply derived from it. In Kant's view the reference to those normative data cannot possibly be immediate, but is constitutively mediated by the way in which pure practical reason is able to cognize them, that is, is able to become aware of the moral law through autonomous lawgiving. Kant thus combines a substantial realism about the moral law with a quite different view about moral obligation, which in fact builds the core of his new conception.

---

36 Cf. Korsgaard (1996, pp. 35 f.).

37 Bojanowski denies that Kant's view can be regarded as a case of substantial realism. However, he lists a number of aspects on which it would appear that it can be, after all. In fact, Bojanowski does remark that "Kant and the substantial realist both agree that moral cognition is a case of 'immediate' cognition (5:29). Kant also agrees with the substantial realist in thinking that the 'data' ('datis'), the given, is not something cognized by us empirically" (Bojanowski 2012, p. 15). On the other hand, Bojanowski argues that "Korsgaard's procedural realism does not go far enough. Practical reason does not simply cognize some procedure or criterion for distinguishing between good and bad maxims. What I cognize is not a mere procedure for making choices, but the good itself. Since this is not an appearance, but a noumenon, Kant's position shares with substantial realism the conviction that practical cognition is cognition of an object that is independent of the arbitrary choices of individual subjects" (Bojanowski 2012, p. 18). The significant differences separating Kant's view from substantial realism are: that (a) Kant understands these "data," as "given by the activity of reason itself, rather than by some source external to it" (Bojanowski 2012, p. 15, cf. p. 17), and (b) that Kant maintains that "the existence of this object depends on individual, empirical subjects" (Bojanowski 2012, p. 18). On my reading, both these differences depend on Kant's new conception of moral obligation, through which he aims at emending traditional moral realism, thereby profoundly modifying it.

The complexity of his view with regard to the terms of current debates also stands out clearly if we consider another distinction between weaker realism, which holds that moral properties are independent of any particular experience, but are "waiting to be perceived," and stronger realism, which holds that moral properties are not constituted by the possibility of a (human) response.[38] Kant holds a stronger realist view regarding the fundamental moral law, since he argues that it is independent of any response at all. On the other hand, his view on moral obligation cannot be construed as a form of realism, even of the weaker kind, because, if moral obligation does not presuppose any particular interest and is cognizable by every moral agent as such, neither moral obligation nor any other moral notion are "waiting to be perceived," according to Kant. All of them are in fact dependent upon the activity of reason. A further significant weakness of the characterization of Kant's view as irrealist is that it obscures this crucial point, namely, that the standards of moral cognition do not lie in the correspondence to external facts but that they arise from the activity of reason.

The interpretation I am putting forward can be further clarified by pointing out an analogy with Kant's view in the theoretical domain. In spite of the differences between morality and knowledge, the combination of a realism of the moral law with a non-realist account of moral obligation suggests an analogy with Kant's perspective on the theoretical use of reason, which helps us see the multi-layered combination of realism and non-realism in his conception of the foundations of morals. As the analogy with the theoretical domain shall suggest, the non-realist aspect can be characterized as idealist, to use a Kantian term that allows a clearer contrast with the elements of realism within Kant's position without implying that they should be seen as mutually exclusive.[39] Kant seems to follow his German contemporaries in that he never uses the notions of realism and idealism with regard to morals, mostly employing these terms only for metaphysical and epistemological views.[40] Nevertheless, I believe that these terms can be safely applied here to show how Kant's view on the foundations

---

38 Cf. Dancy (1986).
39 Bojanowski (2012) has also proposed to understand Kant as an idealist about morality, but on partially different grounds than those that I suggest here. He argues that Kant is committed to moral idealism because he holds that the practical use of reason and practical cognition aim at bringing their objects about (see esp. Bojanowski 2012, pp. 18 and 21; cf. KpV: 15, 46). He therefore insists more on the opposition between idealism and realism.
40 One exception is Kant's contrast between idealism and realism about natural ends in KU: 391 ff.

of morals merges theses holding the mind-independent character of some elements and theses holding the mind-dependent character of others.[41]

If empirical realism in epistemology is the view that our judgments correspond to something real in the world[42] in accordance with the common understanding of the objectivity of knowledge, Kant defends in moral philosophy the idea that moral judgments correspond to what he sometimes calls the constitution (*Beschaffenheit*) of the action.[43] Lying is fundamentally wrong, and it would be so even if it would have never been disapproved or never have been regarded as the violation of a principle. Moral realism is vindicated if we are able to explain how the moral subjects are capable of such judgments about the moral worth of actions.

In theoretical philosophy, transcendental idealism centers on the thesis that the forms through which we are able to have knowledge of objects are not derived from the nature of things and that the features of objects are not represented as belonging to the things in themselves.[44] In practical philosophy, Kant analogously maintains that the criteria of moral judgment and the moral notions like 'good' and 'bad' are not acquired by an insight into the nature of things, but are obtained by the practical use of reason. Like the pure concepts of understanding are "self-thought a priori principles of our cognition" (KrV: B167), the basic criterion of morality, that is, the categorical imperative, is self-given, i.e.,

---

[41] By using 'idealism,' I do not mean to imply any significant contrast with the more often used label 'constructivism.' Insofar as it maintains the mind-dependent character of moral principles, constructivism, in its Kantian version, can be construed as a form of idealism, in the sense I am using the term here. (For a detailed comparison between the labels of idealism and constructivism and their implications, see Rauscher 2015, pp. 23 ff.). Still, it is important to underscore a difference between 'idealism' and 'constructivism.' Unlike idealism, constructivism should be not understood in opposition to realism, as has been often pointed out against realist-minded critics of constructivism and constructivist interpretations of Kant, since constructivism as a general view about morals does not intend to deny every kind of reality to moral principles and values (see Bagnoli 2011 and Rauscher 2015). I have discussed the relationship between Kant's view and moral constructivism in Bacin (2013b). See also Sensen (2013).

[42] Cf. KrV: A375, A491/B520.

[43] Cf. e.g. NK: 39. Although I am largely in agreement with Rauscher's reading, I do not follow him in adopting the qualifications 'empirical' and 'transcendental' for realism and idealism (see Rauscher 2015, pp. 19 ff. and 244 ff., as well as his chapter in the present volume), since I suspect that they might be equivocal with regard to practical philosophy. When Kant mentions empirical realism, the qualification is referred to the realm of possible experience, which is not directly relevant in the practical use of reason. Also using 'transcendental' in this context would require examining Kant's remarks on the separation between transcendental philosophy and practical philosophy. (I discuss the issue in Bacin 2006, pp. 159–164.)

[44] Cf. e.g. KrV: A27 f./B44.

self-legislated in the practical use of pure reason. Kant's conception is thus characterized by an idealism about obligation. Following the parallel with theoretical philosophy, here I call idealism the view that moral obligation is dependent on some (necessary or constitutive) operation of the agent's mind, so that there is no such thing as moral obligation outside the dimension of finite rational subjects as co-legislating the moral law. The obligation not to lie arises only from the practical necessity to recognize that in virtue of the fundamental moral law, lying is wrong. Accordingly, we know that lying is wrong only through the unconditional command not to lie. An account of moral obligation as dependent on pure practical reason is, for Kant, the key to preserving an account of moral demands as objective, necessary and not dependent on any contingent human interest or desire, which can be called in turn a realism of the contents of common moral thought.

One remarkable, yet underappreciated aspect of Kant's idealist conception is that it rejects the talk of moral properties as inappropriate or merely superficial. In this respect Kant's view appears more strongly antirealist than Hutcheson's or Hume's, since both of them had stressed the analogy between moral properties and secondary qualities, as I mentioned before. The so-called moral properties are in fact, for Kant, just the outcome of the imposition of principles.[45] Drawing on a voluntarist conception, Kant holds that concepts as 'good' cannot be construed as designating natural, mind-independent properties, but only as determining a moral qualification of actions through obligation, that is, through the legislation of autonomy. 'Good' is a predicate that we ascribe to actions whose maxims conform to the categorical imperative and are thus recognized as universally valid.[46] Therefore, while Kant aims at a stronger position than merely maintaining the reality of moral distinctions, he does not go so far as holding that such distinctions directly correspond to mind-independent qualities.[47]

The distinction between levels of realism and levels of idealism in Kant's conception would be incomplete, however, if it did not include the strong

---

45 See also Rauscher (2015, p. 4).
46 Cf. KpV: 68f. Against Stern (2012, pp. 35ff.), thus, I do not hold Kant's view to be compatible with value realism.
47 In the terms suggested by Gill (2006, p. 296), Kant is certainly not merely an anti-egoist realist, but he is not a traditional "Ptolemaic realist" either, since he does hold that "moral properties exist independently of the human mind and that our moral judgments represent those properties accurately." His distinctive view introduces a mediation regarding our access to the real ground of moral distinctions, which are not merely reflected in our moral concepts and judgments.

realism about the moral law as the fundamental law of practical reason, which I have already pointed out. Since Kant strongly holds to the idea that the fundamental law of practical reason is independent from any mind's activity, he can argue that the access to the same moral law allows finite rational beings to cognize, if only partially, God's mind, much like previous rationalists had maintained. However, Kant's solution to the epistemological issue of traditional moral realism entails a modification of that thesis about the moral law. While there is an important conceptual distinction between moral law and categorical imperative, there is no corresponding real difference at hand, since finite rational beings can cognize the moral law only as the categorical imperative through its bindingness. Kant's realism about the moral law is inseparable from his idealism about obligation. Since this connection centers on the thesis that the moral law is the fundamental law of practical reason, which can be cognized only by virtue of the autonomy of practical reason, I suggest that it would be appropriate to call this a practical realism of the moral law.

This brief reconstruction of the different aspects of Kant's position concerning the foundations of morals shows how it cannot be regarded as an instance of either moral realism or moral antirealism in their simplest variants. On the contrary, as I have argued, an appropriate understanding of Kant's view has to take into account that his basic philosophical aim is largely convergent with traditional realism and with several of its assumptions. Kant's view is the position of a moral realist who believes that traditional moral realism is unable to solve the central issue of practical philosophy, that is, to vindicate moral obligation while holding to the basic tenets of moral realism. At the same time, it is at least equally important to realize that his philosophical strategy is different and that it is not only novel but also especially significant, since this strategy contributes to the solution of the main issue of clarifying the source of moral obligation, adopting solutions that are incompatible with traditional moral realism. Since this non-realist or idealist strategy provides the core of Kant's answer to the moral question of the validity of moral obligation, the idealist component has a priority and in fact modifies the fundamental moral realism. Kant's conception revolves around the central innovation of a non-realist account of moral obligation in terms of the autonomy of pure practical reason. This is what allows Kant to defend realist theses.

As his solution to the central problem of moral obligation combines elements of realism with elements of mainly voluntarist descent, Kant's position cannot be simply ascribed to one or the other camp according to the neat division made by Shaftesbury. If Kant is certainly not a "nominal moralist," he does not intend to explain that morality is "really something in it-self, and in the nature of Things" either. His view could be characterized as an idealist version of moral realism or, more specifically, as the combination of a strong realism about the moral law with an idealist account of moral obligation.[48]

Literature

Kant

ED	Das Ende aller Dinge, AA 8
G	Über den Gemeinspruch: Das mag in der Theorie richtig sein, taugt aber nicht für die Praxis, AA 8
GMS	Grundlegung zur Metaphysik der Sitten, AA 4
JL	Jäsche Logik, AA 9
KpV	Kritik der praktischen Vernunft, AA 5
KrV	Kritik der reinen Vernunft, AA 3 (B) und 4 (A)
KU	Kritik der Urteilskraft, AA 5
MC	Moralphilosophie Collins, AA 27
MM	Moral Mrongrovius, AA 27
MM II	Moral Mrongrovius II, AA 29
MS	Die Metaphysik der Sitten, AA 6
MSV	Metaphysik der Sitten Vigilantius, AA 27
NK	Nachschrift Kaehler (Immanuel Kant: *Vorlesung zur Moralphilosophie*. Herausgegeben von Werner Stark mit einer Einleitung von Manfred Kühn, Berlin/New York 2004.)
Päd	Pädagogik, AA 9
PPP	Praktische Philosophie Powalski, AA 27
R	Reflexionen, AA 14–19
UDG	Untersuchung über die Deutlichkeit der Grundsätze der natürlichen Theologie und der Moral, AA 2

English translations are taken from the series *The Cambridge Edition of the Works of Immanuel Kant*, Cambridge University Press (1992 ff.).
All page and line numbers in parentheses refer to the so-called Akademie-Ausgabe (AA), i.e., to *Kant's gesammelte Schriften*, herausgegeben von der *Königlich Preußischen Akademie der Wissenschaften*, Berlin: Walter de Gruyter (1900 ff.).

Secondary Literature

Ameriks, Karl (2003): *Interpreting Kant's Critiques*. Oxford: Oxford University Press.

---

[48] I would like to thank Jochen Bojanowski, Robinson dos Santos, Pat Kain, Lara Ostaric, Fred Rauscher, Dieter Schönecker, Oliver Sensen, and Melissa Zinkin for helpful comments on a draft of this paper.

Bacin, Stefano (2006): *Il senso dell'etica. Kant e la costruzione di una teoria morale*. Bologna/Napoli: Il Mulino.

Bacin, Stefano (2013a): "Legge e obbligatorietà: la struttura dell'idea di autolegislazione morale." In: *Studi Kantiani* 26, pp. 55–70.

Bacin, Stefano (2013b): "Kant: ragioni e limiti del costruttivismo morale." In: Carla Bagnoli (ed.): *Che fare? Nuove prospettive filosofiche sull'azione*. Roma: Carocci, pp. 101–128.

Bacin, Stefano (2018): "Autonomy and Moral Rationalism: Kant's Criticisms of 'Rationalist' Moral Principles (1762–1785)" In: Stefano Bacin/Oliver Sensen (eds.): *The Emergence of Autonomy in Kant's Moral Philosophy*. Cambridge: Cambridge University Press.

Bagnoli, Carla (2011): "Constructivism in Metaethics." In: Edward N. Zalta (ed.): *The Stanford Encyclopedia of Philosophy* (on the web).

Barbeyrac, Jean (1735): "Jugement d'un anonyme sur l'original de cet abrégé." In: Samuel Pufendorf: *Les Devoirs de l'Homme et du Citoien*. Vol. II., pp. 379–435. (English translation in: Ian Hunter/David Saunders (eds.): Samuel Pufendorf. *The Whole Duty of Man, According to the Law of Nature*. Indianapolis: Liberty Fund, 2003, pp. 267–305.)

Baumgarten, Alexander Gottlieb (1757): *Metaphysica*. Editio tertia. Halle: Hemmerde.

Baumgarten, Alexander Gottlieb (1760): *Initia philosophiae practicae primae*. Halle: Hemmerde.

Baxley, Anne Margaret (2012): "The Problem of Obligation, the Finite Rational Will, and Kantian Value Realism." In: *Inquiry* 55, pp. 567–583.

Bojanowski, Jochen (2012): "Is Kant a Moral Realist?" In: *Kant Yearbook* 4, pp. 1–22.

Clarke, Samuel (1738): *The Works of Samuel Clarke*. 4 vols. London: Knapton.

Dancy, Jonathan (1986): "Two Conceptions of Moral Realism." In: *Proceedings of the Aristotelian Society*. Supplementary 60, pp. 167–187.

Enoch, David (2011): *Taking Morality Seriously: A Defense of Robust Realism*. Oxford: Oxford University Press.

Gill, Michael B. (1998): "On the Alleged Incompatibility Between Sentimentalism and Moral Confidence." In: *History of Philosophy Quarterly* 15, pp. 411–440.

Gill, Michael B. (2006): *The British Moralists on Human Nature and the Birth of Secular Ethics*. Cambridge: Cambridge University Press.

Gill, Michael B. (2007): "Moral Rationalism vs. Moral Sentimentalism: Is Morality More like Math or Beauty?" In: *Philosophy Compass* 2, pp. 16–30.

Hume, David (1739–1740): *A Treatise of Human Nature*. (Edited by David F. Norton/Mary J. Norton. Oxford: Oxford University Press, 2000.)

Irwin, Terence H. (2004): "Kantian Autonomy." In: *Royal Institute of Philosophy Supplement* 55, pp. 137–164.

Irwin, Terence H. (2009): *The Development of Ethics. A Historical and Critical Survey*. Vol. III: *From Kant to Rawls*. Oxford: Oxford University Press.

Irwin, Terence H. (2015): "Shaftesbury's Place in the History of Moral Realism." In: *Philosophical Studies* 172, pp. 865–882.

Kain, Patrick (2004): "Self-Legislation in Kant's Moral Philosophy." In: *Archiv für Geschichte der Philosophie* 86, pp. 257–306.

Klotz, Christian (2001): "Gesetzesbegriffe in Kants Ethik." In: Volker Gerhardt/Rolf-Peter Horstmann/Ralph Schumacher (eds.): *Kant und die Berliner Aufklärung. Akten des IX. Internationalen Kant-Kongresses*. Vol. III. Berlin/New York: Walter de Gruyter, pp. 55–62.

Korsgaard, Christine M. (1996): *The Sources of Normativity*. Cambridge: Cambridge University Press.
Krasnoff, Larry (2012): "Voluntarism and Conventionalism in Hobbes and Kant." In: *Hobbes Studies* 25, pp. 43–65.
Leibniz, Gottfried Wilhelm (1703): *Méditation sur la notion commune de la justice*. (English translation in: Patrick Riley (ed.): *Leibniz. Political Writings*. Cambridge: Cambridge University Press, 1972.)
Ludwig, Bernd (1997): "Die ‚praktische Vernunft' – ein hölzernes Eisen? Zum Verhältnis von Voluntarismus und Rationalismus in Kants Moralphilosophie." In: *Jahrbuch für Recht und Ethik* 5, pp. 9–25.
Meier, Georg Friedrich (1764): *Allgemeine practische Weltweisheit*. Halle: Hemmerde (Reprint Hildesheim/New York: Olms, 2008.)
Rauscher, Frederick (2002): "Kant's Moral Anti-Realism." In: *Journal of the History of Philosophy* 40, pp. 477–499.
Rauscher, Frederick (2015): *Naturalism and Realism in Kant's Ethics*. Cambridge: Cambridge University Press.
Reath, Andrews (2006): *Agency and Autonomy in Kant's Moral Theory. Selected Essays*. Oxford/New York: Oxford University Press.
Reath, Andrews (2012): "Kant's Conception of the Autonomy of the Will." In: Oliver Sensen (ed.): *Kant on Moral Autonomy*. Cambridge: Cambridge University Press, pp. 32–52.
Sensen, Oliver (2013): "Kant's Constructivism." In: Carla Bagnoli (ed.): *Constructivism in Ethics*. Cambridge: Cambridge University Press, pp. 63–81.
Shaftesbury, Anthony Ashley Cooper, Third Earl of (1711): *Characteristics of Men, Manners, Opinions, Times*. (Edited by Douglas Den Uyl. Indianapolis: Liberty Fund, 2001.)
Shaftesbury, Anthony Ashley Cooper, Third Earl of (1745): *Die Sitten-Lehrer, oder Erzehlung philosophischer Gespräche, welche die Natur und die Tugend betreffen*. Translated by Johann J. Spalding. Berlin: Haude und Spener.
Skorupski, John (2010): *The Domain of Reasons*. Oxford: Oxford University Press.
Skorupski, John (2012): "Aristotelianism and Modernity: Terence Irwin on the Development of Ethics." In: *European Journal of Philosophy* 20, pp. 312–337.
Star, Daniel (2013): "Moral Metaphysics." In: Roger Crisp (ed.): *The Oxford Handbook of the History of Ethics*. Oxford: Oxford University Press, pp. 818–842.
Stern, Robert (2012): *Understanding Moral Obligation. Kant, Hegel, Kierkegaard*. Cambridge: Cambridge University Press.
Suárez, Francisco (1612): "Tractatus de legibus ac Deo legislatore." In: *Opera omnia*. Paris: Vivès 1856–1878. Vols. V-VI. (English translation in: *Francisco Suárez. Selections from Three Works*. Prepared by Gwladys L. Williams/Ammi Brown/John Waldron. Oxford: Clarendon Press 1944.)
Watkins, Eric (2010): "The Antinomy of Practical Reason: Reason, the Unconditioned and the Highest Good." In: Andrews Reath/Jens Timmermann (eds.): *Kant's Critique of Practical Reason. A Critical Guide*. Cambridge: Cambridge University Press, pp. 145–167.
Watkins, Eric (2014): "What is, for Kant, a Law of Nature?" In: *Kant-Studien* 105, pp. 471–490.
Whewell, William (1852): *Lectures on the History of Moral Philosophy in England*. London: Parker.

Wolff, Christian (1733): *Vernünfftige Gedancken von der Menschen Thun und Lassen zur Beförderung ihrer Glückseligkeit* (Deutsche Ethik). 4th edition. Franckfurt/Leipzig. (English translation of selections in: Jerome B. Schneewind (ed.): *Moral Philosophy from Montaigne to Kant*. Cambridge: Cambridge University Press, 2003.)

Wolff, Christian (1736): *Philosophia prima sive ontologia methodo scientifica pertractata qua omnis cognitionis humanae principia continentur*. (Reprint edited by Jean École. Hildesheim/New York: Olms, 1962.)

Wolff, Christian (1751): *Vernünfftige Gedancken von Gott, der Welt und der Seele des Menschen, auch allen Dingen überhaupt* (Deutsche Metaphysik). (Reprint Hildesheim: Olms, 1983.)

Wolff, Michael (2009): "Warum das Faktum der Vernunft ein Faktum ist. Auflösung einiger Verständnisschwierigkeiten in Kants Grundlegung der Moral." In: *Deutsche Zeitschrift für Philosophie* 57, pp. 511–549.

Wright, Crispin (1992): *Truth and Objectivity*. Cambridge: Harvard University Press.

Jochen Bojanowski
Why Kant Is Not a Moral Intuitionist

Abstract In this paper, I argue against the view, most eloquently advocated by Dieter Schönecker, that Kant is what I call a "sensualist intuitionist." Kant's text does not accommodate a sensualist intuitionist reading; the fact of reason is cognized by reason, not intuition. I agree with Schönecker that the feeling of respect for the moral law makes us feel its obligatory character, but I disagree that this feeling constitutes cognition of the normative content of the moral law. We do not cognize the validity of the moral law through feeling. I argue instead for what I take to be the standard view: We feel through respect for the moral law the limiting and humiliating *effect* that rational cognition of the moral law has on our sensibility.

* * *

Introduction

In "Kant's Moral Intuitionism," Dieter Schönecker holds that Kant is an intuitionist with respect to the "validity of the moral law" (Schönecker 2013b, p. 2). The intuitionism ascribed to Kant by Schönecker is of a particular kind; it provides us with knowledge of the moral law's normative force and is an intuition through feeling rather than reason, i.e., the feeling of respect for the moral law. Moreover, it is only through the feeling of respect that we are able to cognize our moral obligations. Many Kantians will be baffled by this claim; Kant explicitly says that the moral law is a "synthetic a priori proposition that is not based on *any* intuition, either pure or empirical" (KpV: 31; my emphasis).[1] Ascribing any sort of intuitionism to Kant (be it sensual or rational) is therefore likely to strike many as misguided. Moreover, since Kant holds that respect for the moral law "serves [...] *only* as an incentive to make this law its maxim" (KpV: 76; my emphasis), ascribing a cognitive rather than motivational role to the feeling of respect does not seem very plausible to begin with.

However, Kant also says: "What I cognize immediately as a law for me, I cognize with respect" (GMS: 401, note). And in another passage, Kant maintains that "[t]he dissimilarity of determining grounds (empirical and rational) is made

---

[1] For the list of abbreviations of Kant's works, see the "Literature" section of this paper.

known by [...] the feeling of a respect [...] for the moral law" (KpV: 92). These passages are, at least *prima facie*, grist to Schönecker's mill; they seem opposed to the merely motivational account of respect, and they seem to support Schönecker's cognitivist reading. I therefore believe that Schönecker's Kant deserves to be taken seriously. His view challenges some of our most familiar assumptions not only about Kant's moral epistemology, and with it his fact of reason claim, but also about his moral psychology. As I aim to show, careful consideration of Schönecker's Kant reveals important lessons about practical cognition and practical normativity in Kant.

In this paper, I will first lay out, in broad strokes, what I call Schönecker's "sensualist intuitionism." I distinguish it from other kinds of intuitionism and then turn to what Schönecker takes to be the main implications of Kant's fact of reason claim. My claim is that Kant's text does not accommodate the sensualist intuitionist reading suggested by Schönecker; the fact of reason is cognized by reason, not intuition. The feeling of respect for the law makes us *feel* the obligatory force of the categorical imperative, but this does not mean that we *cognize* or *know* immediately that we are morally obliged through the feeling of respect for the moral law. I agree with Schönecker that the feeling of respect for the moral law makes us feel its obligatory character, but I disagree that this feeling constitutes cognition of the normative content of the moral law. We do not cognize the validity of the moral law through feeling; instead, we feel through respect for the moral law the limiting and humiliating *effect* that rational cognition of the moral law has on our sensibility. The two passages at KpV: 92 and GMS: 401 are the best textual evidence Schönecker can find for his intuitionism, but I will show why there is a very plausible reading available that entitles us to resist the cognitivist reading. Respect for the moral law does not play an epistemological role; rather, as the traditional reading has it, its role is motivational. Interpretative questions aside, this does not necessarily mean that Schönecker is wrong on philosophical grounds, of course. His Kant might be philosophically better than Kant himself. In the final section, I will show why this is not the case. I will argue that we should resist Schönecker's sensualist intuitionism because it cannot adequately account for the cognition of practical normativity.

I

The moral intuitionism ascribed to Kant by Schönecker is the view that "we cognize immediately through feelings the validity of the moral law" (Schönecker

2013a, p. 2). This feeling presents "a certain kind of self-evidence, [the][2] crucial phenomenological aspect of which is *givenness*." The non-intuitionist, by contrast, holds "that there is a way to demonstrate by strength of argument that it is rational to obey moral laws (The Golden Rule, Contractarianism, something along these lines)" (Schönecker 2013b, p. 2). This definition registers four fundamental features of Schönecker's intuitionism: We intuit the validity of the moral law through (i) a feeling; we experience the feeling as (ii) given; and this validity is presented to us as both (iii) self-evident and (iv) non-inferential.

Let me note at the outset that the intuitionism Schönecker ascribes to Kant is not in line with what is known in metaethics as "rational intuitionism." Rational intuitionists like Clarke, Price, and Moore also endorse some sort of self-evidence claim; according to their brands of *rational* intuitionism, however, we disapprove of an action because it has an objective moral property. On their views, moral goodness is given to us not through feeling but through a non-inferential *intellectual* kind of seeing. If Schönecker's Kant is right and the normative content of moral judgment is grounded in feeling, we don't seem to be entitled to claim that we have *knowledge* of it. For how can we claim that these judgments are objective if *feeling* directly reveals them to us? On the face of things, Schönecker's intuitionism is a non-cognitivist view, and we can distinguish it from rational intuitionism by calling it *sensualist intuitionism*. It is certainly surprising to find a Kantian position that lies on the sensualist side of the divide; given that Schönecker wants to ground moral obligation in feeling and explicitly distances himself from the "rationalism" (Schönecker 2013a, p. 2) ascribed to Kant by some interpreters, however, "sensualist intuitionism" may in fact be the appropriate term. This also makes clear why Kant's claim that the cognition of the moral law is "not based on any intuition" cannot be held against Schönecker's view, for the intuition in Schönecker's intuitionism is not an intuition (*Anschauung*) in Kant's sense but a feeling brought about by reason.

Schönecker might nonetheless disagree with my representation of his position. He might object that I overlook a crucial distinction: that between content and validity. Schönecker explicitly says that we do not "cognize the entire content of the general CI or of specific imperatives [...] by feeling. [...] It is not that the moral law is valid *because* we have that feeling." The view Schönecker develops is that we only *know* that the categorical imperative "really *is* a command" because it is cognized "by the feeling of respect" (Schönecker 2013b, p. 4). Thus he suggests a different way to make this distinction. The categorical imperative has two aspects: its "command" character and its "formal

---

[2] All insertions in square brackets by the author.

content (that *which* we are obliged to do, in short: the universalization)." According to Schönecker, the latter aspect is "descriptive," the former "normative" (Schönecker 2013a, pp. 13 f.). Schönecker does not really say much about the descriptive content or the relation between the descriptive and the normative content. I will return to this topic in the final section below.

We are now in a position to distinguish Schönecker's intuitionism from another kind of Kantian intuitionism, which has been defended most recently by Robert Audi. Audi attempts to supplement Ross's intuitionism with Kant's categorical imperative. Kantian ethics tends to be too abstract; it does not seem to give us enough guidance when it comes to concrete moral decisions. Ross's multitude of moral principles, by contrast, seems to lack the necessary unity. In supplementing Ross's ethics with Kant's, Audi hopes to arrive at a theory that is both "close to our moral practice" (Audi 2001, p. 602), like the Rossian principles, and unified through the Kantian moral principle.[3] Thus in contrast to Schönecker, Audi's Kantian intuitionism is not a justification of the obligatory character of the categorical imperative. Instead, rational intuition of the categorical imperative as the fundamental principle of morality is the unifying feature that explains how each of the particular principles can count as moral knowledge.[4] In Schönecker's terms, Audi's intuitionism is an epistemology of the descriptive content of our moral judgments, while his own intuitionism is an epistemology of the "normative content" of morality (Schönecker 2013a, p. 14). As will become evident in the final part of this paper, it is unlikely that the traditional rational intuitionist would accept this distinction, and nor is it convincing. Before I turn to this more fundamental philosophical question, however, I first want to consider key differences between Schönecker's account and what we find in Kant's texts.

II

The intuitionism Schönecker ascribes to Kant is meant to be an articulation of Kant's claim that the moral law is a "fact of reason." Hence his intuitionism also provides a new intuitionist reading of the fact of pure reason claim. In particular, Schönecker takes this claim to have three implications, the first of which is the following:

---

[3] For a response to Audi, see Bagnoli (2009).
[4] See Audi (2001, p. 602).

1. "The factum theory explains our insight into the binding character of the moral law; it is a theory of justification" (Schönecker 2013b, p. 3).

I read this proposition as speaking to the justificatory aspect of the fact of reason claim, i.e., the fact of reason is an attempt to *justify* the validity of the binding character of the moral law. This view goes against a standard interpretation, according to which Kant, in giving up on the deduction he had attempted in *Groundwork* III, thereby abandoned justifying the moral law altogether. This is very controversial territory, and we don't need to explore it in any depth here. I agree with Schönecker on one important point: Since the fact of reason claim is a *reason* to believe that morality is not illusory, it can be understood as a justificatory claim. Yet this does not mean that Schönecker and I agree on the exact content and epistemic character of that claim. This brings us to what Schönecker takes to be the second implication:

2. "In our consciousness of the CI, the moral law is immediately given in its unconditional and binding validity" (Schönecker 2013b, p. 3).

Schönecker views the gallows example as an elucidation of the fact of reason claim in general. In particular, he takes it to provide textual support for the implication that the categorical imperative is given immediately. The gallows example "does not describe in any detail *how* the pleasure-seeker becomes aware of the dimension of *you ought*; he merely says that 'he is aware that he ought to do it.'" The "it," Schönecker goes on, "refers back to the act of overcoming his love of life." The pleasure-seeker ought to overcome his love of life because the moral law forbids him to "bear false witness against an honorable man." The main point is that our experience of moral obligation does not involve "a pure and abstract knowledge regarding the validity of the moral law." Instead, the pleasure-seeker "experiences" the moral ought "through a specific *you ought* in the specific imperative." Hence, Schönecker concludes, "[a]lthough Kant writes in conclusion that the pleasure-seeker cognizes freedom through '*the* moral law,' our cognition of the moral law [...] is therefore *not* to be understood as an immediate abstract insight into the *you ought* of the CI *in general*. [...] Kant does not describe the pleasure-seeker as someone who is aware of the CI, as it is formulated in § 7 as the 'fundamental law'" (Schönecker 2013b, pp. 15 f.).

Let me first briefly comment on the substantial philosophical point before I say something about the argumentative context of the gallows passage. Schönecker's interpretation suggests a false alternative: Either our ordinary cognition of moral obligation is the cognition of the "fundamental law of practical reason" that Kant puts forward in §7 or we cognize moral obligation by experiencing the force of specific moral principles in the immediate circumstances. Schönecker rightly rules out the first option. The philosopher establishes the "fundamental law of practical reason," which is the result of the definitions, theorems, and problems in sections 1–6. One might even say that the formal principle is *constructed* out of those definitions, theorems, and problems. According to Kant, no one in the history of philosophy before him had articulated this principle explicitly. And yet, Kant argues, this principle governs everyone's particular moral judgments.

Schönecker's second option suggests that we are conscious of moral obligation independently of this general principle. The point is that, while we might not have an articulated understanding of the fundamental law of reason, it can still determine our particular moral judgments in much the same way that logical rules of inference determine our reasoning without our being able to articulate them explicitly. The overlooked alternative, however, is that the pleasure-seeker's experience of moral obligation may be dependent on his consciousness of the practical universality of his maxim. The principle Kant articulates in §7 is the form of every particular moral judgment; hence we might say that all particular moral judgments, to the extent that they express practical knowledge, are expressions of the formal principle of morality. I grant that Kant does not make this explicit in the gallows example, but this is because the passage concerns something very different. This comes out more clearly when we shift our focus to the argumentative context and goal of the gallows passage, which brings me to my second point.

Schönecker wants us to read the gallows example in such a way that it elucidates "how we are to conceive givenness" (as Schönecker (2013b, p. 14) puts it), or the "non-inferential character" of moral obligation. Yet the context of this passage and Kant's explicit remark suggest otherwise: Kant brings up the gallows example in the second *Critique* in the Remark after §6. But that Remark is not only a Remark to §6; in fact, §5 and §6 must be read in conjunction. Both sections pose a "problem," as the title of the section indicates. The problem in each section concerns the relation between a free capacity of volition and the moral law. The first problem can be read as follows: If a capacity of volition is determined by lawgiving form (i.e., the moral law), how must this capacity be constituted? The conclusion and solution is that the capacity of volition must be a free capacity of volition. The second problem is almost a reversal of the first: If the capacity of volition is free, which law can determine it necessarily? The answer to this question is that the "lawgiving form" (as contained in the maxim) must be the determining ground.

In the Remark to § 5 and § 6, Kant first re-endorses the reciprocity thesis from *Groundwork* III and then raises the crucial question, namely "from what our *cognition* of the unconditionally practical law *starts*, whether from freedom or from the practical law" (GMS: 447). As we know, his answer is that it starts from the moral law. In fact, Kant holds that "one would have never ventured to introduce [transcendental] freedom into science [i.e., philosophy], had not the moral law and with it practical reason, come in and forced this concept upon us" (KpV: 30). We need not consider the details of his argument here. The important point for our purposes is that the gallows example is used as verification from ordinary experience of the cognitive order of freedom and the moral law. As Kant puts it, "experience also confirms this order of concepts in us" (KpV: 30). So the gallows example does not serve to elucidate the fact of reason claim. Rather, its argumentative function is to confirm the cognitive primacy of the moral law over freedom.

Schönecker might concede this point, but he might still insist that there is something about moral experience to be learned from the gallows example. This is surely true, but the account of moral experience in the gallows example is also very limited. It is limited to the inferential relation between moral obligation and freedom. Kant does not want to explain how we come to *know* that we are obliged to *x*. Rather, Kant's point in the gallows example is that we infer from our consciousness of moral obligation our own absolute freedom. Cognition of moral obligation cannot be separated from consciousness of the universality of our maxim. Notice, in the quoted passage above, that Kant does not say that the moral law and respect for the law "forced this concept upon us." Instead, Kant says that "the moral law and with it practical *reason*, [came] in and forced this concept upon us." The gallows example is supposed to "confirm" this claim (KpV: 30; my emphasis). The intuitionism Schönecker ascribes to Kant holds that we grasp the categorical imperative through feeling. Yet if the gallows example is supposed to "confirm," as Kant explicitly says, that "practical *reason*" (KpV: 30; my emphasis) forces this concept upon us, it can hardly be read as establishing that *feeling* forces moral obligation upon us.

It is therefore no surprise that Schönecker finds it difficult to relate the gallows example back to a claim Kant makes in the Remark to § 6:

"We become immediately aware of the moral law (as soon as we draw up maxims of the will for ourselves) [...]"

My interpretation of this claim is roughly in line with Schönecker's: The form of a maxim as a fundamental principle of practical reason (or rational agency) involves a claim to its rationality. In adopting a maxim, I become immediately aware of the form of practical reason, i.e., practical universality. This is precisely the demand of the categorical imperative. Schönecker believes that this reading is in tension with the gallows example because the latter is precisely *not* concerned with the question of testing our maxims. As I pointed out earlier, however, the point of the gallows example is to elucidate not the cognition of moral obligation but the inferential relation between moral obligation and freedom ("ought" implies "can"). In order to make this point, Kant does not need to elaborate in detail on the mental acts involved in moral obligation.

The passage quoted above leads to an even more direct argument against Schönecker's interpretation of Kant's factum claim. Kant explicitly asks the question (Schönecker also quotes this passage): "[H]ow is consciousness of that moral law possible?" Kant's answer is: "We can become aware of pure practical laws just as we are aware of pure theoretical principles, by attending to the necessity with which reason prescribes them to us and to the setting aside of all empirical conditions to which reason directs us" (KpV: 30). Schönecker believes that both features, necessity and the setting aside of all empirical conditions, "are clearly revealed in the gallows example: the absolute validity must be obeyed even at the potential cost of one's own death; and the purity of the moral law is revealed by the way in which it commands us independently of the most powerful conceivable inclination and even against such an inclination [...]" (Schönecker 2013b, p. 20). This interpretation strikes me as correct. Yet Schönecker does not explain what "necessity" and the "setting aside of all empirical conditions" involve. A maxim is practically necessary if it is universalizable, i.e., if its determining ground is the idea of practical universalizability and not a given desire. This is precisely what the so-called "universalization test" brings out. In other words, consciousness of practical necessity involves consciousness of the practical universality of one's maxim and cannot be had independently of it. If this is correct, then what Schönecker views as the final implication of the fact of reason claim must also be called into question:

> 3. "The unconditional validity of the CI is given in the feeling of respect" (Schönecker 2013b, p. 3).

The main textual support for this claim is found in the following passage:

> The dissimilarity of determining grounds (empirical and rational) is made so recognizable [*kenntlich gemacht*] by this resistance of a practically lawgiving reason to every meddling inclination, by a special kind of *feeling*, which, however, does not precede the lawgiving of practical reason but is instead produced only by it and indeed as a constraint, namely, through the feeling of a respect such as no human being has for inclinations of whatever kind but does have for the law; and it is made known so saliently and so prominently that

no one, not even the most common human understanding, can fail to see at once, in an example presented to him, that he can indeed be advised by empirical grounds of volition to follow their charms, but that he can never be expected to *obey* anything but the pure practical law of reason alone. (KpV: 92, partly my translation)

The reformulation of this main claim reads as follows:

The dissimilarity of empirical and moral (of empirical and rational) determining grounds of the will is made known by or through the feeling of respect for the law. (Schönecker 2013b, p. 24)

Schönecker (or Mary Gregor) translates "kenntlich gemacht" as "made known" in the longer passage quoted above. This rendition suggests that the feeling of respect gives us *knowledge*. In knowing, I assert that something is true. When I take something to be true, I take it to be "both subjectively and objectively sufficient" (KrV: B850). A true judgment is "necessarily valid for everyone" (ibid.). However, in feeling respect for the moral law, I do not assert anything at all. How could I then be in a state of knowing? Schönecker might respond that this is precisely what is peculiar about the feeling of respect for the moral law; it is a cognitive feeling, a feeling that conveys knowledge. Here are two reasons that speak against this claim, however. First, it would be rather surprising if Kant, believing that the feeling of respect for the moral law plays a cognitive role in moral agency, did not explicitly reflect on that role. If the feeling is special not only because it is brought about by reason but also because it is itself an act of cognition, one would expect Kant to reflect on its peculiarity. Moreover, we would expect Kant to explain how the claim that respect is a cognition is compatible with his claim that sensations are merely subjective and fundamentally distinct from cognitions, which are objective.[5] Instead, what Kant does explicitly claim is that the moral law is a feeling brought about by reason,[6] and the role Kant ascribes to this feeling is clearly motivational rather than epistemological.[7]

Second, in the same passage Schönecker quotes at length, Kant also speaks about feelings that don't have their origin in reason. And even here Kant holds:

[A]nything empirical that might slip into our maxims as a determining ground of the will *makes itself known* at once by the feeling of gratification or pain that necessarily attaches to it insofar as it arouses desire. (KpV: 92)

---

5 See KrV: B376.
6 See KpV: 73.
7 See KpV: 76.

So if "kenntlich machen" is read in terms of acquiring knowledge, then this knowledge acquisition is not reserved for the feeling of respect for the moral law. Instead, we *know* (as Schönecker would put it) that our maxim is empirically determined by the feeling of pleasure or pain that the determining ground arouses in us. So if we read "kenntlich machen" as "coming to know," the claim Schönecker needs to endorse is more general: We can acquire knowledge "intuitively," through mere feeling. But how is this claim compatible with Kant's claim that knowledge acquisition (i.e., cognition) needs both intuition and concepts?

> Our cognition arises from two fundamental sources in the mind, the first of which is the reception of representations (the receptivity of impressions), the second the faculty of cognizing an object by means of these representations (spontaneity of concepts); through the former an object is *given* to us, through the latter it is *thought* in relation to that representation (as a mere determination of the mind). Intuition and concepts therefore constitute the elements of our cognition, so that neither concepts without intuition corresponding to them in some way nor intuition without concepts can yield a cognition. (KrV: B74)

Schönecker might respond that Kant's claim that the moral law is a fact of reason is very peculiar and obviously in tension with Kant's two-component view from the first *Critique*. He might concede that he does not have an answer as to how the two-component view is compatible with the fact of reason claim while maintaining that we only face this problem once we properly appreciate that the fact of reason is cognized through sensible intuition. However, as I have pointed out above, there is nothing peculiar in this regard about respect for the moral law. Kant also says that we "come to know" (as Schönecker translates "kenntlich machen"), through the empirically given feelings of pleasure and pain, any empirical determining ground "that might slip into our maxims." Hence, an appeal to the supposed epistemic uniqueness of the fact of reason will not do the job here.

Let me illustrate my point with the following example. Consider the maxim "I will borrow money even if I know that I cannot pay it back." This maxim has a determining ground that is empirical. In adopting this maxim I become aware, through feeling, that the determining ground is the pleasure I feel in taking possession of that money. Now let us consider the universalizable form of this maxim: "I will borrow money only if I know that I can pay it back." As we saw in the passage quoted above, Kant's claim is that the feeling of respect for the moral law makes us aware of the "dissimilarity of determining grounds (empirical and rational)." In considering the universalizable form of this maxim, we are aware that the determining ground is *not* a given feeling of pleasure but rather the mere thought of the practical universalizability of the maxim, i.e., the thought that my maxim can be endorsed by all rational beings. However, this does not mean that we cognize the "normative content," as Schönecker puts it (Schönecker 2013a, p. 14), through respect for the moral law. Kant never says, not even in this passage, that we cognize moral obligation through the feeling of respect. Nor does he say that we cognize the moral law through it. All he says is that, through the feeling of respect, the difference between a rational and an empirical determining ground "is brought so clearly to our attention" (KpV: 92, my translation) that even the most common human understanding cannot deny it. Schönecker does not acknowledge the intensifier in the phrase "*so* kenntlich gemacht." As a result, he holds that it is *only* through respect that we know the difference between the determining grounds. But this is not what Kant says in this passage. Even if it were, it still does not entitle us to the claim that we know through the feeling of respect that we ought to adopt the rational determining ground and reject the empirical one. The reason why we ought to reject the empirical determining ground is that it is not practically universalizable, and hence acting on this maxim might be good for me but not good without limitation, i.e., universally good. And it is only through our rational awareness of the idea of practical universalizability, which is normative with respect to our inclinations, that we then *feel* respect for the moral law. In other words, we can become empirically aware through feeling that we do in fact have two distinct determining grounds: one humiliating, the other elevating. Yet this does not mean that we cognize the obligatoriness of the moral law through feeling. It only means that our rational cognition of the moral law as binding has an effect on our feeling, and that this experience allows us to feel the obligatory character of the moral law. In saying that the feeling of respect is the original cognition of the moral law, Schönecker therefore puts the cart before the horse.

The end of the central passage at KpV: 92 does not give us any evidence to the contrary. Here, Kant adds that even the most common human understanding will "see at once, in an example presented to him, that he can indeed be advised by empirical grounds of volition to follow their charms, but that he can never be expected to *obey* anything but the pure practical law of reason alone." The relevant example might be precisely the kind we have just considered. Consideration of such an example is not a matter of mere intuition through feeling; we must know whether a principle is practically universalizable. And determining whether a principle is universalizable is a matter not of feeling but of reason: I need to know whether the principle is valid only for me, for some others, or for everyone. I cannot know this without knowing what my end is, and I also need to know whether I am making an exception for myself in adopting that end. Schönecker seems to think that these are non-normative operations, or that we at least do not cognize them as normative. It is only "through respect for the moral law [that we] cognize the normative content" (Schönecker 2013a, p. 14). As I have indicated, this view in fact gets Kant's theory backwards. We cannot cognize the validity of the moral law through feeling; instead, we feel through respect for the moral law the limiting and humiliating *effect* of rational cognition of the moral law on our sensibility.

We are now in a position to deal with the passage quoted in the introduction, which seems to offer strong textual support for Schönecker's reading: "What I cognize immediately as a law for me, I cognize with respect" (GMS: 401, note). Schönecker takes this passage to imply that it is *through* respect that we cognize the moral law immediately. However, the "with" is ambiguous here; it can be read in an instrumental and a non-instrumental sense. Schönecker interprets it in an instrumental sense. Much like the sentence "I read the book with my glasses," Kant's sentence can be interpreted as saying that the feeling of respect is an epistemic instrument with which we access the moral law: "I cognize the moral law with (i.e., by means of) respect." Yet there is another, non-instrumental way to read this sentence. Consider, for instance, the sentence "I welcome you with great pleasure." Here, pleasure is not an instrument in the act of welcoming; rather, the welcoming is accompanied by the feeling of pleasure. I suggest that we read Kant's sentence accordingly. The "with" in "What I cognize immediately as a law for me, I cognize with respect" does not need to be read in an instrumental sense. We do not need respect as an instrument or a tracking device in order to cognize the normative content of the moral law. Instead, Kant can be read as saying that respect necessarily accompanies our cognition of the moral law. It *necessarily* accompanies our cognition of the moral law because it is the "effect" of the moral law, as Kant goes on to say in the same footnote. And since the moral law is not some mind-independent entity, but rather a concept of reason, Kant holds that the feeling is "self-caused" (*selbstgewirkt*) (GMS: 401, note). I agree with Schönecker that the feeling of respect for the moral law makes us *feel* its obligatory character, but I disagree that this feeling amounts to *cognition* of its normative content. I think that the two passages at KpV: 92 and GMS: 401 are the best textual evidence Schönecker can find for his intuitionism. I hope to have shown why there is an alternative reading available. I would suggest that this alternative is also more in line with Kant's explicit claim that respect for the moral law "serves [...] *only* as an incentive to make this law its maxim" (KpV: 76; my emphasis).

III

Schönecker's main claim is that we cognize the "normative content" (Schönecker 2013a, p. 13) of the moral law through the feeling of respect. Its descriptive content, by contrast, is cognized by reason. Schönecker claims that the moral law is merely descriptive for a fully rational agent. For finite rational beings, the moral law also has normative content.[8] In this final section, I will show why, interpretative questions aside, Schönecker's main claim strikes me as philosophically unsound.

In order to get a better grip on the relation between reason and sensibility in rational agency, we first need to get clear on the distinction between finite and infinite rational agency:

> [For finite rational beings] the law has the form of an imperative, because in them, as rational beings, one can presuppose a *pure* will but, insofar as they are beings affected by needs and sensible motives, not a *holy* will, that is, such a will as would not be capable of any maxim conflicting with the moral law. Accordingly the moral law is for them an *imperative* that commands categorically because the law is unconditional; the relation of such a will to this law is *dependence* under the name of obligation, which signifies a *necessitation*, though only by reason and its objective law, to an action which is called *duty* because a choice that is pathologically affected (though not thereby determined, hence still free) brings with it a wish arising from *subjective* causes, because of which it can often be opposed to the pure objective determining ground and thus needs a resistance of practical reason which, as moral necessitation, may be called an internal but intellectual constraint. In the supremely self-sufficient intelligence, choice is rightly represented as incapable of any maxim that could not at the same time be objectively a law, and the concept of *holiness*, which on that account belongs to it, puts it, not indeed above all practical laws, but rather above all practically restrictive laws and so above obligation and duty. (KpV: 32)

Kant claims that for finite agents the moral law has the "form of an imperative." His argument for this claim runs as follows. A finite rational agent (let's call him Ā, where the bar represents his finitude) is finite because his capacity of volition is "pathologically affected" by sensibility. This "brings with it a wish arising from subjective causes" which can be "opposed to" the moral law. The wish is opposed to the moral law if it cannot be willed as practically universal. Hence these wishes need "a resistance of practical reason," which Kant calls "intellectual constraint," in order to be brought in line with the moral law (the idea of practical universality). Thus finite rational agents have a choice between

---

8 See also Schönecker (2015, pp. 181 ff.).

their particular desires (or wishes), given to them by their sensibility, and what they consider to be good not only in particular (for them) but in general (good for every rational agent), i.e., good from the standpoint of reason. Infinite rational agents, by contrast, are not affected by sensibility. They don't have a choice between what is only good for them in particular and what is good for everyone; they only want what is practically universalizable. Hence we have to think of such an agent as morally "holy" (let's call her Å, where the halo represents her holiness). The concepts of "restrictive laws" and "obligation" are incompatible with a being that is in fact holy. Thus Schönecker is clearly right; only because finite rational agents are affected by sensibility does the notion of an "imperative" or an "intellectual constraint" apply to them. Let's call this the obligation-implies-finitude claim. Not only is the obligation-implies-finitude claim obviously philosophically correct, but there is also no question here that both Kant and Schönecker's Kant hold this view. Yet the claim endorsed by Schönecker's Kant is more ambitious. He also holds that Ā cognizes his obligation – the "normative content," as he puts it – through feeling. It is this more ambitious claim that is philosophically unattractive, and also incompatible with Kant's view.

Let me begin with the distinction between the normative and the descriptive. Schönecker's Kant claims that the moral law is a normative principle for Ā, while it is merely descriptive for Å. This distinction is misleading, however. Schönecker is right that from a third-person perspective no action of Å's is contrary to the moral law. In this sense, the moral law "describes" Å's action. However, this is not an adequate characterization of Å's consciousness of the moral law. Å is not simply conscious of what she in fact wants to do; she also cognizes her action, Φ, as rational, i.e., as practically universal. Schönecker seems to think that since Å does not have any inclination, and hence cannot but act rationally, it is impossible for her even to *conceive* of deviating from her course of action. But why should Å not be able, for example, to conceive of the possibility of Ā? Why is it impossible for her to represent her actions as good even if she herself is not tempted (or is even unable to be tempted) to do the opposite? Å does not act like a machine programmed to act in accordance with some law of which she is unconscious. Instead, Å (like Ā) acts *from the representation* of the moral law. In other words, Å's Φ-ing is brought about by her cognition of what is practically universal, i.e., formally good. I agree with Schönecker that Å does not represent the moral law as an imperative directed to herself, but this does not mean that Å's representation of the moral law lacks "normative content." If by "normative content" we mean that Å knows that her Φ-ing is good and that not Φ-ing would not be good, then her practical cognition has normative content. It is therefore more appropriate to say that for Å the categorical imperative takes the indicative mood: "I want to act from universal laws." The relevant cognition, however, is not merely a description of what she wants. In cognizing what she wants, Å also cognizes Φ as good. So while I do believe that we should endorse the obligation-implies-finitude claim, I don't believe that we should also endorse the claim that only finite beings have knowledge of the good.

Schönecker might respond that he can leave this point untouched. The main point of his argument is that Ã represents the moral law as an imperative, cognized through the feeling of respect. But is it? Let's return to our example. Ã has adopted the maxim of borrowing money even when he knows that he cannot pay it back. He knows that this maxim is not practically universalizable, i.e., he judges this maxim to be good merely for him and not unconditionally (or generally). So what Ã knows here is that his particular maxim is a mere maxim and does not have the form of a practical law. Hence it cannot be a principle of universal (rational) volition. Schönecker seems to hold that this knowledge is merely descriptive, or at least not yet normative, because we only "know" or "comprehend" that the moral law is normative through the feeling of respect. This strikes me as incorrect. When Ã is conscious that his particular wish or maxim is not at the same time a universal law, he thereby also *knows* that he *ought* not to act on it. The knowledge of his practical obligation is knowledge of his particular wish or desire under the universal principle. He knows that the particular wish or desire he is considering acting on cannot become a principle of universal (rational) volition. He therefore *knows* that this maxim is wrong (universality is the form of knowledge). To be sure, he does not become conscious of obligation through reason alone; we need to have particular desires or wishes that are not practically universal in order to consider ourselves morally obliged. The obligation-implies-finitude claim holds: Only because there can be a tension between our particular wishes and what we will in general does the notion of obligation gain any traction. But this does not mean that we cognize our obligation immediately through feeling. The cognition that our particular volition is not universalizable does have a painful effect on our sensibility; it restricts our self-love and strikes down our self-conceit.[9] As we have just seen, however, this feeling is not the source through which we access moral obligation. Respect for the moral law is only "produced by reason"; it serves not "for appraising actions and certainly not for grounding the objective moral law itself, but *only* as an incentive to make this law its maxim" (KpV: 76; my emphasis). To put this idea in contemporary terms, the role played by respect for the moral law is motivational, not epistemological. There is no doubt that Å does not know

---

9 See KpV: 73.

what it feels like to be morally obliged. You need to be Ā in order to know what it feels like to be morally obliged. Or, to put it more simply, you need to be able to feel in order to know what it feels like to be morally obliged. This seems trivial, but the claim that this feeling is also the ground of the cognition through which we know that we are morally obliged is not trivial, and it doesn't seem to me that we have reason to think it true.

Conclusion

In this paper, I have attempted to show that we should resist Schönecker's sensible intuitionism on both philological and philosophical grounds. Let me outline, in closing, what I suspect Kant's response to Schönecker's sensible intuitionism would be. My fundamental philosophical worry can be located early on in Schönecker's initial characterization of the non-intuitionist alternative. He writes that the non-intuitionist holds "that there is a way to demonstrate by strength of arguments that it is rational to obey moral laws" (Schönecker 2013b, p.2), and he views "The Golden Rule" as just such an argument. Since there is no argument of this sort to be had, Schönecker argues that we ought to endorse intuitionism. But the intuitionism he proposes is not rational intuitionism, which would give us immediate rational knowledge of what we ought to do; rather, his intuitionism is sensible intuitionism, which is supposed to give us immediate knowledge, through feeling, not of *what* we ought to do but *that* we are morally obliged to do it. I agree with Schönecker that Kant does not attempt to give an argument for why it is rational to obey the moral law.[10] This does not commit Kant to sensible intuitionism, however. Rather, Kant's project is to articulate a principle that is constitutive of moral cognition. This principle is the moral law, which is the form of all of our particular moral judgments. In practical judgment, as in theoretical judgment, we make a knowledge claim – a claim to the judgment's universality. Moral cognition is knowledge of what is good universally, i.e., good without limitation. Knowledge of the good takes the form of obligation if it is possible for an agent to do what is merely good for him but not good without limitation. Asking why I *ought* to do what I know to be universally good rather than merely good for me is like asking why I ought to judge that "S is P" rather than "S is not-P" if I know that "All S's

---

[10] However, it is not immediately clear to me how Schönecker can think that the categorical imperative is not also such an argument if the Golden Rule can be derived from the categorical imperative (GMS: 430).

are P." Schönecker believes that the non-intuitionist is in need of an argument here. In fact, however, he is not. The finite rational agent knows of his moral obligation "as soon as [he] draws up maxims" (KpV: 29), i.e., as soon as he judges practically. He knows this not immediately through feeling, but through the self-consciousness of practical reason. The feeling of respect for the moral law comes into play because in practical judgment I do not simply determine an object as good or evil; rather, I determine my own volition. By determining my own volition, I bring the object of my practical cognition into existence. Yet practical cognition can only be causally efficacious because the cognition of the good necessarily "produce[s]" (KpV: 76) the feeling of respect for the moral law. Hence respect for the moral law makes acting for the sake of duty possible. This is the old story with which we are long familiar; it is worth preserving both because it is philosophically more attractive than sensible intuitionism and because it is faithful to Kant's own words.

Literature

Kant

GMS   Grundlegung zur Metaphysik der Sitten, AA 4
KpV   Kritik der praktischen Vernunft, AA 5
KrV   Kritik der reinen Vernunft, AA 3 (B) and 4 (A)

English translations are taken from the series *The Cambridge Edition of the Works of Immanuel Kant*, Cambridge University Press (1992 ff.).
All page and line numbers in parentheses refer to the so-called Akademie-Ausgabe (AA), i.e., to *Kant's gesammelte Schriften*, herausgegeben von der *Königlich Preußischen Akademie der Wissenschaften*, Berlin: Walter de Gruyter (1900 ff.).

Secondary Literature

Audi, Robert (2001): "A Kantian Intuitionism." In: *Mind* 110/439, pp. 601–635.
Audi, Robert (2005): *The Good in the Right: A Theory of Intuition and Intrinsic Value*. Princeton NJ: Princeton University Press.
Bagnoli, Carla (2009): "The Appeal of Kantian Intuitionism." In: *European Journal of Philosophy* 17/1, pp. 152–158.
Schönecker, Dieter (2013a): "Das gefühlte Faktum der Vernunft. Skizze einer Interpretation und Verteidigung." In: *Deutsche Zeitschrift für Philosophie* 61/1, pp. 91–107.
Schönecker, Dieter (2013b): "Kant's Moral Intuitionism: The Fact of Reason and Moral Predispositions." In: *Kant Studies Online*, pp. 1–38.

Oliver Sensen
Kant's Constitutivism

Abstract In this paper, I argue that Kant is neither a realist nor an antirealist constructivist, as these two positions are usually understood. I first trace Kant's argument that morality must be grounded in autonomy, or in an a priori law of one's own reason. I then sketch why Kant's morality is not based on a value, and classify Kant's position in terms of contemporary distinctions. Kant's position is not moral realism, according to my view, because morality does not exist independently of an activity of (human) reason. On the other hand, Kant also does not adhere to a standard form of constructivism because morality is not based upon human desires – whether they be actual desires or desires one would have under an ideal perspective. Instead, morality is a necessary construction since the supreme moral law is constitutive of how reason operates. One is subject to the moral law independently of what one desires. I suggest calling this position 'transcendental constitutivism.'

* * *

Introduction

Kant's positions hardly ever fit neatly into one of the prominent dichotomies in philosophy.[1] For instance, one can ask: 'Is Kant a rationalist or empiricist, a compatibilist or an incompatibilist, a subjectivist or an objectivist?' In all of these cases the answer seems to be: 'neither,' and in this paper I shall argue that it is the same if one asks: 'Is Kant a moral realist or constructivist?'

Of course, terms such as 'realism' or 'antirealism' are used very differently in the literature, and some of these usages will fit Kant's position while others do not. But in its most distinctive form, moral realism postulates moral entities or properties that exist independently of any human stance,[2] i.e., independently of any human choices. Examples would be moral laws written in heaven, or non-natural properties that supervene upon natural properties: In this sense, to say that the environment has value would literally mean that there is a precious entity out there in nature. Kant, I will argue, rejects the idea that

---

1 Cf. Wood (1984, p. 73).
2 Cf. Shafer-Landau (2003, p. 15).

there is a moral reality independently of an activity of reason. On the other hand, he is also not clearly an antirealist, especially in the form that is most often ascribed to him (especially by John Rawls and several of his students): constructivism. According to many forms of constructivism, morality is *arbitrarily* created by human beings, and we could also change it at will. Kant does not believe that morality is up to our discretion, or based on deliberate human decisions. In these terms, Kant seems to be neither a realist nor an antirealist constructivist in ethics. But what, then, is his meta-ethical position, and how can we best classify it?

In the following I shall start with a positive account of Kant's meta-ethics, what I take to be Kant's central idea, his Categorical Imperative (Section 1). From there I shall look at alternative candidates that might be thought to ground his ethics: respect for persons (Section 2), value (Section 3), and dignity (Section 4), before I shall make a suggestion for how we should classify his position (Section 5). I have given several of these arguments – and reviewed the literature – more extensively elsewhere.[3] My aim here is to bring the results together, and reflect upon the proper classification of this position. Kant's position, I shall argue, is that morality is not a property, but an activity of reason, and since the activity is constitutive of pure reason, I shall call the position 'transcendental constitutivism.'

Section 1: The Categorical Imperative

What is Kant's main contribution to moral philosophy? What makes him distinctive in contrast to, for instance, Hume and Aristotle? I shall argue that Kant's central idea is an element that he borrows from his theoretical philosophy.[4] As an indication of my claim, consider the following: In 1781 Kant published the first edition of the *Critique of Pure Reason*. These 856 pages are followed by a popular introduction to the work, the *Prolegomena*, in 1783. Only then does he publish the *Groundwork to the Metaphysics of Morals*, which takes up 77 pages in the academy edition of his collected works, before going back to work on the second edition of the *Critique of Pure Reason*. In the first *Critique*, Kant argues for what he takes to be a radically new approach, and in the *Groundwork* he says that we have to apply the same idea (see below).

---

3 Cf. especially Sensen (2011, 2013, 2015).
4 For a similar approach see Rauscher (2015).

Kant seems to have believed that his new insight would solve moral problems as well.[5] What is this revolutionary approach?

The central point Kant wants to make in his *Critique of Pure Reason* is that human beings are not merely passive observers when they cognize the world. Kant argues that the mind is not just like a photo camera, trying to mirror as adequately as we can a ready-made world out there. Such a conception, Kant argues, cannot explain how we can know anything empirically, for we could not know whether our representations of things resemble those things outside of us: "If we treat outer objects as things in themselves, it is quite impossible to understand how we could arrive at a knowledge of their reality outside us, since we have to rely merely on the representation which is in us" (KrV: A378).[6] Kant is an indirect realist. We are not in direct contact with the world, but our knowledge of it is always mediated by mental representations. If we just have access to representations of the world, images of reality in our head, how do we know that the images resemble reality?

But the traditional conception of knowledge, according to which we passively represent a ready-made world, can also not explain how we could know anything of objects by pure thought, the traditional project of metaphysics. Kant's revolutionary proposal is that we are not merely passive observers in cognizing nature, but that our mind (partly) constitutes how reality appears to us. If our mind constitutes how reality appears to us, and we can identify this constitution, then we can know something of the appearance of objects prior to experience: "I do not see how we could know anything of the latter [objects][7] *a priori*; but if the object (as object of the senses) must conform to the constitution of our faculty of intuition, I have no difficulty in conceiving such a possibility" (KrV: Bxvii). The first *Critique* is Kant's attempt to work out this revolutionary approach: "We must therefore make trial whether we may not have more success in the tasks of metaphysics, if we suppose that objects must conform to our knowledge" (KrV: Bxvi).

The central task of the *Critique of Pure Reason* is to find and establish the elements we bring to cognition, and delineate what we can and cannot know. The elements include space and time as forms of intuition,[8] and categories such as substance and causality.[9] We can have objective and universal knowledge, e.g., in physics, because those elements are not gained by

---

5 Tom Hill suggested this way of understanding Kant's motivation for the *Groundwork* to me.
6 For the list of abbreviations of Kant's works, see the "Literature" section of this paper.
7 All insertions in square brackets by the author.
8 Cf. KrV: A41/B58.
9 Cf. KrV: A80/B106.

experience, but lie a priori in our epistemic faculties, and we all apply the same elements. Kant's argument is that experience could not yield necessity, for experience only proves that something is the case, not that it must be the case; likewise, experience cannot yield universality, it only provides a limited number of cases.[10] The only way that something can be necessary and universal knowledge is if it lies a priori in our cognitive faculties: "Necessity and strict universality are [...] secure indications of an *a priori* cognition" (KrV: B4). If we can demonstrate that an element of our cognition is necessary, e.g., that we need space to think of something as being distinct from us, we identify it as an a priori element of our cognition.

The crucial point is that Kant applies *the same basic idea* to morality.[11] Kant starts out the *Groundwork* by asking early on: "is it not thought to be of the utmost necessity to work out for once a pure moral philosophy, completely cleansed of everything empirical [...]?" (GMS: 389). The idea is that morality should be necessary, and universally valid, not just for human beings but even for all rational beings as such: "And how should laws of the determination of *our* will be taken as laws of the determination of the will of rational beings as such [...] if they were merely empirical and did not have their origin completely a priori in pure but practical reason?" (GMS: 408). In order to be valid for all rational beings, morality cannot be based upon our limited experience, but must be found in practical rationality itself which all rational beings share. As in his theoretical philosophy, he wants to find the a priori elements that already lie within reason, and he calls this enterprise 'metaphysics' too: "A metaphysics of morals is therefore indispensably necessary [...] for investigating the source of the practical basic principles that lie a priori in our reason" (GMS: 390).

But this metaphysics is not speculation about non-sensible objects, the kind of special metaphysics Kant wrote the 856 pages of the first *Critique* to reject. Rather it is a metaphysics of morals, and as in the general metaphysics of the *Critique of Pure Reason*, its aim is to find the a priori elements that already lie a priori in pure reason: "metaphysics [...] must measure out the whole sum of rational cognition of this kind" (GMS: 412). Therefore, "a system of a priori cognition from concepts alone is called *metaphysics*" (MS: 216). A metaphysics of morals is a system of a priori insights about morality.

---

[10] Cf. KrV: B3.
[11] The common idea is that there are a priori principles. But of course there is a different direction of fit: We use theoretical principles to cognize the world, practical principles to change the world. Theoretical principles constitute the world as it appears, moral principles prescribe how it should be. (I thank Elke E. Schmidt and Dieter Schönecker for prompting me to clarify the difference.)

It is crucial that this metaphysics does not aim to find non-sensible objects, but "to set forth in their generality (*in abstracto*) these concepts as they, along with the principles belonging to them, are fixed a priori" (GMS: 409). Kant's moral philosophy is therefore not based on any non-natural properties, but is merely concerned with the principle and commands reason produces out of itself: "such a completely isolated metaphysics of morals, mixed with no anthropology, theology, physics, or hyperphysics and still less with occult qualities (which could be called hypophysical), is [...] an indispensable substratum of all [...] cognition of duties" (GMS: 410). We already got a glimpse of his argument, that only such a system can ground a necessary and universal morality. Only if morality is not based on any hyperphysical (non-natural) properties one has to experience can morality "be firm even though there is nothing in heaven or on earth from which it depends or on which it is based" (GMS: 425). On Kant's account, there is nothing on heaven or earth which grounds morality, but it is an *activity* of reason: "all moral philosophy is based entirely on its pure part [...] [it] gives to him, as a rational being, laws a priori" (GMS: 389).

As in his theoretical philosophy, Kant therefore holds that a proposition can only be necessary and the same for all if it lies a priori in reason: "from what has been said it is clear that all moral concepts have their seat and origin completely a priori in reason, and indeed in the most common reason just as in reason that is speculative in the highest degree" (GMS: 411). But what does it mean that morality is grounded a priori in reason?

1.1 The Categorical Imperative as Supreme Practical Principle

The central concept of Kant's moral philosophy is – in accordance with what has just been said – an a priori law, the supreme moral principle, or (for human beings) the Categorical Imperative: "*act only in accordance with that maxim through which you can at the same time will that it become a universal law*" (GMS: 421). So what does it mean that this law is a priori? Where does it come from, and what is its basis? For instance, is it an insight of reason with which it discovers that universalizing is the best way to preserve peace and harmony among human beings? Or is it an a priori insight into a non-sensible order such as discovering that human beings have a value, and we therefore should universalize?

The crucial point is that this principle is not based on an insight, on discovering something else. It is an "a priori proposition that is not based on any intuition, either pure or empirical" (KpV: 31), but something "our own cognitive faculty [...] provides out of itself" (KrV: B2). Kant conceives of it as a direct command of reason, an activity of a capacity human beings have: "Pure reason [...] gives (to the human being) a universal law which we call the *moral law*" (KpV: 31), One can picture it like an innate idea, a principle we are already born with, and that already guides our reasoning prior to any discovery we make.

However, strictly speaking, Kant does not believe that the principle is innate either. Instead, "philosophy is to manifest its purity as sustainer of its own laws, not as herald of laws that an implanted sense or who knows what tutelary nature whispers to it, all of which [...] can still never yield basic principle that reason dictates and that must have their source entirely and completely a priori" (GMS: 426). The reason is that if the Categorical Imperative were an innate principle, implanted by a Creator or – we can add – internalized during the process of evolution, the moral imperatives would "lack the necessity that is essential to their concept." They would merely have a "subjective necessity, arbitrarily implanted in us" (KrV: B168). If one principle became innate over the process of evolution, a different principle would have been innate under different circumstances, and the Categorical Imperative would not be strictly necessary.

Instead, Kant says about a priori principles that they are "initially acquired" (ÜE: 222). The moral law makes itself heard "as soon as we draw up maxims of the will for ourselves" (KpV: 29). This means that reason comes up with the imperative itself, creates it spontaneously when it becomes active: "reason does not give in to those grounds which are empirically given, but with complete spontaneity it makes its own order according to ideas [...] according to which it even declares actions to be necessary" (KrV: A548/B576).

The idea that reason is the source of its own law is what Kant calls 'autonomy,' or: "the property [*Beschaffenheit*] of the will by which it is a law to itself" (GMS: 440). In the first instance, autonomy is a doctrine about the origin of principles. It describes that a priori principles arise out of a rational being's own faculty:

> In regard to the faculties of the soul in general, insofar as they are considered as higher faculties, i.e., as ones that contain an autonomy, the understanding is the one that contains the *constitutive* principles *a priori* for the *faculty of cognition* [...]; for the *faculty of desire* it is reason, which is practical without the mediation of any sort of pleasure. (KU: 196)

Kant argues that autonomy must be the ground of morality because only in this way can there be necessary and universal obligation: "*heteronomy* of choice, on the other hand, not only does not ground any obligation at all but is instead opposed to the principle of obligation and to the morality of the will" (KpV: 33). Why is that? Again, Kant starts out from the general view of what morality is like. We hold morality to be necessary and universal: "Everyone must grant that a law, if it is to hold morally, that is, as a ground of an obligation, must carry with it absolute necessity; that [...] the command [...] does not hold only for human beings, as if other rational beings did not have to heed it" (GMS: 389). He then argues that *all* other groundings of the moral law yield heteronomy, and that heteronomy cannot ground obligation. Why do all other theories yield heteronomy?

The idea is that all other ways of grounding the moral law would be dependent upon a desire in order to motivate us to comply with the law. But if we are following our desires, it is "nature that gives the law" (GMS: 444), and we are not following our own law, but a law of nature: heteronomy. But why are all other theories based upon desires? The reason is that "if one thought of him only as subject to a law (whatever it may be), this law had to carry with it some interest by way of attraction or constraint, since it did not as a law arise from *his* will; in order to conform with the law, his will had instead to be constrained by *something else* to act in a certain way" (GMS: 432f.). If the law comes from God or society, then one would need to be motivated by hope or fear "of power and vengefulness" (GMS: 443) of the lawgiver. If one sees morality as based on feelings of happiness or moral sentiments, the theories are by definition based on feelings. But why can a feeling not ground morality?

The reason is that feelings are relative and contingent, they "by nature differ infinitely from one another in degree," and therefore cannot "furnish a uniform standard of good and evil" (GMS: 443).[12] Therefore, Kant holds that – whoever wants morality to be necessary and universal – must agree with his account of the source of the moral law: "By explicating the generally received concept of morality we showed only that an autonomy of the will unavoidably [...] lies at its basis. Thus whoever holds morality to be something [...] must also admit the principle of morality brought forward" (GMS: 445).[13]

So far, this is only a conditional justification. *If* one wants morality to be necessary and universal, it must be grounded in autonomy. But is there more to be said? Can one also show that there really is such a law, and can one explain why reason comes up with this law and not another? Why does reason put forth this law, and does it? As in his theoretical philosophy, Kant's answer is indirect. We do not know why reason comes up with this law: "all human insight is at an end as soon as we have arrived at basic powers or basic faculties" (KpV:

---

[12] One could object that the feeling of respect for the moral law is an exception. But, first, it is not clear whether it is a feeling at all, cf. Zinkin (2006) and Schadow (2012), but, second, Kant explicitly denies that it discovers or grounds the moral law (cf. TL: 399f., MM II: 625–627). The only thing it lets us discover is whether our own motives are pure (cf. KpV: 91f.).
[13] For a more thorough discussion of the previous, see Sensen (2013).

47). But what we can do is to look for elements that are necessary – as he did for time, space, substance and causality, among others, in the *Critique of Pure Reason:* "We can become aware of pure practical laws just as we are aware of pure theoretical principles, by attending to the necessity with which reason prescribes them to us" (KpV: 30). If an element is necessary, it is a priori.[14]

In order to support his claim that we can become aware of a necessary principle, Kant presents the following example of the 'gallows.' Imagine a prince demands that you give false testimony against an innocent and honorable man, who would then lose his life. Imagine further that no desire speaks in favor of the moral action: If you refuse, you and your family will be punished, you will lose your influence at court, along with everything you hold dear, including your life, and so on. Similarly, suppose you do not believe in an afterlife, that you do not expect a revolution to follow upon your demise, and that you are not a person who desires to be moral etc. Kant assumes that – even if no desire speaks in favor of refusing to give false testimony – everyone will judge the action to be morally wrong; the man is innocent after all.

But Kant does not introduce the gallows example to make the case that everyone has a direct knowledge of what is right and wrong, and that it does not need any further evidence. Rather he uses it to prove freedom, and grounds morality on freedom. His point is that the judgment about the wrongness of the action lets one discover that one *could* refuse to give false testimony. The agent "must admit without hesitation that it would be possible for him" (KpV: 30). If this is the case, then one assumes that one could act independently of one's desires – since one has assumed that *no* desire speaks in favor of the action – and determining oneself independently of desires is freedom. The moral judgment therefore lets one discover that one assumes freedom: "He judges, therefore, that he can do something because he is aware that he ought to do it and cognizes freedom within" (KpV: 30).

In the next step of the argument, Kant uses the assumption of freedom to justify morality. Freedom is considered to be a causality, and Kant sees laws as an essential feature of causality: "the concept of causality brings with it that of laws" (GMS: 446). The only law that could be a law of freedom (understood as independence from desires) is one that abstracts from all desires and ends adopted on account of desires. What remains is the mere form of the law, which demands universality and is the same as the Categorical Imperative: "what, then, can freedom of the will be other than autonomy, that is […] to act on no other maxim than that which can also have as object itself as universal law.

---

14 Cf. again KrV: B3f.

This, however, is precisely the formula of the categorical imperative" (GMS: 446 f.; cf. GMS: 402, KpV: 29).[15]

1.2 The End in Itself Objection

One could object against what I have said so far that it is contradicted by the *Groundwork* passage leading up to the Formula of Humanity,[16] where Kant says: "The ground of this principle is: *rational nature exists as an end in itself*" (GMS: 428 f.), and where he draws a parallel, saying that relative ends ground hypothetical imperatives, while an end in itself – something whose existence has an absolute worth[17] – grounds a categorical imperative. Does this not introduce a very different justification, in which a value of human beings grounds the Categorical Imperative?

It is not clear that it does. For the passage can be read in very different ways, and does not necessarily contradict the interpretation given above. First, the passage does not specify in which sense an end in itself grounds the Categorical Imperative. For instance, does Kant talk about a metaphysical grounding relation, a justifying or motivating ground? Second, and more importantly, the passage does not explain what exactly is meant by 'end in itself.' It does not, for instance, specify 'end in itself' as a hyperphysical value property, but it seems that such a conception would be needed in order to contradict my previous interpretation. Third, if one looks beyond this particular *Groundwork* passage, it seems that 'end in itself' has a much more innocent meaning, and actually supports the reading I gave above. Here is why.[18]

If a few lines of text do not specify what Kant means by 'end in itself,' and in which sense it is supposed to be the ground of the Categorical Imperative, then one has to look at other passages in order to clarify the concepts, and one has to look at the wider context of the passage, i.e., the question Kant wants to address. What is his question? The passage about ends in themselves begins right after Kant's discussion of the Formula of Law of Nature and its examples. Kant says that he has shown that duty must be expressed in a categorical imperative, but that he has not yet shown whether there really is such an imperative.[19] He goes on: "The question therefore is this: is it a necessary law *for all rational*

---

15 For a more detailed defense of this interpretation, see Sensen (2015).
16 See GMS: 427–429.
17 I will discuss Kant's usage of 'absolute value' in Section 3 below.
18 I defend the following answer much more fully in Sensen (2011, pp. 96–113).
19 Cf. GMS: 425.

beings always to appraise their actions in accordance with such maxims as they themselves could will to serve as universal laws?" (GMS: 426) In other words: The question is whether we have reason to assume that the Categorical Imperative is a necessary law for every rational being.

Kant goes on to say that in order to answer this question one has to demonstrate a priori that the principle is connected with the concept of a will of a rational being as such. This is why he must make a step into metaphysics, i.e., the a priori connections between moral concepts (see above). If one can demonstrate that the Categorical Imperative follows a priori from the concept of a rational will, then every rational being is under this law. The connection between rational nature and the imperative is that rational nature exists as an end in itself: "The ground of this principle is: *rational nature exists as an end in itself*" (GMS: 428 f.). But how and why is this the case?

Kant immediately continues by saying that a human being necessarily regards himself as an end in itself, and – since there is the connection between an end in itself and the imperative – the imperative is therefore a subjective principle for this human being. "But every other rational being also represents his existence in this way consequent on just the same rational ground that also holds for me;* thus it is at the same time an *objective* principle" (GMS: 429). In the footnote Kant says that he will give the reasons for this claim in the third section of the *Groundwork*. There he argues that everyone has to regard him- or herself as free, and that freedom is the ground of the Categorical Imperative.[20] Could it be that 'end in itself' means 'freedom'?

This is how Kant himself specifies it: "as an end in itself [...] – as free with respect to all laws of nature, obeying only those which he himself gives" (GMS: 435). Kant expresses this connection more clearly in the lectures *Naturrecht Feyerabend*.[21] In virtue of freedom one is not just determined by laws of nature, one is not a means to the end of another (nature), but is oneself an end. This is the descriptive content of the expression 'end in itself.' An end in itself possesses freedom. Now the expression also has a normative component. What is an end in itself should be treated as an end in itself. But this is not a self-standing argument. It might be a popular shorthand argument in certain times and circumstances.[22] But try to make the same argument in another contexts: 'What is a desk should be treated as a desk,' or 'what is a roach should be treated as a roach.' What does this mean? It is not self-explanatory, but any

---

20 Cf. GMS: 446–448.
21 Cf. NF: 1320, 1322.
22 On this see Bacin (2015).

such statement would rely on a suppressed premise. (Kant's premise, I hold, is the Categorical Imperative.)

We can now go back to the *Groundwork* passage. If one substitutes 'freedom' for 'end in itself,' the sentence reads loosely: 'The ground of this principle is: *rational nature possesses freedom*.' I have to regard myself as free, and since freedom is the ground of the Categorical Imperative, the imperative is a subjective law for me. But since I have to lend the idea of freedom to every other rational being also, the imperative is at the same time a principle for all rational beings. This was the question Kant meant to answer. The end in itself passage therefore does not introduce a hyperphysical value – as Kant has said we are not permitted to introduce – nor does it contradict the story given above. Freedom is a causality, every causality needs a law; the law of freedom abstracts from all matter, so only the form of the law remains.[23] The moral law is therefore a descriptive law of purely rational beings: It describes how their reason functions. Only to beings that can be tempted by inclinations does this law appear as an imperative: "this 'ought' is strictly speaking a 'will' that holds for every rational being under the condition that reason in him is practical without hindrance" (GMS: 449).

The Categorical Imperative is a direct command, an action, of our pure reason.

Section 2: Respect for Persons

If one takes a step back from the *Groundwork* for a moment – since it employs a unique method by beginning with common moral cognition rather than starting with it's real foundation – what I have said so far should not be surprising. Whenever Kant explains his own theory directly: in the third section of the *Groundwork*, in the section on prior concepts to the *Metaphysics of Morals*,[24] his theory and practice essay 'On the Common Saying,' as well as his *Lectures on Ethics*, the key concepts are 'Categorical Imperative,' 'duty,' and 'freedom,' not 'respect for persons,' 'value,' or 'dignity.' It is a combination of factors that made Kant scholars turn away from the first three concepts: a sense that

---

23 Postulating freedom does not contradict Kant's exclusion of hyperphysical properties for two reasons: (1) He never says that we can know freedom; we are merely justified in assuming it for practical purposes, i.e., in order to act: 'Ought implies Can'; (2) in virtue of being a causality, freedom is a relation: "if A, then B," not an intrinsic property. (I thank Elke Schmidt and Dieter Schönecker for raising this objection.)
24 See MS: 221–228.

the Categorical Imperative itself is empty, the worry that it rests on a panicky metaphysics, and in general the fear that it is too cold and abstract. I believe that all these charges can be met,[25] but my aim here is to interpret Kant's views that these other concepts: respect for persons, value, and dignity, are not foundational, but play important roles in spelling out the Categorical Imperative. I shall start with respect for persons.

If one holds that persons should be respected, it is natural to believe that this requirement is grounded in what the other is like.[26] However, Kant often surprises, and turns our common understanding around by proposing a revolution, and this is also the case here, as I shall argue. The first thing to notice is that he employs two notions of respect. One is the moral feeling of respect for the law that is so familiar from the first section of the *Groundwork* and the third chapter of the *Critique of Practical Reason*. It is a feeling of esteem that appears involuntarily if one is confronted with an example of a morally good will: "before a humble common man in whom I perceive uprightness of character in a higher degree than I am aware of in myself *my spirit bows*, whether I want it or whether I do not" (KpV: 76f.). Kant calls this form of respect "*reverentia*" (TL: 436).

But this is different from the "*respect* to be shown to others," which is "not to be understood as the mere *feeling* that comes from comparing our own *worth* with another's" but is a "*maxim* of limiting our self-esteem" (TL: 449). Kant calls this form of respect "*observantia*" (TL: 462), or "respect in a practical sense" (TL: 449).[27] Respect in this sense is therefore a maxim one should adopt of "not exalting oneself above others" (TL: 450), of not thinking of oneself as something better. Why should one adopt this maxim?

Kant says that it is commanded by the Formula of Humanity: "The duty of respect for my neighbor is contained in the maxim not to degrade any other to a mere means to my ends" (TL: 450). This formula runs: "*So act that you use humanity, in your own person as well as in the person of any other, always at the same time as an end, never merely as a means*" (GMS: 429). But what is important to note is that this is a *categorical* imperative too. The command is always valid, and independently of what one wants. In virtue of being a categorical imperative, it too must rest on a direct a priori command of one's own reason: "This principle of humanity [...] is not borrowed from experience

---

[25] Cf. Sensen (2014 and 2015).
[26] Cf. Watkins/FitzPatrick (2002).
[27] The two forms of respect correspond to what Darwall calls "appraisal" and "recognition respect" (cf. Darwall 1977).

[...] because of its universality [...] so that the principle must arise from pure reason" (GMS: 430 f.). Strict universality is a sure sign of an a priori principle.[28]

Kant states explicitly that he puts forth the Formula of Humanity as "tantamount" and "at bottom the same as the basic principle" (GMS: 437 f.):

> For to say that in the use of means to any end I am to limit my maxim to the condition of its universal validity as a law for every subject [Formula of Universal Law] is tantamount to saying that the subject of ends, i.e. the rational being itself, must be made the foundation of all maxims of actions, never merely as a means, but as the supreme limiting condition in the use of all means, i.e. always at the same time as an end [Formula of Humanity]. (GMS: 438)

He explains why they are tantamount in the following passage from the second *Critique:*

> [...] every will [...] is restricted to the condition of agreement with the *autonomy* of the rational being, that is to say, such a being is not to be subjected to any purpose that is not possible in accordance with a law that could arise from the will of the affected subject himself; hence this subject is to be used never merely as a means but as at the same time an end. (KpV: 87)

If I should be able to will that my maxim could become a universal law, I should not act on a maxim that could not spring from the will of another, as this law would not be universal. One therefore respects another as equal if one does not act on a non-universalizable maxim. In other words: The main formulation of the Categorical Imperative commands not to make an exception for oneself to a law one recognizes as objectively necessary.[29] The second formulation demands not to exalt oneself above others.[30] In order to follow Kant's directive that the two are meant to be the same, one has to interpret him as proposing that one exalts oneself above others if one makes an exception for oneself (laws are for others, one does not have to obey them), and that when one makes an exception for oneself, one is thereby exalting oneself above others. The central content of the two is the same, even if they provide two different methods for deriving particular duties.

But what is important for our purposes is that Kant's views on respect for persons (*observantia*) do not introduce a separate justification of morality. One should respect others because it is commanded by a law of one's own reason:

---

28 Cf. again KrV: B3f.
29 See GMS: 424.
30 See TL: 450.

> For I can recognize that I am under obligation to others only insofar as I at the same time put myself under obligation, since the law by virtue of which I regard myself under obligation [the Categorical Imperative] proceeds in every case from my own practical reason; and in being constrained by my own reason, I am also the one constraining myself. (TL: 417 f.)

Even the requirement to respect others is in the first instance a command of my own reason. This means that Kant places duties prior to rights. The duty of the agent to respect someone is prior to the right of the victim:

> But why is the doctrine of morals usually called (especially by Cicero) a doctrine of *duties* and not also a doctrine of *rights*, even though rights have reference to duties? – The reason is that we know our own freedom (from which all moral laws, and so all rights as well as duties proceed) only through the *moral imperative*, which is a proposition commanding duty, from which the capacity for putting others under obligation, that is, the concept of right, can afterwards be explicated. (MS: 239)

What this means is that a victim can claim a right by reminding the agent of *his* duty which his own reason lays on him:

> [...] the other, having a right to do so, confronts the subject with his duty, i.e., the moral law by which he ought to act. If this confrontation makes an impression on the agent, he determines his will by an Idea of reason, creates through his reason that conception of his duty which already lay previously within him, and is only quickened by the other, and determines himself according to the moral law. (MSV: 521)

The Formula of Humanity, and the requirement to respect others, therefore do not rest on different foundations. According to Kant, they follow from the same a priori law laid out in Section 1 above.

Section 3: Value

In my discussion of the *Groundwork* passage that leads up to the Formula of Humanity (in Section 1.2), I postponed the discussion of value. However, does Kant not say in that passage that the Categorical Imperative is grounded in an absolute worth of human beings? The passage runs: "But suppose there were something the *existence of which in itself* has an absolute worth [...] then in it [...] would lie the ground of a possible categorical imperative" (GMS: 428). Later he says that "without it nothing of *absolute worth* would be found anywhere; but if all worth were conditional [...] then no supreme practical principle [...] could be found anywhere" (GMS: 428). So does this mean that all human beings possess an absolute value property that grounds the Categorical Imperative?

What is value? In order to be a distinctive claim that offers a different picture from the one I gave above (in Section 1), it is not enough to say that value is what we in fact do value, based on our preferences. Preferences differ, and do not yield a necessary and universal morality (see above). It is also not enough to say value is something that we should value – since then one needs a different account of why one should value other human beings. Finally, if one does not believe that value is simply identical with a natural property (such as pleasure or health etc.), then one needs to conceive of value as a non-natural or hyperphysical property. Kant might conceive of value as a "transcendental kernel" (Rosen 2012, p. 31).

However, the *Groundwork* passage does not specify absolute worth as a hyperphysical property all human beings possess. There is no passage in Kant's works that specifies value in this way. But there are unmistakably explicit passages that support my view that Kant cannot conceive of value this way. In this section I argue for four claims: (1) Kant rejects the idea of hyperphysical properties; (2) he does not believe that all human beings have an absolute worth; (3) he positively construes value differently, and (4) he gives an argument that rules out that value as such a property could ground morality.[31]

(1) Even in the *Groundwork* Kant rules out that there are any hyperphysical properties that ground morality.[32] Kant puts it more strongly in the first *Critique* where he sums up his results by saying: "we cannot cook up [...] a single object with any new and not empirically given property [...]. Thus we are not allowed to think up any sort of new original forces, e. g., an understanding that is capable of intuition of its object without sense" (KrV: A770/B798). Kant would be schizophrenic to rule out such properties in 1781, to repeat the rejection at the beginning of the *Groundwork* passage, and then to postulate the opposite two pages later, before forgetting about it in the third section of the book, and repeating that we cannot assume such properties in 1787. But this is not all. There are at least three other reasons why he does not put forth such a conception.

(2) The second reason why I believe that Kant does not put a hyperphysical value at the foundation of his morality is that he does not ascribe an absolute value to all human beings as such, but only to a good will. Kant famously opens the first section of the *Groundwork* by saying: "It is impossible to think

---

31 On Kant's conception of value see also Horn (2014, pp. 98–110).
32 Cf. again GMS: 410, 425.

of anything at all in the world, or indeed even beyond it, that could be considered good without limitation except a *good will*" (GMS: 393). This is not an isolated passage where what once seems impossible later becomes the norm. Instead, we find the same message expressed throughout his work, for instance, in the *Critique of the Powers of Judgment:* "Only through that which he does without regard to enjoyment [...] does he give his being as the existence of a person an absolute value" (KU: 208, similarly 443). Human beings do not possess an absolute value, but they acquire it by their actions:

> Thus good or evil is, strictly speaking, referred to actions [...], and if anything is to be good or evil absolutely (and in every respect and without any further condition), [...] it would be only the way of acting, the maxim of the will, and consequently the acting person himself [...], but not a thing. (KpV: 60)

Therefore not everyone has an absolute worth. There are human beings who appear to be unworthy: "I cannot deny all respect to even a vicious man as a human being; [...] even though by his deeds he makes himself unworthy of it" (TL: 463). What this suggests is that value is not the reason why one should respect others. Think about it: (i) Only a good will has absolute value;[33] (ii) not all human beings have a good will,[34] but (iii) all human beings should be respected.[35] Value is not the reason why one should respect others.[36]

But even if one agrees with me so far, one could argue that a good will creates a hyperphysical value property, and that Kant understands value this way.[37] I believe that this extra step is not necessary (it is not clear what is gained by it), and it seems to be ruled out by the same passages I quoted under (1). But Kant also says that the good will "consists just in the principle of action being

---

33 See GMS: 393.
34 See TL: 463.
35 See GMS: 429.
36 But if 'absolute value' means 'should be pursued unconditionally,' does this not mean that (iii) could be reformulated as "all human beings have an absolute value," thereby leading to a contradiction with (i)? (I thank Elke Schmidt and Dieter Schönecker for this objection.) This is not the case because they would mean the same, and then there is no contradiction. However, the argument still demonstrates that value is not the foundation of moral requirements, and this is my point here.
37 Cf. Bojanowski (2015). As I understand it, Patrick Kain would argue that value is prior to morality, Schmidt/Schönecker that it is simultaneous with the moral law, and Bojanowski that it follows from a good will. However, the question is always the same: What is this value ontologically, where does Kant specify it this way, and how does this fit with passages where he seems to rule out that value is a separate property?

free from all influences of contingent grounds" (GMS: 426, cf. 437). He does not seem to add a hyperphysical property.

(3) But what, then, is the meaning of 'good' or 'value' for Kant? He does use these concepts, and they must have a function even if they are not the name for a hyperphysical property. It seems to me that Kant is a prescriptivist about value. On this view, 'good' is another way of saying what reason deems necessary: "the will is a capacity to choose *only that* which reason [...] cognizes as practically necessary, that is, as good" (GMS: 412). To put it differently: Under an ontological X-ray, the only thing one sees is a prescription of reason. There is no additional value property. There are rational beings, and those cognize something as necessary and usher prescriptions. If reason cognizes something as necessary as a means, e.g., to take a plane if one wants to get to Australia quickly, then it ushers a hypothetical imperative. But if it commands something as necessary under all circumstances, e.g., not to treat someone as mere means, then it commands categorically:

> Since every practical law represents a possible action as good [...], all imperatives are formulae for the determination of action that is [...] good in some way. Now, if the action would be good merely as a means *to something else* the imperative is *hypothetical*; if the action is represented as *in itself* good, hence as necessary in a will in itself conforming to reason, as its principle, *then it is categorical.* (GMS: 414)

To use an expression such as 'is good' or 'has value' is therefore a shorthand for saying that reason judges something to be necessary. To add that it has 'absolute' or 'inner' value is to say that reason judges the action to be necessary under all circumstances, and independently of one's inclinations: "The word *absolute* is now more often used merely to indicate that something is valid of a thing considered *in itself* and thus *internally [innerlich]*" (KrV: A324/B381). Absolute value therefore does not exist independently of the moral law which commands absolutely: "For, nothing can have a worth other than that which the law determines for it" (GMS: 436).

This view is confirmed if one looks at my final point, that Kant argues that no value could be the foundation of morality.

(4) Kant does not even discuss a theory according to which value is a hyperphysical property under the heading of "all possible" moral theories.[38] But he gives an argument that rules out that *any* value could be the ground of morality. The argument is similar to the one I discussed in Section 1 above.[39]

---

38 Cf. KpV: 39 f., GMS: 440–444.
39 For a more thorough discussion see Sensen (2011, pp. 14–52).

Imagine that we want to defend the view that there are non-natural, hyperphysical value properties that ground morality. How could we know such properties? Kant argues that all knowledge begins with the senses.[40] So, if the value is not a physical property one can discover with the five senses, the only sense left is a feeling: "If the concept of the good is not to be derived from an antecedent practical law but, instead, is to serve as its basis, it can be only the concept of something whose existence promises pleasure" (KpV: 58). But feelings are relative and contingent and cannot ground a universal and necessary moral law, as we conceive of morality: "From the feeling of a sensation that may be different in every creature, no generally valid law can be derived for all thinking beings, and that is how the moral principle must be constituted" (MM II: 625).

Kant's result is that – paradoxically as it sounds – it is not a value that grounds the moral law: "*the concept of good and evil must not be determined before the moral law [...] but only [...] after it and by means of it*" (KpV: 62f.). This is not a statement that appears within a minor discussion about a tiny aspect of valuing, but it concerns the most fundamental question of method, and ties it back explicitly to his argument of autonomy: "This remark, which concerns only the method of ultimate moral investigation, is important [...] all the errors of philosophers [...] they should first have searched for a law that determined the will a priori and immediately [...] their principle was in every case heteronomy" (KpV: 64).

So if Kant uses an expression such as 'has absolute inner value,' we cannot assume that he has a hyperphysical property in mind. Value is dependent upon the Categorical Imperative,[41] the account I gave in Section 1 still stands.

Section 4: Dignity

The same objection against my interpretation that has been raised in terms of value could be raised in terms of dignity. Is it not the case that one should

---

[40] Cf. KrV: B1.
[41] Notice that this is even true for the *Groundwork* passage that leads up to the Formula of Humanity. There Kant says that if nothing of absolute worth would be *found*, then no imperative *could be found* (cf. GMS: 428). This passage talks about an epistemic relation. But this is compatible with the law being the metaphysical ground of value: 'If there is a Categorical Imperative, then there is value. Now no value is found, therefore no Categorical Imperative is found.' This *Modus Tollens* confirms my interpretation.

respect others because they have a dignity?⁴² Here I will confine myself to brief remarks.⁴³ Kant sometimes seems to equate 'dignity' and 'unconditional worth,' when, for instance, he uses expressions such as: "In the kingdom of ends everything has either a *price*, or a *dignity*. [...] inner worth, i.e. *dignity* [...] dignity, i.e. unconditional, incomparable worth" (GMS: 434–436). However, as we have seen above (in Section 3), absolute worth is not the ground of moral requirements, including the requirement to respect others. So even if Kant were to use 'dignity' and 'absolute value' interchangeably, this would not prove that he intends to ground morality this way. But Kant's usage of 'dignity' is even more complicated than that.

First, Kant uses 'dignity' in all sorts of contexts. He talks about the "dignity of mathematics" (KrV: A464/B492), the "dignity of a teacher" (Rel: 162), or the "dignity of a monarch" (SF: 19). All these have dignity, but only a good will has absolute value,⁴⁴ therefore 'dignity' does not mean 'value' in these instances. Furthermore, if dignity were to mean 'absolute value,' then we all would need to study mathematics, become teachers and monarchs. How to explain this? The answer, I believe, is that Kant uses an older concept of dignity. Notice that he often specifies it with the Latin *dignitas*: "dignity (*dignitas interna*)" (TL: 436), "*dignity (dignitas)*" (TL: 462), and he explicitly endorses what he takes to be a Stoic conception of dignity.⁴⁵ What is the older conception of dignity?

In the Roman conception of *dignitas*, the term described a rank (as well as the qualification to occupy that rank, and the esteem one might get from observers). It is a relational term that expresses that one thing is higher than another on a certain scale. In this sense a monarch can be elevated over his subjects in terms of power, mathematics over other disciplines in terms of being more purely a priori, and a teacher in the classroom. Notice that none of these instances are moral examples. The term '*dignitas*' by itself is not a moral term.⁴⁶

Now, one could object that Kant uses a different notion of dignity in the *Groundwork* passage on dignity and price (GMS: 434–436), as well as in the passage on the duty against false humility (TL: 434–436). Maybe in those passages he defines 'dignity' as an absolute value. The problem with this thesis is that even in those contexts Kant specifies dignity as "prerogative" (GMS: 438), and "sublimity" (GMS: 440), which are again relational terms of rank and

---

42 Cf. TL: 462.
43 For an extensive discussion see Sensen (2011).
44 Cf. GMS: 393.
45 Cf. Rel: 57, note.
46 Cf. Sensen (2011, pp. 152–164).

distinction. Furthermore, if one takes the contexts of these passages into account, and focuses on the question Kant wants to answer, it becomes clear that he is not trying to ground morality in a hyperphysical value.

In the first passage of these passages on dignity (GMS: 434–436) Kant asks why a morally good being obeys the Formula of Autonomy, and the answer is that one does not do it out of inclinations or in order to get an advantage, but out of the dignity of morality. Kant asks again: "what is it, then, that justifies a morally good disposition [...] in making such high claims?" (GMS: 435) In other words, the passage is not about the respect owed to others (*observantia*), but the "immediate respect" (*reverentia*) one feels for a morally good will. It is a question about the proper moral motivation. Now it could be that Kant introduces a new version of dignity (out of the 111 times Kant uses the term, only seven appear next to 'value'), but this reading would miss what this passage is about. Kant wants to say that one should be moral because moral value is "raised above all price" (GMS: 434), and 'dignity' is exactly the term he uses to express that something is elevated in this way.[47]

The second passage on dignity (TL: 434–436) is also about "*reverentia*" (TL: 436). It concerns the respect one feels for the moral aspect that is within oneself. It is not a question of why one should respect others (*observantia*), but Kant argues that one should not lower oneself into servility towards others. The reason is that one is equally capable as anyone else to acquire what is of absolute value, namely a good will. Therefore one should not lower oneself into servile spirit, or compare one's non-moral merits with others, but esteem the moral aspects within and aim for a good will.[48]

Finally, there is a third passage in which Kant might be said to base the requirement to respect others on a dignity they possess (TL: 462). However, in that passage Kant immediately goes on to make dignity dependent upon the requirement to respect others. He says: "Humanity itself is a dignity; for a human being cannot be used merely as a means [...] but must always be used at the same time as an end. It is just in this that his dignity (personality) consists, by which he raises himself [...] over all *things*" (TL: 462). Notice that what Kant wants to express is that human beings are raised over things, and that they are raised because – "for" – they should be respected, not that they should be respected because they have dignity. The reason why one should respect others, we have seen (see Sections 1 and 2), is that it is commanded by the Categorical Imperative.

---

[47] For a longer defense of this claim see Sensen (2011, pp. 180–191).
[48] For a more textual discussion see Sensen (2011, pp. 192–202).

Section 5: Kant's Constitutivism

I therefore conclude that the basis of Kant's moral philosophy is an a priori law of one's own reason. It is an activity of reason, something reason does spontaneously and out of itself (not something it discovers) that grounds morality. How would one classify such a position?

I shall start with a contemporary proposal by Russ Shafer-Landau.[49] He distinguishes three possible metaphysical theories: (1) nihilism: there is no morality, (2) constructivism: morality is constructed by human beings, and (3) moral realism: morality exists independently of any particular human stance.[50] He then divides constructivism into three further possibilities: Morality might be constructed by the preferences of one human being: subjectivism (2.1); it might be constructed by the conscious decision of a group of people: relativism (2.2), or it might be what is consciously endorsed from an ideal standpoint, such as a standpoint of impartiality or from behind a veil of ignorance: ideal contract theories (2.3).[51]

However, Kant's position as I have characterized it does not seem to fit into any of the contemporary alternatives.[52] Kant is not a nihilist (1), for he believes that morality exists. He is also not a moral realist (3) in the sense defined here, since morality would not exist independently of the standpoint of pure reason. So, for Kant morality is dependent upon a particular human stance. But it is also not constructed consciously, whether by one person, many people, or under ideal conditions (2). This can be brought out with Shafer-Landau's objection against constructivism. He poses a Euthyphro-style dilemma against constructivism, and particularly 2.3.[53] If one assumes that morality is constructed under ideal conditions, the ideal conditions are either moral in nature, or they are not. If they are not moral requirements, then there should not be any expectation that the results will have a moral quality, the ideal standpoint might endorse genocide, or reject that one need to help others. But, Shafer-Landau asserts, if the ideal conditions are moralized, then they are dependent upon an external morality, and this would be Realism (3).

However, the argument is not sound since there is a neglected alternative. It could be that the ideal conditions are moral in nature, but that the moral stan-

---

49 Cf. Shafer-Landau (2003).
50 Cf. Shafer-Landau (2003, pp. 15–17).
51 Cf. Shafer-Landau (2003, pp. 41–45).
52 Verbal confirmation by Shafer-Landau.
53 Cf. Shafer-Landau (2003, pp. 41–43).

dard does not originate in an outside moral reality. For if it is commanded by one's own pure reason to take up the ideal standpoint, e.g., to ask yourself whether you could will your maxim as a universal law, then the moral standard does not depend upon an external reality independently of a human stance. Rather it is generated by a human (rational) stance, namely a law of one's own reason. Without the existence of pure reason, there would not be any morality. But pure reason generates a *moral* requirement.

I therefore propose a different classification of moral theories that includes the Kantian position sketched above. My model works with a set of binaries. One can ask: 'Does morality exist?' If one says 'no,' one is a nihilist (i); if one answers 'yes,' it leads to a new question. The new question is: 'Is morality constructed by humans (or rational beings in general)?' If one answers 'no,' one is a moral realist (ii); 'yes' leads to the next question: 'Is it constructed by more than one person?' 'No': subjectivism (iii), 'yes' specifies constructivism further: 'Is morality constructed under ideal conditions?' 'No': relativism (iv), 'yes' distinguishes Kant from contract theories: 'Is it pre-consciously dictated by one's own reason?' 'No': contract theories (v), 'yes': Kant. This model can be further refined as needed, but it makes room for the Kantian position within the contemporary framework.

According to my interpretation, Kant holds a particular form of constructivism. Morality is the result of something pure reason does. Without it, there is no morality on his view. But it is not a form of constructivism many realists would object to. Because it is not an arbitrary construction, and one cannot change moral commands at will. Pure reason dictates the moral law independently of what one wants. It is a principle that is constitutive of how pure reason operates.[54] I therefore propose to label Kant's position 'constitutivism.'

However, there are several possible versions of constitutivism as well. Christine Korsgaard has proposed that there cannot be a particularist willing, but that in order to want anything at all, one has to follow the Categorical Imperative, and that this further implies that one has to respect others.[55] However, on my reading of Kant, the Categorical Imperative is not constitutive of an empirical willing. One can consciously and responsibly choose an immoral action. But hopefully this person "still has enough conscience to ask himself" (GMS: 422) whether the action is morally right. The Categorical Imperative is only constitutive of pure reason, which is the background check once we draw

---

54 Cf. KU: 196f.
55 Cf. Korsgaard (2009).

up maxims for ourselves,[56] but it is not involved in our empirical willing. One could say that it is constitutive of the (pure practical) will [*Wille*], not choice [*Willkür*].

In order to distinguish my interpretation from Korsgaard's, I will classify Kant's position as 'transcendental constitutivism.'[57]

Literature

Kant

GMS Grundlegung zur Metaphysik der Sitten, AA 4
NF   Naturrecht Feyerabend, AA 27
KpV Kritik der praktischen Vernunft, AA 5
KrV Kritik der reinen Vernunft, AA 3 (B) and 4 (A)
KU   Kritik der Urteilskraft, AA 5
MM II Moral Mrongovius II, AA 29
MS   Die Metaphysik der Sitten, AA 6 (*Vorrede* und *Einleitung in die Metaphysik der Sitten*, 205–228)
MSV Metaphysik der Sitten Vigilantius, AA 27
Rel Die Religion innerhalb der Grenzen der bloßen Vernunft, AA 6
SF   Der Streit der Fakultäten, AA 7
TL   Metaphysische Anfangsgründe der Tugendlehre, AA 6
ÜE   Über eine Entdeckung, nach der alle neue Kritik der reinen Vernunft durch eine ältere entbehrlich gemacht werden soll, AA 8

English translations are taken from the series *The Cambridge Edition of the Works of Immanuel Kant*, Cambridge University Press (1992 ff.).
All page and line numbers in parentheses refer to the so-called Akademie-Ausgabe (AA), i.e., to *Kant's gesammelte Schriften*, herausgegeben von der *Königlich Preußischen Akademie der Wissenschaften*, Berlin: Walter de Gruyter (1900 ff.).

Secondary Literature

Bacin, Stefano (2015): "Kant's Idea of Human Dignity: Between Tradition and Originality." In: *Kant-Studien* 106, pp. 97–106.
Bojanowski, Jochen (2015): "Kant on Human Dignity." In: *Kant-Studien* 106, pp. 78–87.
Darwall, Stephen L. (1977): "Two Kinds of Respect." In: *Ethics* 88/1, pp. 36–49.

---

56 Cf. again KpV: 29.
57 I would like to thank Elke E. Schmidt and Dieter Schönecker for their very helpful comments on an earlier version of this paper.

Horn, Christoph (2014): *Nichtideale Normativität*. Frankfurt: Suhrkamp.
Korsgaard, Christine (2009): *Self-Constitution*. Oxford: Oxford University Press.
Rauscher, Fred (2015): *Naturalism and Realism in Kant's Ethics*. Cambridge: Cambridge University Press.
Rosen, Michael (2012): *Dignity: Its History and Meaning*. Cambridge, MA: Harvard University Press.
Schadow, Steffi (2012): *Achtung für das Gesetz*. Berlin/Boston: Walter de Gruyter.
Sensen, Oliver (2011): *Kant on Human Dignity*. Berlin/Boston: Walter de Gruyter.
Sensen, Oliver (2013): "Kant's Constructivism." In: Carla Bagnoli (ed.): *Constructivism in Ethics*. Cambridge: Cambridge University Press, pp. 63–81.
Sensen, Oliver (2014): "Universalizing as a Moral Demand." In: *Estudos Kantianos* 2, pp. 169–184.
Sensen, Oliver (2015): "Die Begründung des Kategorischen Imperativs." In: Dieter Schönecker (ed.): *Kants Begründung von Freiheit und Moral in* Grundlegung *III*. Paderborn: Mentis, pp. 233–258.
Shafer-Landau, Russ (2003): *Moral Realism*. Oxford: Oxford University Press.
Watkins, Eric/Fitzpatrick, William (2002): "O'Neill and Korsgaard on the Construction of Normativity." In: *Journal of Value Inquiry* 36, pp. 349–367.
Wood, Allen (1984): "Kant's Compatibilism." In: Allen Wood (ed.): *Self and Nature in Kant's Moral Philosophy*. Ithaca: Cornell University Press, pp. 73–101.
Zinkin, Melissa (2006): "Respect for the Law and the Use of Dynamical Terms in Kant's Theory of Moral Motivation." In: *Archiv für Geschichte der Philosophie* 88/1, pp. 31–53.

About the Authors

Stefano Bacin is Assistant Professor of History of Philosophy at the University of Milan. His research focuses mainly on Kant's moral philosophy and on the history of ethics in the 18th and 19th century.

Jochen Bojanowski is Associate Professor at the University of Illinois at Urbana-Champaign. He primarily works on moral and political philosophy.

Robinson dos Santos is Professor of Philosophy at the Universidade Federal de Pelotas, Brazil, and Visiting Scholar at the University of Siegen. His main interests are in Kant's practical philosophy (especially moral value, dignity, prudence, and responsibility) and metaethics.

Christoph Horn is Professor of Ancient and Practical Philosophy at the University of Bonn. His main historical interests concern Plato, Aristotle, and Kant; his systematic topics are mainly ethics and political philosophy.

Patrick Kain is Associate Professor of Philosophy at Purdue University. He has worked on Kant's ethics, epistemology, and philosophy of religion, and is currently interested in philosophical and psychological questions about human dignity and autonomy.

Lara Ostaric is Associate Professor at Temple University and Humboldt Fellow at the University of Leipzig. She specializes in Kant and German Idealism and is interested in moral teleology, metaphysics, and epistemology and their relation to aesthetics.

Frederick Rauscher is Professor of Philosophy at Michigan State University. His research focuses on Kant's metaethics as well as on Kant's social and political philosophy.

Elke Elisabeth Schmidt is Master of Philosophy and Research Assistant in the Department of Philosophy at the University of Siegen. She works on Kant's ethics, philosophy of love, and metaethics.

Dieter Schönecker is Professor of Practical Philosophy at the University of Siegen. His main interests are in Kant's practical philosophy, metaethics, and philosophy of religion.

Oliver Sensen is Associate Professor of Philosophy at Tulane University and Vice President of the North American Kant Society. He mainly works on Kant's ethics and issues of autonomy, dignity, as well as respect.

Melissa Zinkin is Associate Professor of Philosophy at Binghamton University (SUNY). She specializes in Kant and is currently working on Kant's *Critique of Judgment* and the concept of depth.

Subject Index

aesthetic, transcendental   10
agent   3 ff., 7 – 10, 12 – 16, 18, 23 ff., 36, 39 f., 46, 61, 72, 77, 83 f., 96, 163, 171, 173, 191 f., 194 f., 204, 210
– empirical moral agent   4, 7, 12 ff., 16
– transcendental moral agent   4 f., 7 ff., 14 f.
analysis   9 f., 72
– empirical level of analysis   9 f., 13
– transcendental level of analysis   9 f., 13
animality   79, 86, 127
animals   48, 128, 131, 146
Anthropologie in pragmatischer Hinsicht   47, 52, 57, 63, 146, 151
antirealism, moral   3 f., 15 – 18, 24, 28, 45 f., 49, 56 f., 92 f., 95, 97, 100, 103, 108 f., 150, 155 – 158, 168, 173 f., 197 f.
a priori   4, 6 f., 12, 18, 28 f., 31, 34, 37, 50, 55, 71, 83, 87, 93 ff., 102 f., 150, 160, 172, 179, 199 – 202, 204, 206, 208 f., 214 f., 217
author   105, 113, 162, 164,
– author of obligation → obligation
– author of the law → law
autonomy   9 f., 13, 18, 34, 37, 46 f., 70 f., 77, 81, 83, 87, 93, 105, 119 – 129, 131, 148 f., 162 f., 167 f., 170, 173 f., 197, 202 ff., 209, 214, 216

capacity   6 f., 9, 23 f., 32, 47 ff., 51 f., 55, 61 f., 70, 79 f., 85, 100, 107, 110, 119 f., 126, 128 – 131, 140, 146, 162, 184, 191, 202, 210, 213
categorical imperative → imperative
categories of the understanding   6 f., 9, 21, 28, 45, 199
causality   11 f., 15, 54, 61, 81, 95, 106, 123, 126, 149, 195, 199, 204, 207
– law of causality   11, 123, 204, 207
character   22, 46, 51, 54, 56 f., 60 – 63, 111, 124, 160 f., 164, 166 ff., 172, 179 – 184, 189 f., 208
cognition   6 ff., 10 ff., 15 f., 23 f., 28, 31 f., 38, 53, 59 f., 63, 74, 87, 100 – 104, 106 – 111, 113 f., 150, 159 f., 162 f., 166 – 170, 172, 179 ff., 183, 185 – 190, 192 – 195, 199 – 202
– common rational moral cognition   87, 125, 158, 168 f., 173, 187, 189, 201, 207
– moral cognition   24, 76, 104, 125, 157, 159 f., 162 ff., 167 f., 170 f., 194, 207
– practical cognition   24, 32, 91 ff., 97, 102 – 109, 115, 150, 160, 163, 169 ff., 180, 192, 195
– theoretical cognition   87, 91 f., 102 – 105, 107 f., 160
cognizer   6 ff., 10 f., 14 f., 28, 31, 38, 67, 70
color   12, 16
commensurability   138, 140
common rational moral cognition → cognition
constitutivism   120, 197 f., 217 ff.
constructivism   17 f., 21 – 28, 30 f. 33, 36, 39 f., 46, 55, 59, 120, 135, 147 ff., 172, 197 f., 217 f.
copernican revolution   158
cosmopolitanism   47, 49, 56 f., 61

deduction   5 f., 70 f., 82 f., 183
– empirical deduction   5 f.
– metaphysical deduction   9
– transcendental deduction   5 ff., 9, 11, 93
depth   21, 33, 183
descriptive term   165
desire   14, 34, 72, 81 – 85, 87, 123 f., 160, 173, 186 f., 192 f., 197, 202 ff.
dignitas interna   141, 215
dignity   36, 67 f., 78 – 81, 85, 87 f., 119 – 123, 128 – 137, 139 – 149, 198, 207 f., 214 ff.
– human dignity   80, 119 f., 133
– two-level model of dignity   129 ff.
disposition, moral   29 f., 79, 91 f., 94 f., 97 f., 101, 124, 131, 216
divine command conception of morality   158, 164, 167

elevation 79, 120, 130, 145 f., 189, 215 f.
empirical 3–7, 9–15, 17 ff., 50, 55, 70, 83, 87, 96, 99, 101 ff., 105, 107 ff., 112, 114, 167, 170, 172, 179, 186–189, 200 f., 218 f.
- empirical idealism → idealism
- empirical level of analysis → analysis
- empirical moral agent → agent
- empirical moral idealism → idealism
- empirical moral realism → realism
- empirical realism → realism
end 3, 5, 8, 12 ff., 17, 26, 32, 34, 37–40, 46 f., 50–55, 57, 59–62, 69, 71–79, 83–86, 94, 96 f., 100 f., 104 f., 108, 111, 113 ff., 121 f., 124, 127 ff., 131–137, 139 ff., 144 f., 149, 158, 160, 171, 189, 203–206, 208 f., 215 f.
- end in itself 9 f., 25 f., 67, 69, 71–80, 119–123, 127–136, 138–141, 144 f., 149, 205 ff.
- existent end 72, 76
- objective end 67, 72 ff., 78, 80 f., 121 f.
- realm of ends 37, 46, 127 f., 130
- subjective end 72 f., 121 f.
Ende aller Dinge 57, 158
epistemology 68, 87, 150, 159, 172, 180, 182
equality 132, 137–141, 209
essentialism 47
experience 3–12, 23 f., 28 ff., 34, 45 f., 49 f., 53, 57 ff., 83, 96, 99, 102, 107, 111, 114 f., 150, 159, 162, 166 f., 169, 171 f., 181, 183 ff., 189, 199 ff., 208
- moral experience 8 f., 18 f., 36, 185
- object of experience 11, 21, 28 f., 36, 45

fact of reason 5, 87, 102, 179 f., 182 f., 185 f., 188
faith → *Glaube*, moral
feeling 21, 23 f., 29–32, 34, 36 f., 40, 58, 78, 82 f., 85 f., 93, 140, 142 f., 179 ff., 185–195, 203, 208, 214
- moral feeling 24, 123, 148, 208
formula of humanity → humanity

freedom 5, 7 ff., 17, 80–83, 87 f., 95, 104–107, 126 ff., 131 f., 139, 146, 148–151, 165, 183, 185 f., 204, 206 f., 210
- free will → will

gallows example 183–186, 204
Glaube, moral 3 ff., 7–19, 21–25, 27–32, 34–39, 45–48, 52 f., 57 ff., 62, 68 f., 71, 75, 79, 81 f., 85 f., 91–103, 105–116, 119–125, 128, 130–133, 138–142, 145–150, 155–175, 179–184, 187, 191, 194, 197–204, 206 f., 210, 212–219
- rational necessity of moral *Glaube* 91 f., 108
God 13, 59, 75, 86, 91, 94–102, 104–107, 112 f., 115, 124, 147, 150, 157 f., 161, 163 ff., 174, 203
Golden Rule 181, 194
good 8 ff., 13, 15 f., 25, 28, 32 f., 49, 52, 56, 58 f., 62, 68 ff., 76, 79–84, 87, 92–97, 99, 102 f., 106–109, 111, 113 ff., 123–128, 131, 137, 143, 147, 149, 156, 160 f., 170, 172 f., 189, 192–195, 203, 212 ff., 216
- absolute good 79, 84, 124 f.
- good will → will
- highest good 9 f., 59, 62, 84, 93–97, 102, 106 f., 109, 111, 113 ff.
ground 10, 15, 33, 53, 67, 69–81, 83–87, 91 f., 95 f., 98 f., 101–106, 108, 111 ff., 116, 120 ff., 125, 128 ff., 141, 149, 151, 159 f., 162 ff., 168, 171, 173, 179 ff., 184, 186–189, 191, 194, 198, 201–207, 210 f., 213–217
- grounding of the moral law 67, 69, 203
- objective ground 67, 70 ff., 76, 81, 85–88, 98–101, 103, 121
Grundlegung zur Metaphysik der Sitten 9, 13 f., 17, 23, 28 ff., 33, 37 f., 48, 62, 67–83, 85–88., 93, 119, 121–131, 134 ff., 143 ff., 147, 158, 161 ff., 165 f., 179 f., 183, 185, 190, 194, 198–216, 218

highest good → good
history 45, 47–62, 156, 168, 184

holiness   69 f., 86 f., 94, 124, 131, 163, 191 f.
– holy will → will
homo noumenon   123, 132 f.
homo phaenomenon   133
human being   8, 10, 14, 17 f., 48–52, 55, 57, 59, 61 f., 67 f., 70, 75, 79 ff., 85 f., 88, 94, 111 ff., 119 f., 122 f., 126–149, 166, 186, 198–203, 205 f., 210 ff., 216 f.
human dignity → dignity
humanity   9 f., 14 f., 25 f., 36, 38 f., 48 f., 51, 56 ff., 61, 67, 69, 75 ff., 79 f., 84–87, 123, 127 f., 130 f., 133, 140 f., 143 f., 146, 208, 216
– formula of humanity   26, 39, 71, 73, 75 ff., 81, 83, 205, 208 ff., 214
humiliation   29, 34, 179 f., 189 f.
hyperphysics   201, 205, 207, 211–214, 216
hypothetical imperative → imperative

idea   6, 9, 17, 26 f., 37, 45–57, 59 f., 63, 69, 71 f., 78, 80, 86, 91 ff., 105 ff., 113 ff., 122 f., 126, 131 f., 138, 140, 147, 150, 158, 163, 167, 172, 174, 186, 189, 191, 193, 197 f., 200, 202 f., 207, 210 f.
– presupposition of the objects of the ideas   91 f., 95, 129
idealism   3 ff., 7, 10, 13, 15 f., 19, 28, 157, 171–174
– empirical idealism   14 f., 16
– moral idealism   3–20
– refutation of idealism   11, 45
– transcendental idealism   5 f., 14, 19, 45, 50, 110, 162, 172
Idee zu einer allgemeinen Geschichte...   47–52, 54–57, 59
immortality   91, 94 f., 102, 104, 106 f., 112, 115, 150
imperative   69 ff., 73 f., 77, 80, 104 ff., 108 f., 124 f., 163, 166, 181, 183, 191 ff., 202, 205 ff., 210, 213 f.
– categorical imperative   5, 9 f., 14 f., 19, 21, 28 f., 31, 36 ff., 67, 70 f., 73 f., 76 f., 83, 87, 95, 104, 106, 120–124, 128 ff., 148, 150, 163, 166, 168, 172 ff., 180–183, 185 f., 192, 194, 198, 201 f., 204–211, 214, 216, 218

– hypothetical imperative   72, 108, 121 f., 205, 213
imputability   129
inclination   9, 23, 29, 33 ff., 70 ff., 75, 78, 124, 186, 189, 192, 207, 213, 216
innate   202
instinct   62, 79, 128
intelligible world → world
intrinsic property → property
intuition   6, 10 ff., 18 f., 29, 34, 37 f., 45, 101 ff., 105, 107 ff., 112, 115, 150, 179–182, 188 f., 199, 201, 211
– a priori forms of intuition   21, 29, 34, 37
– intuitionism   8, 13, 179–182, 185, 190, 194 f.
– intuitionist, sensualist   68, 179–182, 194 f.
irrealism, cognitive   168 f.

Jäsche Logik   38, 102 ff., 116, 160

Kritik der praktischen Vernunft   9, 29 f., 40, 67, 69, 75, 81–87, 88, 91–95, 97, 102, 104 f., 107, 109 ff., 111, 115, 121, 131, 143, 147, 150, 158, 160, 162 f., 165–169, 171, 173, 179 f., 185 ff., 189 ff., 193, 195, 201–205, 208 f., 212 ff., 219
Kritik der reinen Vernunft   4 ff., 8–12, 21, 28–31, 34, 37 f., 45, 48 52–55, 45, 49, 54, 59, 82, 91, 93, 97–104, 106, 115, 150, 165, 172, 187 f., 198–202, 204, 209, 211, 213 ff.
Kritik der Urteilskraft   49, 52, 54, 59, 62, 91–94, 96–106, 108–116, 163, 171, 202, 212, 218

law   11 ff., 23, 28 ff., 33 ff., 51, 53, 57, 59, 61, 67–79, 81 f., 85–88, 94 f., 101, 104 f., 111, 113 f., 121–125, 128, 132, 141, 143, 148, 150, 158–168, 170, 174, 179 f., 183–187, 189–193, 200–210, 213 f., 218
– a priori law   197, 201, 210, 217
– *author of the law*   162, 164
– grounding of the moral law → ground
– law of causality → causality

- moral law   3 ff., 7, 9 f., 12 ff., 16 f., 19, 21, 23 f., 28 – 39, 67 – 81, 83 – 88, 93 – 97, 101 f., 104 – 109, 111, 119 ff., 123, 125, 127 f., 131, 143, 148 ff., 155, 158, 161 ff., 165 ff., 169 ff., 173 ff., 179 – 195, 197, 202 f., 207, 210, 212 ff., 218
- normative content of the moral law   179 f., 190
- subject of the moral law → subject
- universal law   3, 37, 70 f., 74, 77 f., 83, 124 f., 127, 193, 201 f., 204, 206, 209, 218
- validity of the moral law → validity

legislation   4, 46, 68 f., 78, 81, 105, 122, 126, 128, 130, 162, 167 f., 173
legislator   86, 104, 162, 164 ff.
love   30, 34, 39, 142 f., 183, 193

maxim   29, 33, 36 f., 39, 70 f., 76 ff., 83, 124 ff., 128, 130, 141 ff., 163, 170, 173, 179, 184 – 191, 193, 195, 201 f., 204, 206, 208 f., 212, 218 f.
measure   103, 132, 135, 138, 140, 200
metaethics   3, 22, 181
metaphysical naturalism → naturalism
metaphysics   6, 9, 10 f., 15, 18, 38, 47 – 50, 53 f., 60, 62, 68, 73 ff., 77, 82, 84 f., 105, 109, 120 f., 125, 131, 145, 148 – 151, 157, 159, 163, 165, 169, 198 – 201, 206 ff.
Metaphysik der Sitten   38, 126, 131, 162, 200, 207, 210
Metaphysik der Sitten Vigilantius   158, 162, 210
Metaphysische Anfangsgründe der Rechtslehre   132
Metaphysische Anfangsgründe der Tugendlehre   38 f., 72, 79, 119, 131 – 138, 140 – 146, 203, 208 ff., 212, 215 f.
method   6, 18, 37, 54, 63, 82 ff., 87, 207, 209, 214
- paradox of method   67 ff., 81 ff., 85 ff.
- transcendental method   6 f., 11
mind-dependence and mind-independence of moral standards   28, 149, 157 f., 168 f., 171 ff., 190
moral   3 ff., 7 – 19, 21 – 25, 27 – 32, 34 – 39, 45 – 48, 52 f., 57 ff., 62, 68 f., 71, 75, 79, 81 f., 85 f., 92 – 98, 101, 105 f., 108 f., 111 – 115, 119 – 125, 128, 130 – 133, 138 – 142, 145 – 150, 155 – 175, 179 – 184, 187, 191, 194, 197 – 204, 206 f., 210, 212 – 219
- moral antirealism → antirealism, moral
- moral disposition → disposition, moral
- moral experience → experience
- moral feeling → feeling
- moral *Glaube* → *Glaube*
- moral idealism → idealism
- moral image realism → realism
- moral law → law
- moral property → property
- moral realism → realism
- moral subject → subject
- moral worth → worth
morality   4, 7 ff., 11 f., 14, 17 ff., 22 – 25, 27 – 33, 35 – 39, 46, 58 f., 67, 70 f., 79 f., 84, 93 ff., 100, 104, 108, 115, 126, 129 ff., 133, 140 f., 150 f., 155, 157 ff., 163, 166, 168, 171 f., 174, 182 ff., 197 f., 200 – 204, 209, 211 – 218
Moral Mrongrovius   6, 158, 162, 203, 214
Moralphilosophie Collins   158, 161 f., 166
motive   22, 33 ff., 39, 72, 78, 158, 161, 191, 203
Mutmaßlicher Anfang der Menschengeschichte   75, 136, 138, 146

Nachschrift Kaehler   158, 162, 166, 172
naturalism   18, 148, 164
natural property → property
nature   6 f., 9, 11, 13 – 19, 21, 26, 33, 36 ff., 47 f., 50 – 57, 61 f., 70 f., 74 f., 78, 86, 92 – 97, 99 ff., 105, 111, 113 – 116, 124, 127 ff., 131, 147 f., 155 – 161, 163, 165, 168, 172, 174, 197, 199, 202 f., 205 f., 217
Naturrecht Feyerabend   127 f., 206
necessity   11, 30, 33, 70 f., 78, 84, 91 ff., 95, 97, 101, 108 ff., 115, 123, 158, 161, 165, 167, 173, 186, 200, 202 ff.
non-natural property → property

object   4, 6 ff., 10 ff., 14 f., 19, 25, 28 f., 32 ff., 37, 45, 53, 70, 72, 75 ff., 81 – 86,

Subject Index — 227

91 f., 94, 98 f., 102 f., 105–109, 112–115, 124, 126, 131, 138–143, 148 ff., 160, 168, 170 ff., 181, 188, 195, 199 ff., 203 ff., 211, 215, 218
– given object   32, 91 f.
– object of experience → experience
objective   7–12, 14 f., 17 f., 25, 45, 60, 63, 69, 71–76, 95, 98 f., 104, 106 f., 113, 122 f., 131, 144, 157 ff., 169, 173, 181, 187, 191, 193, 199, 206
– objective end → end
– objective ground → ground
objectivity   16, 28, 102 f., 108, 159, 172
obligation   17, 19, 68 f., 71, 80, 88, 94, 132, 144, 146, 161–164, 166 f., 173 f., 191–194, 202 f., 210
– author of obligation   162, 164
– moral obligation   155, 159–164, 166 ff., 170 f., 173 ff., 179, 181, 183–186, 189, 193, 195
ontology   15, 18, 45, 82, 148 ff., 212 f.

Pädagogik   162
paradox   82 ff., 214
– paradox of method → method
perception   11 f., 150, 160
perfectionism   47, 52, 80
person   8, 29, 32 f., 40, 57, 75 f., 79, 83–87, 100, 123 f., 127–133, 135, 140–143, 145 f., 192, 198, 204, 207 ff., 212, 217 f.
personality   79, 85 ff., 95, 123, 127, 133, 144, 216
perspective, practical   5, 17 f., 24, 33, 45 f., 51–57, 59, 91 ff., 110, 113 f., 155, 162, 171, 192, 197
philosophy of history   45–50, 52, 56, 59–62
plants   131
Platonism   49, 147
practical reason → reason
Praktische Philosophie Powalski   158, 162
prerogative   146, 215
presupposition (of the objects of the ideas) → idea
price   75, 78 f., 132–135, 137, 141 f., 144, 181, 215 f.

progress   45–48, 52, 56–59, 61, 94 ff., 107, 114
property   10, 12 f., 79, 87, 119, 125 f., 132, 136, 145, 148, 150, 198, 202, 205, 211–214
– intrinsic property   120, 122, 141, 144, 207
– moral property   149, 181
– natural property   211
– non-natural property   120, 147 ff., 164, 197, 201, 211, 214
providence   47

queerness argument   149

rational being   9, 19, 36, 38, 67 f., 70–81, 83, 85–88, 95, 121 ff., 126–131, 135, 144, 149, 157 f., 162 f., 165 ff., 174, 189, 191, 200–203, 206 f., 209, 213, 218
rational nature   36, 67, 71, 73 ff., 79, 120–123, 127 f., 131, 205 ff.
rational worldbeing   132, 137 f.
realism   3 ff., 12 f., 16 f., 19, 24, 26 f., 40, 45 f., 49, 55 f., 68, 91 f., 108, 110, 115, 147, 155 ff., 159 f., 168–174, 197, 217
– definition of moral realism   4
– empirical moral realism   3–20
– empirical realism   10 f., 13 ff., 18, 172
– moderate realism   148
– moral image realism   91 ff., 115 f.
– moral realism   3–7, 10, 15 ff., 19, 22 ff., 35 f., 40, 68 f., 119, 147, 149 f., 155 ff., 159, 161 f., 168 ff., 172, 174 f., 197, 217
– rational necessitation realism   91 ff., 110, 113, 115 f.
– strict realism   147
– strong realism   155, 171, 174 f.
– traditional moral realism   155, 159 ff., 166 ff., 170, 174
– transcendental moral realism   3–20, 172
– transcendental realism   10, 14, 19
– value realism   67 ff., 80 ff., 87 f., 173
reality, empirical   10 ff., 15, 18
reality, objective   4, 10 f., 13 f., 45, 48, 53, 56, 91 ff., 95 f., 104–107, 115 f., 150, 157, 159–163, 165, 168 f., 172 f., 198 f., 218
realm of ends → end

reason   3, 5f., 8ff., 13, 15, 17, 19, 21–26, 28, 30–40, 45–50, 52–56, 59f., 62, 70f., 73, 76–80, 82, 84–87, 91f., 95ff., 99, 101, 104–114, 116, 120f., 123, 127, 129f., 134, 136f., 144, 148ff., 157, 159–162, 164–173, 179–184, 186f., 189–194, 197–204, 206–213, 216ff.
– human reason   8, 55, 59, 113, 157f.
– practical reason   5, 9f., 12, 14–17, 19, 22, 24, 27, 29, 33, 38ff., 62, 67, 69, 80f., 84f., 95f., 98, 102, 107, 109f., 113, 115f., 123, 125, 132f., 148, 150, 162f., 167f., 170, 173f., 184ff., 191, 195, 200, 208, 210
– speculative reason   82, 91f., 96f., 107–110, 150
– theoretical reason   91f., 95, 107–110, 116
recognition   29, 34, 71, 87, 137, 142f., 162, 166, 208
reflective judgment   91ff., 100f., 110–116
refutation of idealism → idealism
Religion innerhalb der Grenzen der bloßen Vernunft   72, 79, 96, 111, 127, 215
respect   10, 21, 23f., 29–40, 48, 60, 73, 83, 85f., 91ff., 97, 99, 104–107, 110, 112f., 115f., 120, 126f., 130ff., 135f., 138–144, 147ff., 156f., 159, 169, 173, 179ff., 185–191, 193, 195, 198, 203, 206–210, 212, 215f., 218

self-esteem   136, 143, 208
sensibility   29f., 82, 97, 123, 125, 179f., 190–193
servility   136, 216
soul   33, 36, 91, 94f., 97, 102, 104–107, 112f., 150, 202
space   4, 10ff., 14, 18f., 29, 45, 104, 121, 199f., 204
spatio-temporal beings   45
species   47f., 51f., 55, 57, 61, 101, 114, 146, 165
speculative reason → reason
Streit der Fakultäten   47f., 59f., 215
subject   7–12, 14, 21, 26ff., 31, 34, 49, 59, 73, 76, 78, 81ff., 85f., 92f., 95, 98f., 105f., 128, 132f., 140, 158, 161f., 165ff., 170, 173, 197, 203, 209f., 215
– moral subject   8, 14, 132ff., 136f., 139f., 144, 146, 162, 167, 172
– subject of the moral law   85–88
subjectiv end → end
sublimity   86, 145, 215
supervenience   150
systematicity   9, 23, 37ff., 53f., 70, 129

teleology   38, 47, 52ff., 59ff., 68, 76, 80, 82, 85, 98ff., 112ff.
theology   47, 95, 104, 201
theoretical reason → reason
time   4f., 9–12, 14, 18f., 29, 37, 45, 48f., 53, 58–61, 68, 70, 76ff., 85f., 96, 100, 116, 121f., 124, 126, 128, 130ff., 135, 144, 147, 149f., 163f., 170, 174, 191, 193, 199, 201, 204, 206–210, 216
transcendental   3–19, 29, 114f., 150, 172, 185, 197f., 211, 219
– transcendental aesthetic → aesthetic, transcendental
– transcendental deduction → deduction
– transcendental idealism → idealism
– transcendental level of analysis → analysis
– transcendental method → method
– transcendental moral agent → agent
– transcendental moral idealism → idealism
– transcendental moral realism → realism
– transcendental condition   3, 9, 11–14, 18
– transcendental realism → realism

Über den Gemeinspruch…   49, 57f.
Über eine Entdeckung…   202
understanding   3f., 6, 11, 21–24, 28, 30–34, 37ff., 54, 58, 97, 113ff., 130, 136, 156ff., 163, 165, 168, 170, 172, 174, 184, 187, 189, 199, 202, 208, 211
– discursive understanding   91f., 114
universality   18, 37, 84, 116, 124, 161, 184ff., 191, 193f., 200, 204, 209
– universal law → law
– universal validity → validity
Untersuchung über die Deutlichkeit…   161

Subject Index — 229

validity   4, 10 ff., 15, 17 ff., 70, 74, 83, 98, 101 f., 106, 124 f., 148, 161, 166, 174, 181, 183, 186
– universal validity   166, 209
– validity of the moral law   77, 179 ff., 183, 190
value   4 f., 7 ff., 12, 14 f., 17, 22, 24 f., 27, 33, 36 f., 39, 45, 60, 67–70, 72, 74 ff., 78–81, 84, 86 f., 119–122, 128, 130–142, 144, 146–149, 156, 172, 197 f., 201, 205, 207 f., 210–216
– absolute value   3, 15, 26, 73 f., 81, 119 f., 122, 129 ff., 137, 144, 146, 148 f., 205, 211 ff., 215 f.
– inner value   67, 88, 120, 131 f., 134, 136 f., 139 ff., 149, 214
– value realism → realism
vocation   8, 57, 62, 80, 82, 85 ff., 145
volition   69, 82, 122 ff., 184, 187, 189, 191, 193, 195
voluntarism   155, 157 f., 164–168, 173 f.

way of thinking   108, 128, 131
will   9 f., 13 f., 19, 22–26, 28 ff., 32 f., 34–38, 62, 69–78, 80–87, 92, 94 f., 100, 104, 108 f., 121–130, 135, 141, 156, 158, 160–167, 185, 187, 191, 200–204, 206–210, 212–215, 218 f.
– free will   3, 10, 25, 126
– good will   22, 28, 30, 36, 62, 71 f., 76, 79 f., 84 f., 87, 121, 123 ff., 128, 130, 208, 211 f., 215 f.
– holy will   69 f., 73, 123 f., 130, 191
– noumenally-good will   123–127, 130, 132 f., 144, 148
– practically-good will   123–130, 142
world   4 f., 8, 12, 15, 18, 24 f., 27 f., 32, 35 f., 45, 53, 58–61, 86, 94 ff., 99, 101 f., 104 f., 107, 112–116, 124 ff., 148, 163, 167, 172, 199 f., 212
– external world   45
– intelligible world   124 ff.
– world of sense   126
– world of understanding   87, 123, 125 f., 150
worth   17, 29 ff., 33 f., 36, 67–75, 77–81, 85 f., 122, 147, 195, 205, 208, 210–215
– inner worth   67, 78–81, 85–88, 128, 215
– moral worth   21, 23 f., 27–36, 38 ff., 172

Index of Persons

Adams, Robert 94, 97, 111, 117
Adelung, Johann Ch. 135
Allison, Henry E. 72, 88
Ameriks, Karl 18, 81, 83, 88 f., 97, 105, 110, 117, 169, 175
Aristotle 47, 52, 198
Audi, Robert 182, 195

Bacin, Stefano 80, 103, 155, 158, 167, 172, 206, 219
Bagnoli, Carla 23 f., 27, 35, 90, 152, 172, 176 f., 182, 195, 220
Baiasu, Sorin 90
Barbeyrac, Jean 163 f., 176
Baumgarten, Alexander G. 162, 165, 176
Baxley, Anne M. 166, 176
Beck, Lewis W. 63, 69, 82, 89
Bird, Graham 117
Bloom, Allan 41
Bojanowski, Jochen 15 f., 24, 27 f., 32, 41, 147, 151, 170 f., 175 f., 179, 212, 219
Bormann, Franz-Josef 152
Broad, Charlie D. 68 f., 89
Brown, Ammi 177

Chiba, Kiyoshi 45, 64
Chignell, Andrew 98 f., 116 f.
Clarke, Samuel 157, 161, 176, 181
Copernicus, Nicolaus 158
Crisp, Roger 177

Dancy, Jonathan 171, 176
Darwall, Stephen L. 208, 219
Darwin, Charles 61
Delaney, Cornelius 117
Den Uyl, Douglas 177
Denis, Lara 151

École, Jean 178
Egger, Mario 41, 152
Ellis, Elisabeth 64
Engstrom, Stephen 24, 32, 41, 90, 117
Enoch, David 40 f., 169, 176

Esser, Andrea M. 147, 151
Euler, Werner 65

Ferguson, Michaele 52, 64
Ferrarin, Alfredo 90
Ferrero, Luca 39, 41
FitzPatrick, William J. 208, 220
Forberg, Friedrich K. 95
Forkl, Markus 147, 151
Formosa, Paul 77, 89
Förster, Eckart 50, 64, 93, 117
Frank, Manfred 47, 53, 64

Gardner, Sebastian 95, 108 f., 117
Garve, Christian 93
Gerhardt, Volker 176
Gill, Michael B. 158, 173, 176
Guyer, Paul 53, 64, 68, 70, 80 f., 89, 97, 117

Hare, John 147, 151
Hebbeler, James 38, 41
Heidemann, Dieter 20
Henrich, Dieter 115, 117
Höffe, Otfried 63 f., 147, 151
Horn, Christoph 45, 53, 61 f., 64, 89 f., 211, 220
Horstmann, Rolf-Peter 174
Hume, David 155, 160, 173, 176, 198
Hunter, Ian 176

Irwin, Terence H. 156, 162, 176 f.

Johnson, Robert N. 69, 84, 89
Josifović, Saša 152

Kain, Patrick 4, 13, 18 f., 46, 67–69, 78, 88 f., 105, 117, 121, 147, 151, 162, 175 f., 212
Kerstein, Samuel 75 f., 89
Kleingeld, Pauline 53, 64
Klemme, Heiner 64
Klotz, Christian 165, 176
Kok, Arthur 152

Korsgaard, Christine M.   22–27, 31–33, 35 f., 38–40, 46, 69, 147, 149, 152, 155, 165, 170, 177, 218–220
Krasnoff, Larry   165, 177
Krueger, James   117
Kühn, Manfred   64, 175
Kutschera, Franz von   147, 152

La Rocca, Claudio   90
Langton, Rae   68, 89
Leibniz, Gottfried W.   119, 157 f., 164, 177
Lipscomb, Benjamin   117
Locke, John   6, 21
Ludwig, Bernd   164, 177

Malibabo, Balimbanga   147, 152
Meier, Georg F.   103 f., 117, 162, 165, 177
Milgram, Elijah   40 f.
Moore, George E.   8, 68, 89, 181
Muchnik, Pablo   117

Neymeyr, Barbara   64
Nietzsche, Friedrich W.   109, 117
Norton, David F.   176
Norton, Mary J.   176

Oksenberg Rorty, Amélie   63 f.
O'Neill, Onora   19, 42, 46, 64, 220
Ostaric, Lara   91, 94, 111, 116 f., 175

Paton, Herbert J.   67, 69, 84, 89
Peterson, Grethe B.   89
Plato   41, 49, 147
Porcheddu, Rocco   147, 152
Pufendorf, Samuel   80, 164, 176

Rauscher, Frederick   2–5, 15, 18, 28, 147, 149, 152, 157, 162, 165, 172 f., 175, 177, 198, 220
Rawls, John   21, 24 f., 38, 41, 46, 64, 68, 82, 86, 89, 147, 149, 152, 176, 198
Reath, Andrews   66, 69, 84, 87 f., 116, 160, 175
Riley, Patrick   177
Rosen, Michael   68, 90, 211

Rousseau, Jean-Jacques   21–23, 30, 32, 35, 41
Ruffing, Margit   90

Saunders, David   176
Sayre-McCord, Geoffrey   3, 21, 90, 68
Schaber, Peter   147, 152
Schadow, Steffi   203, 220
Schilpp, Paul A.   89
Schmidt, Elke E.   34, 40 f., 119 f., 122, 131, 148, 152, 200, 207, 212, 219
Schmidt, James   63 f.
Schmidt, Jochen 64
Schneewind, Jerome B.   69, 82, 88, 90, 178
Schönecker, Dieter   34, 37, 74, 119 f., 122, 127, 131, 146, 148, 152, 175, 179–195, 200, 207, 212, 219 f.
Schumacher, Ralph   176
Sensen, Oliver   14, 19 f., 39, 69, 79 f., 85, 87, 90, 120, 122, 127, 129 f., 135, 145–149, 152, 169, 172, 175–177, 197 f., 203, 205, 208, 213, 215 f., 220
Shafer-Landau, Russ   147, 152, 197, 217, 220
Shaftesbury, Earl of   156 f., 174, 176 f.
Skorupski, John   156, 169, 177
Sommer, Andreas U.   64
Spalding, Johann J.   157, 177
Star, Daniel   159, 177
Stern, Robert   4, 20, 68, 74 f., 90, 164, 166, 173, 177
Steup, Matthias   42
Stoics   47, 52, 90, 215
Street, Sharon   4, 20
Suárez, Francisco   163–165, 167 f., 177

Timmermann, Jens   75, 79, 90, 118
Timmons, Mark   90, 152
Tuschling, Burkhard   65

Vaihinger, Hans   95

Waldron, John   177
Ware, Owen   29, 42
Watkins, Eric   36, 42, 165, 169, 177, 208, 220

Wetzstein, Verena   152
Weyand, Klaus   56, 64
Whewell, William   156, 177
Whiting, Jennifer   90
Willaschek, Marcus   94, 117 f.
Williams, Gwladys L.   177
Wolff, Christian   119, 161–163, 165, 178
Wolff, Michael   65, 178
Wood, Allen   17 f., 37, 67, 80, 97, 127, 147, 197, 220
Wright, Crispin   155, 178

Yovel, Yirmiyahu   53, 59, 65

Zagzebski, Linda   31, 42
Zalta, Edward N.   41, 176
Zanetti, Véronique   47, 53, 64
Zimmermann, Bernhard   64
Zinkin, Melissa   21, 30, 175, 203, 220